"Chiefs and Generals *assembles a stellar cast of authorities to personify the western Indian wars in terms of leaders on both sides. This is a highly readable and authoritative anthology that captures* people, events, and competing perspectives."

Robert M. Utley,
author of *The Indian Frontier*
and *Custer: Cavalier in Buckskin*

CHIEFS & GENERALS

NINE MEN WHO SHAPED THE AMERICAN WEST

CHIEFS & GENERALS

NINE MEN WHO SHAPED THE AMERICAN WEST

EDITED BY

RICHARD W. ETULAIN & GLENDA RILEY

FULCRUM PUBLISHING
GOLDEN, COLORADO

Library of Congress Cataloging-in-Publication Data

Chiefs and generals : nine men who shaped the American West / edited by Richard W. Etulain and Glenda Riley.
    p. cm.
  Includes index.
  ISBN 1-55591-462-4 (pbk. : alk. paper)
  1. Indians of North America—Kings and rulers—Biography. 2. Generals—United States—Biography. I. Etulain, Richard W. II. Riley, Glenda, 1938-
  E89.C45 2004
  978'.02'0922—dc22

2004012371

ISBN 1-55591-462-4

Printed in the United States of America
0 9 8 7 6 5 4 3 2 1

Editorial: Lori Kranz, Katie Raymond
Design: Jack Lenzo
Cover illustrations: Jack Lenzo

Fulcrum Publishing
16100 Table Mountain Parkway, Suite 300
Golden, Colorado 80403
(800) 992-2908 • (303) 277-1623
www.fulcrum-books.com

CONTENTS

SERIES FOREWORD

Along with the editors of *Chiefs and Generals*, Fulcrum Publishing is proud
to be the publisher of the Notable Westerners series. The books in this series
explore the real stories behind the personalities and events that continue to
forge our national character. Other books in the series include *By Grit &
Grace*, *With Badges & Bullets*, *The Hollywood West*, and *Wild Women of the
Old West*.

The American West—land of myth, epitome of the independent
American spirit. When we think of the men and women who influenced the
West, we tend to think in terms of caricatures, of larger-than-life heroes and
heroines. Notable men and women have always loomed large on the open
and wide landscapes of the American West. From the earliest Native
American leaders to more recent westerners, these influential people have
attracted the attention of travelers, historians, and writers. Often, such visitors focus on how these heroes and heroines of the region were important in
shaping and reshaping images of the West.

Editors Richard W. Etulain and Glenda Riley draw on their long experience in western history and their wide associations with western historians
of varied racial, ethnic, gender, and social backgrounds. To these books, contributors bring expertise in their fields, knowledge of significant individuals,
and lucid writing styles. The result is a variety of essays providing insight
into the movers and shakers of a unique region of the United States. The
American West not only helped form the American national character, but
continues to provide an endless source of fascination for Americans and
non-Americans alike.

 ACKNOWLEDGMENTS

The editors would like to thank several people and organizations for their help and support in preparing this book. First of all, we are much indebted to the contributors for taking the time from their full schedules to prepare essays for this collection. Their professionalism and insightful analyses are particularly appreciated.

Richard W. Etulain would like to thank the Center for the American West at the University of New Mexico for supporting his research. He is also indebted to Cindy Tyson of the Center and Judith Austin, formerly of the Idaho State Historical Society for assisting him with the preparation of this book.

Glenda Riley would like to thank Ball State University, especially the Bracken Fund, for research support, and Ellyn Bigrope of the Apache Cultural Center in Mescalero, the staff of the Geronimo Springs Museum in Truth or Consequences, the staff of the Center for Southwest Research of the Zimmerman Library at the University of New Mexico in Albuquerque, volunteers at the Lincoln County Historical Museum, James Kunestses of the Mescalero Indian Reservation in Mescalero, and writer Linda Sánchez. Those who reviewed her essay and made suggestions include Donna McFadden and Jeffery Hanson in the Cultural Historic Preservation Office at the Mescalero Indian Agency in Mescalero.

Finally, the editors wish to indicate their appreciation to Bob Baron, Sam Scinta, Marlene Blessing, Dan Forrest-Bank, Katie Raymond, and Faith Marcovecchio of Fulcrum Publishing for their encouragement and aid.

Richard W. Etulain
Professor Emeritus of History
University of New Mexico

Glenda Riley
Alexander M. Bracken Professor Emerita of History
Ball State University

INTRODUCTION
RICHARD W. ETULAIN

The history of the American West overflows with lively, notable characters. From the earliest Indian leaders to the most recent headline figures, the region's heritage is replete with memorable men and women.

Often, these notable leaders emerged in contacts with western competitors. Sometimes these contests were within the confines of one group, at other times with outsiders. Such is the case with the nine lives treated here. Their careers as Native American or white military figures took on greater meaning and significance in their encounters with members of their own society as well as with leaders of foreign cultures.

These biographical essays deal with important lives even as they illuminate larger cultural contexts. Clearly, these nineteenth-century men played especially significant roles in the encounters between Native American and Euro-American military leaders on the western frontier.

The present volume, the fifth in Fulcrum's Notable Westerners series, both follows and diverges from the successful format of previous books in this biographical series. Here, rather than limit life stories of individuals from one society, profiles illustrating two cultures—Native American and white—are presented. The essays are organized so as to give balanced coverage of these opposing societies. Even though the middle section obviously illustrates clashes between chiefs and generals, this is not a book devoted entirely to conflict. Writers have been urged to see their subjects within their own communities and as opponents of others. In addition, the editors have asked authors to approach their characters analytically—neither as saints nor as devil figures. Contributors have done an outstanding job in achieving this desired balance.

The first section of this collection includes probing essays on two well-known Indian leaders, Red Cloud and Victorio. In his interesting and clearly written essay, Robert Larson, the author of a superb book-length biography of Red Cloud, treats the central role of this notable Indian leader. At first, Red Cloud became known as an outstanding war chief; later, during the final years of armed conflict on the American frontier and the first years of reservation life, he tried to maintain the impossible balance between Indian needs and white and governmental policies and demands. The next essay, by Glenda Riley, deals with the Apache chief Victorio. As Riley points out, Victorio attempted to protect his family and other tribal members from attacks from the U.S. military as well as from encroaching settlers. For Riley, in her sympathetic and appealing essay, Victorio deserves continued attention as a "seeker of peace and [a] master strategist."

The next four essays illustrate how chiefs and generals often gained expanding reputations as leaders in conflicts with opponents. In the first paired set of essays, Richard Etulain and Richard Ellis treat the differences between Chief Joseph of the Nez Perce and the pursuing general O. O. Howard. Etulain describes Joseph's attempts to hold on to tribal lands and, failing that, to serve as camp leader in his tribe's heroic retreat and tragic defeat. Conversely, Ellis depicts Howard as a flawed military leader who misstated Nez Perce ideas and actions to protect his own inadequate diplomatic leadership. Ellis comments revealingly on Howard's shifting attitudes and actions before war broke out against the Nez Perce in the early summer of 1877.

The following two essays, focusing on Geronimo and George Crook, also elucidate the lives of two major figures through their competitions with opponents. In his smoothly written sketch of the Apache leader, L. G. Moses details Geronimo's lifelong struggles for survival—against demanding southwestern landscapes, with Mexicans raiding from the south, with the American army and American settlers, and with reservation life at Fort Sill, Oklahoma. Moses also clearly delineates the revulsion/attraction Americans have felt for this Indian leader, sometimes labeled "the last renegade." Perhaps the army leader who understood Geronimo best was George Crook, whom Darlis Miller labels a "humanitarian general" in her essay. Drawing on her extensive work in western military history, Miller convincingly argues that Crook knew Indians and their cultures, championed Indian rights, understood how to deal with "army politics," and enjoyed the help of his supportive wife in his "rise to military prominence." As she also shows, Indian opponents trusted Crook; he kept his word with them.

The final three essays deal with well-known military leaders. In the first of these, Shirley Leckie, author of a superb biography of Elizabeth "Libby" Custer, presents a balanced, probing portrait of George Armstrong Custer. She points out that Custer, introduced to the concept of "total war" in the North's defeat of the South in the Civil War, attempted to employ that policy in fighting Indians on the frontier. Custer, like most of his contemporaries, believed Indians must give up their cultures and be assimilated into American society. If they refused to do so, Custer argued, the U.S. military should force them into line. Leckie concludes her portrait by showing how the "total war" policy has been reversed, with many Indians reasserting rights to their lands and ways of life.

Next, Durwood Ball depicts Ranald Mackenzie as a frontier military leader in many ways similar to George Custer. Equally committed to frontier military life, Mackenzie overcame early predictions of failure to become a stern, demanding leader of soldiers against Indian tribes of the southern plains. As Ball points out in his thorough, factual essay, Ranald Mackenzie was indefatigable, as excessively demanding of himself as he was of his men. Like Custer, Crook, and Nelson Miles, Mackenzie epitomizes the frontier military man sworn to the task of fighting Indians.

The closing essay, Robert Wooster's sprightly profile of Gen. Nelson A. Miles, provides a compelling, probing picture of another frontier military leader. As Wooster persuasively demonstrates, Miles was a complicated man. His leadership skills shone brightly in his successful commands against the Sioux, Nez Perce, and Apaches, for example. Yet Miles was also, Wooster writes, "a shameless self-promoter" and "an inveterate booster of things western." Wooster's realistic sketch, drawing on his own book-length study of the general, furnishes readers with a valuable, balanced discussion of Miles.

Taken together, these biographical profiles make up a rewarding, composite portrait of nine military leaders of the frontier and American West. Careful readers will discover how these chiefs and generals arose as leaders of their own cultures and in later conflicts with representatives of opposing societies. By examining competitions within Indian and white groups, as well as conflicts between the two cultures, these essays furnish stimulating, broad-based studies of an important era in American frontier history.

LAKOTA CHIEF RED CLOUD

Formidable in War and Peace

ROBERT W. LARSON

The June 13, 1866, gathering at Fort Laramie of Lakotas, Cheyennes, and Arapahoes, on the one hand, and federal officials and U.S. Army personnel on the other, seemed convivial and surprisingly optimistic given the tensions that marked the western landscape at this time. The members of a recently arrived presidential commission, headed by the self-assured E. B. Taylor, were doing all they could to placate the two Indian leaders at the meeting considered most crucial to any settlement. Yet there was a certain calm confidence among these government officials that brightened the atmosphere at this busy army post along the banks of the Laramie River in what is now eastern Wyoming. Helping the federal commissioners was the capable commandant at Fort Laramie, Col. Henry E. Maynadier, who had been largely responsible for identifying these two key tribal leaders. Maynadier's cooperation was essential if the U.S. Army were to improve and fortify the Bozeman Trail, which connected the Oregon Trail with the Montana goldfields.

The powerful Indian pair who caused Taylor and the other commissioners such concern were Lakota Sioux. One was Red Cloud of the Oglala Sioux, and the other Spotted Tail of the Brulé Sioux. The two men, in Maynadier's opinion, were the most important of all the Lakota leaders; these "two rule the [Sioux] nation," he wrote in a letter to Commissioner of Indian Affairs D. N. Cooley. Of the two, Spotted Tail was the more cooperative. Colonel Maynadier had paved the way for a good relationship with Spotted Tail when he arranged a poignant funeral at Fort Laramie for the Brulé chief's favorite daughter, who had tragically died from a disease. Moreover, a year in prison at Leavenworth several years earlier for an attack on a mail train in retaliation against Lt. John L. Grattan's rash 1854 assault on Conquering Bear's encampment near Fort Laramie had opened Spotted Tail's eyes to the power of these increasingly numerous white intruders pushing relentlessly into the West. Spotted Tail was also less concerned about the fate of the Bozeman Trail because it crossed through choice hunting grounds wrested from the Crows by Red Cloud's Oglala Sioux. The shrewd Brulé chief would have been far more alarmed if the trail had been located in the rich grasslands surrounding the Republican River to the south, where Spotted Tail's Brulé Sioux hunted buffalo with Southern Cheyennes and Cheyenne Dog Soldiers.

Red Cloud's willingness to cooperate was much more in doubt. Yet, he was no stranger to the character and culture of the whites. Much of his earlier life was spent encamped near Forts William and John, two trading posts constructed consecutively on the site of what became Fort Laramie in 1849. As a consequence, he knew many white traders, such as Sam Deon, John Richard, and Nicholas Janis. When the army bought Fort John from the American Fur Company and made it a military post in 1849, Red Cloud also became personally acquainted with many army officers as well as enlisted men. Indeed, Red Cloud's band of Oglalas, called Bad Faces because their allegedly downcast faces made them look bad,* were the last of the independent Sioux bands to take down their tipis and move from Fort Laramie, leaving only a small number of Loafers (Lakota outcasts who had become overly dependent on white largesse and trade) to remain in the shadows of this vital military post.

Red Cloud's warlike reputation, however, brought into question the warmth and sincerity of his white connections. Nevertheless, the fighting skills he developed during his early adult years were not used against settlers but against such enemy tribes as the Crows and Pawnees. Red Cloud, born in May 1821 on Nebraska's Blue Water Creek, approximately 80 miles west of the forks of the Platte River and 130 miles east of what later became Fort Laramie, thrived in a warrior-hunter society that tested its young men and women at a very early age. Danger was not an uncommon experience, particularly for the tribe's younger males who were rigorously trained to meet it. Red Cloud's birth occurred in an especially unsafe neutral hunting ground where the territorial claims of the Pawnees were as strong as those of the Lakota Sioux, who ordinarily hunted on the Dakota plains to the north. Fortunately, the Pawnees, a seminomadic people who lived along the Platte and Loup Rivers in eastern Nebraska, were probably planting their spring corn at the time and did not constitute an immediate threat to Red Cloud's small Sioux band headed by his father, Lone Man.

Red Cloud's father, an *intancan* or peace chief, became an early victim of one of the white man's most pernicious vices, alcoholism, and died of its effects in 1825. Deprived of her husband's support and probably disgraced by the nature of his death, Lone Man's wife, a Soane or Lakota from the

* The explanation is Red Cloud's. Some army officers attributed the name to the band's alleged bad faith.

north called Walks-as-She-Thinks, took Red Cloud and his sister and brother to the camp of Smoke. Smoke, also a Soane and possibly her brother, had moved his band south some years earlier to join the Oglalas who hunted along the Bad River that meandered from the Missouri River westward to the Black Hills. Red Cloud was raised with exceptional care and affection by his maternal uncles and aunts, quite in keeping with the matrilineal focus of Sioux society at that time.

Red Cloud's people migrated south to the Fort Laramie area when the leading Oglala chief, Bull Bear, became convinced that buffalo herds were more plentiful on the central plains than in the north. While he was encamped at Bear Butte near the Black Hills, Bull Bear was approached by John Saville and C. E. Galpin, two traders from Fort William, the first post to be built on the site of Fort Laramie. The two men were eager to boost trade at their new fort and easily persuaded Bull Bear to move his people southward to the Platte Valley. Indeed, during the years 1834 and 1835, about 2,000 Oglalas migrated to the hunting lands along the north fork of the Platte, including Red Cloud's band, still headed by Smoke, who was now called Old Smoke because of his advancing years. Bull Bear's arrogant domination of the Oglala Sioux brought Red Cloud into prominence when he was only twenty years of age. In 1841 a long-standing feud between Bull Bear and Old Smoke erupted into a violent, alcohol-induced episode along the Chugwater, a small creek in southeastern Wyoming, in which Red Cloud, fighting on behalf of Old Smoke, fatally shot Bull Bear in the head. This wrenching incident deeply divided partisans on both sides for many years—they even sought separate hunting grounds—but it gave Red Cloud an unusual prominence for such a young man.

Red Cloud's reputation as the Lakota Sioux's fiercest warrior, until the Battle of the Little Bighorn brought into renown such war leaders as Crazy Horse, Sitting Bull, and Gall, helped him overcome some of the resentment caused by his controversial role in Bull Bear's death. As many as eighty coups were attributed to the powerfully built six-footer. A coup, which occurs when a warrior touches or kills an enemy, was the most coveted prize sought by a warrior in hand-to-hand combat. According to one of his comrades-in-arms, American Horse, the fearless Oglala warrior killed four Pawnees single-handedly in one engagement. In another battle, Red Cloud killed a Crow boy herding fifty horses and then killed the zealous leader of a pursuing Crow party who was determined to recover these horses. The aggressive warrior was so fierce in battle that many opponents, and even rivals in his own tribe, accused him of excessive cruelty. This charge was probably an unfair one given the survival economy that forced most Plains

Red Cloud was still the Lakota Sioux's most effective leader when this picture was taken around the year 1880. (Photograph by Charles M. Bell, courtesy of the Colorado Historical Society)

tribes during the mid-nineteenth century to struggle for control of the buffalo ranges and the horses necessary to ensure that control. Moreover, the great pride that almost all Plains warriors took in excelling in battle, at whatever cost, was certainly not confined to Red Cloud.

Army personnel at Fort Laramie who knew Red Cloud were familiar with his prowess in battle. They were also aware that his coups were counted against enemy tribes, not against the army or the settlers the frontier army was sworn to protect. Actually, Red Cloud did not take up arms against the U.S. government until he participated in the Battle of the Upper Platte Bridge on July 25, 1865, two and a half months after Robert E. Lee surrendered his Army of Northern Virginia in the Civil War. Many of the younger Oglala warriors, such as Crazy Horse and Young-Man-Afraid-of-His-Horses, had become incensed by Little Crow's War in 1862 and the infamous Sand Creek Massacre in 1864. Red Cloud, though forty-four years old and well past his prime, became one of the leaders of a large force of Lakota and Cheyenne Indians who attacked a small army garrison on the North Platte, where the city of Casper, Wyoming, now stands. Even though the garrison was not taken, a column of troopers under the command of Lt. Caspar Collins was almost ambushed, costing the lives of Collins and four of his troopers and giving the Indian attackers a triumphant feeling greater than they deserved.

Mostly because of the pressure of these younger warriors, Red Cloud, the leading *blotahunka*, or war chief, of the Oglalas, began to take a more aggressive stance against the influx of settlers and the activities of their military guardians. This position was in sharp contrast to that of the older and more conservative *intancan*, or peace chief, Old-Man-Afraid-of-His-Horses, who wanted to maintain the status quo, despite the outrage felt by tribes throughout the Great Plains over the massacre of Cheyenne and Arapaho women and children at Sand Creek in Colorado Territory.

The mood in Washington began to change during the fall of 1865 when Gen. Patrick E. Conner, who unsuccessfully led three columns of soldiers through Sioux country without fighting a major engagement, became discouraged. His frustration was anticipated, however, by Brig. Gen. John Pope, a mediocre Civil War officer who was given command of the campaign against the western tribes in 1865. On August 23, Pope wrote the new commander of the District of Nebraska, suggesting that the frontier army return to a policy of merely protecting "the security of the overland routes," which included the Oregon Trail and the transcontinental railroad being built west from Omaha. A majority of President Andrew Johnson's cabinet agreed with Pope, as did the chairman of the Senate Committee on Indian Affairs, James R. Dolittle of Massachusetts. Senator Dolittle had authored a bill to send three congressional groups westward to investigate tribal conditions. But the position of the Johnson administration did not preclude travel routes outside the so-called Platte Road; keeping the Bozeman Trail opened for argonauts scurrying northward to the Montana goldfields was still a high priority for the federal government.

With gold fever sweeping through the settlements in the Mississippi River Valley, Red Cloud's attitude became crucial to both civilian and military authorities. Two major questions regarding the Sioux leader's future actions emerged: Would the good feelings he enjoyed toward whites prior to the Battle of Upper Platte Bridge resurface? Or would he become a captive of the increasingly antagonistic mood of his younger warriors? In March 1866, Colonel Maynadier provided the federal government with the kind of news it wanted to hear. After a difficult three-month journey on the seemingly boundless plains north of Fort Laramie, Maynadier's steadfast emissaries had located Red Cloud, and the unpredictable war chief had agreed to negotiate a peace with any presidential commission chosen for that purpose. Moreover, he promised to bring 250 lodges of his followers to the conference, plus representatives of the Northern Cheyenne and Arapaho tribes.

When Red Cloud finally arrived at Fort Laramie, he was given a particularly warm reception by Colonel Maynadier and Vital Jarrot, the Indian agent on the Upper Platte. The independent-minded warrior, now commanding enormous respect, was taken to the telegraph office at the fort. There he received news from Peace Commission leader E. B. Taylor, via the "singing wire," that he would bring a trainload of presents by June 1, 1866, if Red Cloud and his people would meet with the peace commissioners on that day.

On May 30, Taylor and the members of his party reached the fort and were delighted to see that both Red Cloud and Old-Man-Afraid-of-His-Horses were there, along with the friendlier and more predictable Spotted Tail. Five days later the conference was opened with great enthusiasm by the optimistic Taylor, who declared that the U.S. government had not sent representatives to Fort Laramie to purchase land; it simply wanted to "establish peaceful relations" with the tribes on the northern plains. There was a vague reference to the Bozeman Trail in Taylor's remarks: the federal government had also hoped to "make and use" roads through Sioux country "for the emigrants to mining districts of the West." The latter remark foretold serious trouble; Red Cloud and the other Indian leaders at the conference were never briefed about any plan to upgrade or fortify the Bozeman Trail, or the Powder River Road as the federal government preferred to call it.

Unbeknownst to Red Cloud were plans already implemented in Washington to reorganize the military forces on the frontier and open the Powder River country for travel to the coveted Montana goldfields. A force of 700 soldiers from Fort Kearny on the Platte River was already on its way to what many called the Lakota Sioux's last great hunting ground. Their leader, Col. Henry B. Carrington, appointed two months earlier to head up the Mountain District of the newly organized Department of the Platte, arrived at Fort Laramie on June 13 on his way north to fortify the Bozeman Trail. Because the winter of 1865–66 had been such a severe one, making wild game very scarce, federal authorities, who had already won the gratitude of Red Cloud and other leaders by feeding their people, expected no problems connected with Carrington's expedition.

The timing of Carrington's surprise appearance at Fort Laramie could not have been more awkward. When Red Cloud, who had just returned

A busy Sioux village, similar to the nomadic encampments of Red Cloud and his people during pre-reservation days. (Courtesy of the Colorado Historical Society, #F-5948)

from the headwaters of the White River with additional Lakota participants for the conference, encountered Carrington, he expressed shock over the colonel's mission, claiming he had been given no advance knowledge of it. The accounts of Red Cloud's outrage vary, but all seemed to spell doom for the overconfident members of the peace conference. The wife of one of Carrington's officers claimed that Red Cloud indignantly refused to be introduced to the colonel and surprised Carrington with these angry words: "The Great Father sends us presents and wants us to sell him the road, but White Chief goes with soldiers to steal the road before the Indians say Yes or No." The remarks of the muscular and commanding Sioux leader had particular significance because the gifts Taylor had earlier proposed to give the Indians were contingent upon their approval of the government's plan to improve and maintain the Bozeman Trail.

Probably the most accurate testimony regarding Red Cloud's outburst was provided by William Murphy, one of the enlistees in Carrington's well-traveled Eighteenth Infantry force. According to Murphy, Red Cloud gave an impassioned speech before he bolted out of the Fort Laramie conference, accompanied by the once-conciliatory Old-Man-Afraid-of-His-Horses and almost all the followers of both men. That left only Spotted Tail, some of the more peaceful Brulés, and those "friendlies" called Laramie Loafers still willing to sign the controversial peace treaty.

Red Cloud's forceful utterances anticipated the nature of his orations in behalf of the Sioux people for the next quarter of a century, when he was often regarded by the federal government as the chief spokesman for all seven of the Lakota bands or tribes that dominated the northern plains. Insisting that the peace commissioners were treating all chiefs at the conference like children and "pretending to negotiate for a country which they had already taken by conquest," Red Cloud listed the Sioux's grievances before he departed from Fort Laramie. He denounced the army's prevailing strategy of callously crowding his people into an ever-smaller area, forcing his tribe's women and children to face starvation, and punctuated these observations by urging his tribal allies at the conference to fight rather than starve. He concluded his inflammatory remarks with a dire warning against any intrusion into Sioux country and then dramatically stalked out of the conference, leaving a chilling pall over the once-promising peace process.

In the months that followed, Red Cloud showed the army and the frequently baffled federal authorities that his warnings were not to be ignored. Colonel Carrington did push ahead, however, building Fort Phil Kearny in the heart of the Powder River hunting grounds and dispatching two of his infantry companies ninety-two miles northward to build Fort C. F. Smith in that stretch of the Bozeman Trail located in Montana Territory. But these forts were besieged by angry Lakota, Northern Cheyenne, and Arapaho warriors, forcing the soldiers manning the garrisons to feel like prisoners in

Capt. William J. Fetterman, who lost his entire command in a Lakota, Cheyenne, and Arapaho ambush on December 21, 1866, during Red Cloud's War. (Courtesy of the Denver Public Library, Western History Collection, #F-17373)

their own homes. Needless to say, those Montana-bound gold seekers who insisted on using the trail were clearly inviting disaster. The guerrilla fighting initiated by Red Cloud was transformed into a full-scale war, which would later be called Red Cloud's War. On December 21, 1866, Capt. William Judd Fetterman, a brash thirty-one-year-old army officer from Fort Phil Kearny who sported distinctive muttonchop whiskers, pursued a small decoy force led by Crazy Horse into an ambush. This mistake resulted in the loss of his life and the lives of his entire command; the Sioux claimed that one hundred soldiers were killed, but army sources counted about eighty.

Red Cloud and many of his Oglala Sioux would boast for years that he was an active participant in Fetterman's demise, even though many Miniconjou Sioux would deny that Red Cloud was present. Few, however, would question that the strong-willed leader of the new Indian coalition was the chief mastermind of the campaign to thwart the proposed federal road, whether he was at the Fetterman Fight or heading the crucial war councils gathering along the Tongue River east of the Bighorns.

Red Cloud was definitely at the Wagon Box Fight on August 2, 1867. It turned out to be his last military encounter with the U.S. Army. This largely unsuccessful attack against a party of soldiers and woodcutters fortified inside a circle of wagons near Fort Phil Kearny followed by a day the Hayfield Fight, an attack by Cheyenne warriors on a haying party guarded by soldiers from Fort C. F. Smith. The army counted both of these bloody battles as victories, which compensated somewhat for its disastrous defeat in the Fetterman Fight, although the possession of Springfield-Allen breech-loading rifles rather than the slower muzzle-loaders may have made the difference. Nevertheless, the federal government was ready to switch to a peace policy largely because of Red Cloud's stubborn resistance. It was also a matter of priorities. The military reconstruction of the post–Civil War South and the building of the first transcontinental railroad had become more important options.

On July 20, 1867, the U.S. Congress unveiled one of its new priorities. A week and a half before the Wagon Box and Hayfield Fights, Congress created a new Indian Peace Commission. It was composed of prominent military men, such as the hard-bitten Lt. Gen. William Tecumseh Sherman, and prominent civilians, such as the bewigged Indian sympathizer Nathaniel G. Taylor and Missouri senator John B. Henderson, chair of the Senate Indian Affairs Committee. The commission was not only charged to deal with the perplexing Lakota Sioux question but also to cope with the problems of all the major tribes on the Great Plains. When the peace commissioners arrived at Fort Laramie on November 9, however, Red Cloud was not there; only a band of friendly Crows was on hand to greet them. Despite their great disappointment, the commissioners left two special agents from the Indian Bureau to communicate their strong desire to meet and negotiate with Red Cloud during the following summer. One of the agents, H. M. Mathews, later encountered a party of Red Cloud's Bad Faces, which included a warrior who claimed to be Red Cloud's brother. They told the eager emissary that Red Cloud would make peace if the government would abandon its plans to improve the Bozeman Trail and remove the hated forts that guarded it. Although the federal government had known for almost eighteen months that Red Cloud was intransigent on the issue of the forts, it was now ready to act upon this demand as part of its new peace effort.

On March 2 and 3, 1860, Gen. Ulysses S. Grant wrote General Sherman, ordering him to close the forts along the Bozeman Trail. In essence, almost all of Red Cloud's major demands had now been met. Not only were forts like Kearny and Smith to be closed but an enormous tract of land between the Bighorns and the Missouri was set aside for the Lakota Sioux. The eastern portion would be reservation land and the western portion unceded Indian territory where the Sioux could continue to hunt. Moreover, the Lakotas were granted hunting rights along the Republican River and above the North Platte as long as herds of buffalo still roamed there. The promise of rations and annuities for thirty years was also included in this alluring package to significantly sweeten the revised treaty.

With justified confidence, the peace commissioners returned to Fort Laramie on April 10 with these final revisions in what would hereafter be called the Treaty of Fort Laramie of 1868. It was a far more generous arrangement than the one presented to Red Cloud during the earlier Fort Laramie conference. To their bitter disappointment, Red Cloud was not there. The willful Lakota leader declared shortly after that he would not meet with the commission until the Powder River forts were evacuated. Although some in the government were too outraged to concede again to this crafty and stubborn man, the army evacuated Fort C. F. Smith on July 29 and Fort Phil Kearny a few days later. Both forts were torched after the soldiers left, Red Cloud leading the party of warriors who set Fort Smith afire.

Three months later, on November 4, 1868, Red Cloud arrived at Fort Laramie with approximately 125 chiefs and headmen in a party that included his old rival for tribal leadership, Old-Man-Afraid-of-His-Horses. A copy of the revised treaty had been left with the new commandant at the post, Maj. William Dye, who proved to be quite a diplomat. For three days Dye coped with the difficult Oglala leader, who was so sullen at first that he refused to shake hands with Dye and his colleagues. But the patient major went through the treaty point by point, a procedure Red Cloud would later deny ever happened. Even so, the Indian leader, who had stalled the federal government's policies toward the Plains tribes for two and a half years, put his reluctant mark on the treaty document on the very last day. Red Cloud then insisted on having the final word by concluding the negotiations with the kind of long and divisive oration that was becoming his trademark. Despite his lack of enthusiasm, the treaty became Red Cloud's greatest achievement, even exceeding his distinction as being the only Native American leader to force the federal government to back down in a major Indian war.

In the months and years that followed, Red Cloud was to learn that it was one thing to negotiate a treaty and another to implement it. In his final remarks made at Fort Laramie on that fateful November day, he candidly told Major Dye and the other military and civilian negotiators that he would have a difficult time selling the treaty to many of his younger warriors. His efforts to convince the more isolated and intransigent northern Lakota Sioux, such as Sitting Bull and his Hunkpapas, would be equally difficult. Yet Red Cloud's own commitment to peace never wavered. In an 1872 message to a group of northern Lakotas at Fort Peck in Montana, which was delivered by Dr. J. W. Daniels, his agent at the newly established second Red Cloud Agency, he declared, "I shall not go to war with any more whites." Then to reinforce his position, he added, "I shall do as my Great Father says and make my people listen."

Red Cloud's dramatic change of heart was probably due more to his awareness of the strength and numbers that the U.S. government could muster in any future war than to any increase in his respect or affection for these powerful new adversaries. When he signed the 1868 Treaty of Fort

Laramie, the government in Washington managed the affairs of a nation with a population approaching 36 million, while there were probably fewer than 25,000 Lakota Sioux to oppose them.

Red Cloud's first trip to the capital to visit President Grant in 1870 only heightened his realization of the dangers his people would face. Although there are few, if any, direct quotations revealing his awareness, there seems little doubt that this highly intelligent leader, who had been close to whites during his early years at Fort Laramie, was impressed by the power displayed during this first of many trips to Washington. His hosts in the capital made a not-so-subtle point of showing him, and the large Lakota delegation he headed along with Spotted Tail, the impressive arsenal and navy yard at Washington. The curious Sioux delegates saw a fifteen-inch coastal gun at the navy yard that could lob a shell four or five miles down the Potomac. They also observed a flashy display put on by a regiment of smartly attired marines in full-dress parade. In a follow-up trip to New York City that same month, they saw crowds probably greater in size than the entire Sioux Nation, including the Nakota and Dakota Sioux who were found as far east as Minnesota. During a Fifth Avenue parade in their honor, they received an ovation that was in sharp contrast to the hostility toward them felt by so many whites living on the frontier. Red Cloud's speech that night at the famous Cooper Institute also won respect for his people. "The Great Father that made us both wishes peace to be kept; we want peace. Will you help us?"

Red Cloud faced a recurring problem during his two decades of active leadership as the Lakota Sioux's most prominent treaty Indian. It was the inclination of the federal government to alter the treaty he signed at Fort Laramie whenever it stood in the way of settlement or mineral exploitation. When some 15,000 argonauts flocked to the Black Hills after Lt. Col. George Armstrong Custer's discovery of gold in 1874, the army showed a seemingly deliberate laxness in its attempts to expel these intruders from land clearly granted to the Sioux by the Fort Laramie Treaty. When the expected unrest over the Black Hills crisis occurred, particularly among those Lakotas hunting on the treaty-sanctioned unceded Indian territory of eastern Wyoming, the government ordered them to return to their reservations in Dakota Territory by January 31, 1876.

When leaders like Sitting Bull and Crazy Horse defied this order and the Battle of the Little Bighorn resulted in June 1876, Red Cloud was arrested by a force under Col. Ranald S. Mackenzie for unproven allegations that he conspired with these "hostiles." Shortly thereafter, pressure was put on Red Cloud and other treaty Indians to give up the Black Hills, which had been sacred to all Lakota Sioux for three generations. Article 12 of the

Treaty of Fort Laramie, which required the approval of three-fourths of all adult Lakota males to authorize such a land cession, was ignored by a government commission headed by former commissioner of Indian Affairs George W. Manypenny, who oversaw this rather brazen treaty violation.

Red Cloud found throughout these years that he could never relax in his defense of the 1868 treaty. When the Dawes Severalty Act of 1887 was implemented on the Great Sioux Reservation, which still comprised all of western South Dakota outside of the Black Hills plus a small slice of neighboring North Dakota, Red Cloud was in the forefront of the opposition. The federal government in this land cession did adhere to the treaty provision requiring the approval of three-fourths of all the adult Lakota males at the six agencies on the sprawling reservation. The vote on this measure, called the Sioux bill of 1889, allocated tribal lands to individuals, particularly to the heads of families, and opened the rest to outside settlement. The process was designed to create small independent farmers, but it cost the Sioux about half the territory encompassing their original reservation as defined in the Treaty of Fort Laramie.

Red Cloud failed to defeat the Sioux bill, but his agency at Pine Ridge was the only one of the six newly created reservations to deny the government its three-quarter majority of adult males in the heated fight over the bill's ratification. Red Cloud paid an especially heavy price for opposing the disputed severalty measure. The government, at the forceful behest of Secretary of the Interior John W. Noble, decided to punish the man who had been recognized as the chief spokesman for all of his people since the 1860s. American Horse was chosen instead of Red Cloud to head the Lakota delegation sent to Washington in December 1889 for the final conference on the Sioux bill. Moreover, Washington would largely ignore Pine Ridge's leader, now sixty-eight, during the last twenty years of his long and venerable life. Yet, despite Red Cloud's persistence in guarding his people's treaty rights, many of his contemporaries blamed him for agreeing to a treaty that could be violated so often. Indeed, some of the Lakota Sioux today, particularly the younger, more militant ones, still hold him responsible for these violations.

To many members of the federal government, Red Cloud's opposition to changing any of the major provisions of the treaty put him in the camp of the traditional or nonprogressive treaty Indians. His feud with two of his agents, J. J. Saville at the second Red Cloud Agency in northwestern Nebraska during the 1870s and Dr. Valentine T. McGillycuddy at the Pine Ridge Agency in southwestern South Dakota during the 1880s, is an example of what many of his critics viewed as Red Cloud's all-too-typical querulousness and negativism. His differences with Agent Saville, for instance, over the quality of the food rations at the Red Cloud Agency near Fort Robinson led to a three-month investigation by a special commission, selected by the Board of Indian Commissioners in 1875. These intensive hearings at a number of sites featured eighty-seven witnesses and resulted in an 841-page official report. In the end, Saville was acquitted of allegations that he defrauded the government and deliberately cheated the Indians, but the adverse publicity resulted in his resignation four months later.

Red Cloud's feud with Dr. McGillycuddy was even more bitter, lasting throughout this strong-willed agent's seven-year tenure. The disagreements between the mustachioed thirty-year-old McGillycuddy and the much older Red Cloud began during their first meeting in the spring of 1879. At that hopeful gathering, McGillycuddy presented a new map to his charges at the Pine Ridge Agency, emphasizing that Red Cloud's people should spread out and cultivate the fertile valleys that marked the agency's rolling land-scape rather than cluster idly around the new agency's headquarters. Red Cloud promptly rejected this provocative recommendation, insisting that the Great Spirit had created the Lakota Sioux for hunting, not farming. Now the federal government, which had already robbed his people of much of their bountiful lands, wanted to change their identity too. The pattern was set for a seemingly perpetual stalemate. In fact, not long after this dispute, McGillycuddy established an Indian police force over Red Cloud's objections.

Red Cloud's disagreements with Agent McGillycuddy soon deteriorated into a strong mutual dislike. One possible cause for this bitterness was McGillycuddy's resentment over the way Red Cloud had treated the late Crazy Horse. Red Cloud was never close to Crazy Horse, twenty years his junior, and often disagreed with him over efforts to accommodate to the federal government's policies toward the Sioux. When Crazy Horse finally surrendered in the spring of 1877 after his stubborn resistance in the Great Sioux War, Red Cloud and a number of older and undoubtedly jealous Lakota leaders were critical of the popular warrior's defiant conduct as a treaty Indian. Thus, a set of circumstances was created that resulted in Crazy Horse's death at Camp Robinson while being arrested by soldiers on September 5, 1877. McGillycuddy, a former contract physician for the army who had successfully treated Crazy Horse's wife, Black Shawl, for tuberculosis, tried to save Crazy Horse's life from the fatal bayonet wounds he received during this arrest. The agent had always regarded his relationship with Crazy Horse as a special one and probably held Red Cloud at least partially responsible for Crazy Horse's death.

The sharp differences between Red Cloud and McGillycuddy soon generated nationwide publicity. McGillycuddy, ten weeks after his first encounter with Red Cloud, ordered the Benedictine priest, Father Meinrad McCarthy, off the agency's land as Pine Ridge had been designated by the government to be the spiritual monopoly of the Episcopal Church. Moreover, prior to this controversial incident, Red Cloud, supported by twenty-one other chiefs at Pine Ridge, wrote President Rutherford B. Hayes, urging him to replace McGillycuddy with his predecessor, Dr. James Irwin.

During the mid-1880s, Red Cloud grew increasingly alarmed by McGillycuddy's support of the Lake Mohonk Movement. In this movement, such reformers as Sen. Henry L. Dawes and Herbert Welsh, founder of the Indian Rights Association, began to aggressively push for the assimilation of Indians into American society. Red Cloud was in opposition, believing that the individualism and private landownership the reformers emphasized would significantly undermine tribal leadership. In desperation the frustrated chief wrote Secretary of the Interior Henry M. Teller in June 1884, asking for permission to invite to Pine Ridge the more sympathetic Thomas A. Bland of the National Indian Defense Association, one of the few reform organizations to advocate Indian self-determination. An outraged McGillycuddy intercepted the outspoken Bland upon his arrival at the agency and, using members of the Indian police force he had organized, had Bland escorted off Pine Ridge. Both Red Cloud and Dr. McGillycuddy were soon embroiled in the smoldering politics over what should be done with displaced Native Americans no longer roaming freely on the western plains. Although the reformers of the Mohonk movement helped to bring about the individual land allotments of the Sioux bill of 1889, McGillycuddy was removed by the administration of Democrat Grover Cleveland three years earlier for partisan political reasons. The reputations of both Red Cloud and McGillycuddy had no doubt been tarnished by the hard-line positions each took during these years of feuding.

Red Cloud had repeatedly demonstrated his independence at both the Red Cloud and later Pine Ridge Agencies. He chose to become a Roman Catholic in defiance of a federal directive to give the Episcopal Church the conversion mission among the Oglala Sioux. When he and Spotted Tail were invited to the Carlisle Indian Training School in Pennsylvania in 1880 to see how certain selected children from the Pine Ridge and Rosebud Agencies were doing, they were shocked to see them in military blue uniforms and sporting closely trimmed haircuts. To the anger of the school's superintendent, the often-dogmatic Capt. Richard Henry Pratt, the two leaders withdrew these youngsters from the nationally known Indian school.

Although Red Cloud and Spotted Tail would later prefer on-reservation to off-reservation day schools and boarding schools like Carlisle, they remained skeptical of all government-sponsored schools. Red Cloud also sharply criticized those government policies that would change his people from nomadic hunters and grazers to small farmers. His motivation for this opposition was due not only to the reluctance of Red Cloud and most of his people to give up a cherished and centuries-old way of life but also to the hard times that accompanied their difficult transition from a hunting to an agrarian culture. Ironically, one of the South Dakota counties encompassed by Pine Ridge today is the third poorest in the nation.

Red Cloud, during his two decades of leadership, which at times bordered on a preeminence rarely acknowledged in a leader by the staunchly independent Lakotas, took a number of different positions on the issues his people faced. Sometimes his stands were supportive of federal Indian policy, particularly in matters of war and peace. Yet an objective assessment of all of them would clearly disqualify him as a culture broker in the sense that Spotted Tail probably was. Certainly neither of the two Lakota chiefs was as cooperative in this regard as such Sioux leaders as the Hunkpapa Gall and the Blackfeet Sioux John Grass or the famous Comanche chief Quanah Parker.

Still, to categorize Red Cloud as an unbending traditionalist who opposed almost all federal Indian policies would be unfair. His right to insist on strict adherence to the provisions of the Fort Laramie Treaty does not seem unreasonable, even for a vanquished leader. His quarrels with Indian agents, such as Saville and McGillycuddy, were sometimes petty and self-defeating, but he usually knew when to back down. In this regard he was unlike Sitting Bull whose divisive disputes with Agent James McLaughlin at Standing Rock eventually resulted in his death at the hands of Indian police sent by McLaughlin to arrest him in December 1890. Red Cloud's defiance of General Sherman in late 1877, when he halted the migration of some 8,000 Lakotas and Northern Cheyennes eighty miles short of a new reservation proposed by the federal government at the junction of Yellow Medicine Creek and the Missouri River, was unquestionably an audacious act. Yet the fact that Red Cloud and his people finally ended up at Pine Ridge, where their descendants remain today, proves that this decision has definitely withstood the test of time.

The best proof that Red Cloud was neither progressive nor nonprogressive, but straddled both camps, as historian Robert M. Utley has argued, can be found in his controversial role in the events that surrounded the Ghost Dance. When this new Indian religion spread eastward into Sioux country, now divided into six much smaller reservations because of the Sioux bill of 1889, Red Cloud did not discourage the many new converts at Pine Ridge, although he himself elected not to join the activities. As the dancing grew more frenzied and the incantations for a transformed world without whites grew more insistent, however, Red Cloud began to discourage participation in this compelling new faith, which promised all Ghost Dancers the return of their beloved ancestors and those buffalo herds that had once flourished on the plains. Red Cloud was especially disturbed by rumors that U.S. Army forces and adjacent state militias would invade the Sioux reservations. These rumors were prompted by increased fears among whites that the new religion would fan an Indian uprising comparable to that which resulted in the Great Sioux War of 1876–1877. This apprehension was strengthened in mid-November when the inept Indian agent at Pine Ridge, Daniel F. Royer, a politically well-connected, small-town druggist from the newly created state of South Dakota, demanded immediate federal protection against such a possibility.

During these nervous weeks in late 1890, Red Cloud and such peacemakers as Big Road, Young-Man-Afraid-of-His-Horses, Calico, and No Water began meeting to see if they could head off a military showdown with the federal government. In fact, they contacted Big Foot, a wavering Ghost Dancer and Mineconjou leader from the Cheyenne River Reservation near the North Dakota border, and urged him to bring his followers south to the agency headquarters at Pine Ridge to join in meaningful peace discussions. As an intriguing lure they offered Big Foot and his people one hundred horses. But the army misconstrued Big Foot's intentions as he moved southward through the Badlands toward Pine Ridge; the commanding officers of the troops that had moved into South Dakota were convinced that Big Foot and his band were headed toward the Stronghold, a triangular plateau that served as a natural fortress for the Ghost Dance leaders and their most dedicated converts. Instead Big Foot's band was headed toward the Pine Ridge agency headquarters where Red Cloud awaited them. The tragic result of this miscalculation was the Battle of Wounded Knee Creek on December 29, where casualties were disturbingly high, particularly among the Indians; Big Foot and 150 of his followers were killed, along with twenty-five soldiers, not to mention the eighty-nine participants who were wounded in the bloody fray.

Red Cloud, the man who had stalked out of the 1866 Fort Laramie meeting and went on to block the U.S. Army's efforts to build a federal road through the Powder River country, had failed to avert this disaster. Despite his dominant role in bringing about one of the most favorable Indian treaties ever negotiated, the Treaty of Fort Laramie of 1868, he was, by 1890, an aging, nearly blind man largely ignored by the federal government since his opposition to the Sioux bill of 1889. He was, therefore, no longer in a position to help his people during this crisis. To demean his status even more, Two Strike, a bitter Brulé chief and Ghost Dance advocate who resented Red Cloud's peace efforts, kidnapped him and his family on January 9, 1891, less than two weeks after the Wounded Knee fiasco.

Although Red Cloud escaped a week later and the new religion's hard-liners surrendered shortly thereafter, the once-great chief slipped into relative obscurity, at least outside of Pine Ridge. His life became a quiet one; he spent much of his time in a two-story wooden

Red Cloud in his late eighties, assisted by two younger members of his family. (Photograph by J. A. Miller, courtesy of the Colorado Historical Society, #F-5947)

house built in 1879 by the federal government. During his earlier years, he had raised a family of five daughters and a son named Jack, whom Red Cloud had tried unsuccessfully to handpick as his successor; these offspring no doubt brought him comfort during this period of decline. His closest companion, however, was his wife, Pretty Owl. According to Red Cloud's own story, dictated to an old friend in 1893, she had been his longtime mate ever since he playfully struck her with the ramrod of his rifle, as if counting coup, and affectionately said, "You are mine."

With a few exceptions, such as a trip to Washington in 1897, Red Cloud rarely left Pine Ridge and his once-great renown diminished as the years passed. Only a flurry of news stories when he died on December 10, 1909, reminded many of those who had been a part of the Old West of his once-significant presence. Part of the cause for his dramatic decline in importance was the ongoing historical ascendancy of Lakota Sioux leaders like Sitting Bull and Crazy Horse, whose role at the Little Bighorn had brought such glory to their people. Indeed, Red Cloud's name recognition would never match that of these two domineering participants of the Great Sioux War.

Although underrated by many historians, Red Cloud did leave a formidable record of accomplishments during his eventful life. Because of his humble beginnings, largely caused by his father's drunkenness and resulting death, he was forced to achieve his initial recognition through ferocious warfare; his give-no-quarter approach to battle and the bold horse-stealing expeditions he led sometimes brought charges of cruelty against him. Even during the zenith of his amazingly long career, he was often more respected than loved by his people. Yet the steely will he demonstrated as a warrior also made him formidable as a leader. His determination to prevent the military fortification of the Bozeman Trail and his refusal to agree to the Treaty of Fort Laramie until his terms were met probably delayed the settlement of the northern plains for at least a decade. In fact, no sustained efforts to remove the Lakota Sioux from their hunting grounds in Wyoming and Montana occurred until early 1876, almost ten years after Red Cloud had thrust himself into history by abruptly leaving the controversial 1866 conference at Fort Laramie.

Red Cloud was a complex figure. Although never a culture broker who actively blended the Lakota way of life with the life of the victorious white culture that surrounded him and his people, Red Cloud worked consistently, despite serious differences with Indian agents, to keep the peace with both the U.S. Army and those federal authorities in the West given supervisory powers over the vanquished tribes. He did receive credit for his greatest achievement, the favorable 1868 Treaty of Fort Laramie, but even this recognition proved to be a mixed blessing. When the treaty was violated by the loss of the Black Hills in 1876 and the institution of land allotments in the Sioux bill of 1889, Red Cloud was blamed by many of his own people for these developments. Yet his opposition to both changes was forceful, eventually costing him those prerogatives the federal government had bestowed upon him as the chief spokesman for his people. Surely a leader of this caliber deserves a better historical image than the one that has endured since Red Cloud's death in 1909.

APACHE CHIEF VICTORIO

Seeker of Peace and Master Strategist

GLENDA RILEY

As a chief, Victorio led into battle a dwindling number of Apaches desperate to retain a portion of their homelands in southwestern New Mexico, eastern Arizona, and northern Mexico. As a brother, Victorio turned for aid and advice to his warrior sister, Lozen. As a husband and father, he often took with him his family, as well as other women, children, and the aged, to protect them from soldiers.

Rather than becoming overwhelmed, Victorio responded to these demanding roles in two ways. First, until 1878 Victorio repeatedly—and usually unsuccessfully—tried for peace with Anglo leaders, who not only were distracted by their own problems but usually took a dim view of Indians. Second, as he became increasingly disillusioned with Anglos, Victorio concluded that he and his people were better off fighting than suffering the poverty, disease, and slow death of reservations that could be more accurately described as detention camps. In the process, Victorio became a master strategist, developing usual Apache guerilla tactics to an unusually effective level. As Victorio's opponents recognized and remarked upon his abilities and courage, they turned him into a widely respected and inordinately feared figure.

Despite his reputation, however, Victorio has not received as much public interest and scholarly attention as other leaders of his era, notably Cochise and Geronimo. Even Hollywood and television generally overlook Victorio. A snippet of Victorio's story appears in the made-for-TV film *Buffalo Soldiers* but the vignette is brief and biased. Although it is true that little information exists about Victorio's early life and his major campaigns lasted less than two years, the life story of this talented and at times desperate military leader is worth reconstructing, especially to reveal how an Indian leader in search of peace became a key figure in the Indian-white conflicts of the 1870s and 1880s.

This is purported to be the only known photograph of Victorio, but several recent scholars debate whether it is Victorio at all, undated. (Courtesy of the Arizona Historical Society, Tucson, #30371)

Victorio's training as a resistance leader and clever tactician started virtually at birth. Although one legend says Victorio was born to a Mexican family and captured by the Apaches as a child, it is more likely that he was born around 1825 to the Ojo Caliente or Warm Springs Apaches living in New Mexico's Black Range. As a child, Victorio traveled with his highly mobile people, also known as Mimbres Apaches or Mimbreños from the mountains where they camped and hunted. During his youth, he acquired the skills that Apaches had developed during centuries of gathering wild plants, hunting small game such as deer and elk, and trading with settled Indians for grain and other staples.

In addition to learning the arts of hunting, raiding, and warfare, the young Victorio absorbed the Mimbreños' long-standing hatred of Mexicans. This hostility dated back to the early 1500s, when Spanish conquistadors and settlers became the first invaders to upset the balance of Apache economic life. The Spanish also supplied Apaches with horses, making them more effective hunters who could support a larger number of people, as well as swift and deadly fighters. The invaders, however, had no intention of making a place in their new empire for the Apaches. Virtually nowhere in Spanish colonialist discourse was there any suggestion that Apaches were the equal of Spaniards. Rather, Spanish officials often sold captive Apaches as slaves or exiled those they labeled "incorrigibles" to the far reaches of El Norte, the northern frontier. Even Lieutenant José Cortés, who was sympathetic with the Apaches' plight, thought the Indians subhuman. In 1799, he wrote of their "barbarous customs," their "bilious temperament," and their "destructive instinct." Trained in European warfare, Cortés viewed Apache tactics—derived from stalking and surprising wild game—as disorganized, barbaric, and unfair: "their lack of trustworthiness and ignorance of all laws that govern the waging of war have no other source than the natural propensity of the Apaches to steal and to inflict damage on their enemies."

After 1821, when Mexico wrested its independence from Spain, it soon became clear that such notions of Indian inferiority also underlay Mexican policies. Like the Spanish, the newly independent Mexicans hoped to stop Apache raiding and remove the Apache barrier to northward expansion, in part by giving them gifts and gathering them on lands called rancherías. In 1835, when Victorio was about ten years of age, Mexican authorities in Sonora and Chihuahua adopted the practice of their Spanish predecessors in offering cash payments for Apache scalps. Two years later, the principal leader of the Mimbres Apaches, Juan José Compá, and some of his people lost their lives, reportedly to an unscrupulous scalp hunter from Kentucky. Because they believed in avenging deaths, Mimbres warriors retaliated by killing Mexicans in the area, essentially closing down the Santa Rita copper mines.

Victorio soon found reasons to distrust and dislike Anglos who came to the Southwest with similar reductionist ideas regarding Apache society and culture. After the United States took over what is today the American Southwest, first by the Treaty of Guadalupe Hidalgo ending the Mexican War in 1848 and then by the Gadsden Purchase of 1853, numerous Americans arrived. These and other white invaders offered gifts in return for land or, more typically, simply took the land they wanted. Anglos also slaughtered small game, either for sport or purposely to deprive Apaches of sustenance. Understandably, Mimbres Apaches, who by now had grown proficient at seizing animals and at escaping from their enemies or destroying them, resisted Anglo expansion, often using the very firearms they obtained from Anglo traders.

Victorio especially proved himself capable and shrewd. After finishing his military apprenticeship, he often rode with the Mimbreños' primary leader, Mangas Coloradas. By all accounts, Mangas was an imposing and charismatic figure who preferred peace yet often found it necessary to conduct raids and even wage war. In 1849 alone, Mangas Coloradas successfully led his men against American dragoons, meaning heavily armed and often mounted soldiers, near the abandoned copper mines, and attacked so many wagon trains that the mention of his name caused travelers and settlers to avoid the area. Because Mangas Coloradas was unhappy with this way of life, he began talking with John Russell Bartlett, head of the U.S. Boundary Commission based near Santa Rita, about the possibility of a reservation at Santa Rita and the rationing of Indians while they learned to farm.

Victorio shared Mangas's dream of peace, but both men would have been less optimistic had they known that Bartlett's 1852 report, although at points sympathetic with the Mimbres Apaches, described them as "savages" and among the "boldest" of the "depredators." Like the Spanish and

Mexicans before them, Anglo conquerors subscribed to colonialist beliefs that ranked Indians as nearer to animals than to humans. As one military man wrote, the countryside around his post was full of "bear, elk, deer, antelope, turkey, Indians, and other wild game." Such a demeaning characterization would prove useful for those Anglos who wanted Indian lands and wanted quick solutions to the Indian "problem."

Victorio, however, was young and hopeful. In 1853, at Fort Webster, he signed his first treaty. In doing so, he was in good company with other Apaches who had made their marks, such as Ponce, Cuchillo Negro, and Delgadito. In approving the 1853 treaty, apparently a follow-up to an 1852 pact, Victorio and others agreed to become farmers, to adopt Anglo-style legal codes, and to "give up the ancient laws of retaliation." In return, the U.S. government was to teach Apache men to farm and to supply them with food while they were learning. In other words, the subtext of the document required Apaches to jettison a centuries-old way of life and become pseudo-whites, a goal supported by most Anglos who believed that acculturating Indians to white ways was the answer to Indian-white conflict.

Despite the treaty's quixotic goals, Victorio was willing to try. After Mangas Coloradas came to the agency at Fort Webster as well, the two men attempted to abide by the 1853 agreement. Although they found little more than a few rickety buildings meant to serve as an office, a storehouse, and a kitchen, Victorio and Mangas Coloradas urged their followers to join other Apache groups in establishing homes around the fort. The Mimbreños built nearly one hundred lodges only to discover that the farming "instructor" was self-interested and unscrupulous, the land assigned to the Apaches nearly worthless, and government rations inadequate. To make matters worse, small game was nearly depleted in the area. Moreover, illicit whiskey caused numerous free-for-alls in which people got hurt or killed.

Victorio and Mangas Coloradas did what they could. With varying degrees of success, they attempted to restrain the Mimbreños from using their hunting skills to "capture" local horses and mules to provide much-needed meat. From Anglo authorities they repeatedly solicited the promised ration issues, especially corn, tobacco, and knives, and charged officials with failing to uphold treaty arrangements. Eventually, the U.S. Congress failed to ratify the 1853 agreement.

During these years, Victorio grew increasingly puzzled and frustrated. As the numbers of miners, setters, and travelers increased, his people's hunting areas shrank so drastically that they faced malnutrition and even starvation. Victorio did not understand how his people were to survive if the bison and other game were gone, if raids on Anglos' herds were forbidden, and if the U.S. government did not give the rations they had promised. To Victorio it appeared that Anglo officials made colossal promises that were little more than outright lies.

His hopes rose, however, in 1854 when Dr. Michael Steck came to New Mexico to head up an Indian agency at the new Fort Thorn. Steck made clear that he viewed raids as outright stealing and warned that thieves would be "punished" and he would "have nothing to do" with them. But Steck also became a strong advocate for the Indians in his jurisdiction. He saw the Mimbreños as peaceful Indians who had not raided in the U.S. since the Treaty of 1852. If he knew of raids into Old Mexico, he overlooked them. As early as the fall of 1854, Steck informed officials in Washington that the Indians "expected the promises to be fulfilled" and that while they had "endured semi-starvation and destitution ... they can not be expected to do so indefinitely."

The following year, 1855, Apache leaders were called upon to consider yet another treaty, a lopsided one in which the Mimbres and Mescalero Apaches would give 12,000 to 15,000 square miles of their land to the U.S. government in exchange for food and protection. This agreement would leave the Mimbreños and Mescaleros with about 2,000 to 2,500 square miles each for their reserves. Although Mangas Coloradas and Victorio desired peace, they believed the cost was too great, so they refused to sign. Mangas pleaded ill health while Victorio seemed to have vanished, probably leading raids in northern Mexico. In the end, the U.S. Senate refused to ratify the treaty because deposits of iron, lead, copper, and silver would fall into the confines of Mimbres land rather than in the areas given to the U.S. government.

During the remainder of 1855 and in 1856, the situation deteriorated for the Mimbreños. Victorio's fighting men, who by one account numbered approximately 150, were blamed for a series of stock thefts. Other Apache groups, including the Mescaleros and the Mogollons, were also implicated. Steck insisted on a vigorous investigation, which indicated that Mexican bandits had been responsible for a number of the losses. Other culprits were white rustlers and "white Indians," or Anglos who disguised themselves so that their actions would be attributed to Indians. Still, most people thought the Indians were at fault, a belief that led to tragedy. In 1856, a party of jittery white soldiers in search of stock thieves in the Mogollon Mountains attacked a group of peaceful Mimbres, killing one woman and wounding several children. Steck had no reasonable answer for Victorio's question why. Neither could Victorio satisfactorily convince Steck and other Anglos that, according to the Apache code of honor, this death had to be avenged—and soon was.

Each day, Victorio, who operated in a very different kind of culture than did the Anglos, found it harder to control his people. In the Apache political system, leaders and subleaders of a band were usually elected rather than gaining their rank through inheritance. Also, individual warriors were free to join any leader or any given campaign. If a head chief lost his followers, he lost his job. Thus, Victorio wanted to retain his followers while honoring his promises to Anglos. To keep his men from raiding nearby ranches and farms, he relied upon little else than his and Dr. Steck's personal magnetism. Despite such efforts, both men admitted that Mimbreños "stole" horses and mules in New Mexico and traded them in Mexico for food, weapons, ammunition, and other goods. In fact, tensions ran so high that in mid-1857, another innocent group of Mimbres Apaches was attacked by dragoons, this time with six or seven Indians killed, including a chief.

Victorio was nearing desperation. Many of his Mimbreños were starving, ill, and nearly naked. Even the intrepid Mangas Coloradas was aging and frequently unwell. Those who managed to survive the winter of 1857–58 found matters little improved by the spring. In early April, a band of Hispanics from Mesilla assaulted peaceful Indians huddled near Fort Thorn. When Steck reported on the carnage, he said the assailants "indiscriminately butchered" Indians, leaving seven dead and a number wounded. Victorio became even more alarmed the following summer of 1858 when white miners returned to the copper and gold lodes near Santa Rita, which an 1855 treaty had given to the Mimbres. Once more, Steck and Victorio joined forces to quiet the Mimbres and avert disaster.

To Victorio, Anglos were a greater enigma than ever. Although Mimbreños raided for bare survival and refrained from scalping or otherwise mutilating their enemies, most Anglos seemed to hate them beyond human reason. If Victorio could have read white-generated government reports, he might have understood. For instance, one Anglo official, Special Agent George Bailey of the Interior Department, reported in the fall of 1858 that Apaches were "treacherous, bloodthirsty, brutal," with "an irresistible propensity to steal." Moreover, the authorities who were supposed to help the Indians frequently argued about whether reservations or outright genocide would be more cost-effective to the American public.

Given the misunderstanding and violence of the 1850s, it is little wonder that the year 1860 marked a further, and calamitous, downturn in Apache-white relations that would characterize the two groups' contact from then on. The tone was set by a gold discovery on Bear Creek that led to an influx of miners during the early 1860s. The rambunctious mining town of Pinos Altos sprang up and soon included a growing number of gamblers, shills, saloon owners, prostitutes, and others ready to make their living from miners. The Mimbreños' already poor opinion of Anglos was reinforced in late 1860, when a group of twenty-eight Texans from Pinos Altos descended on the Mimbres Apaches, allegedly to retrieve stock taken by the Indians, and killed several Apaches, including the peaceful leader Elias. The latter event marked a turning point for Victorio, who retaliated with violence. He sent out men who not only retrieved the animals but also killed several Texan herdsmen in the process.

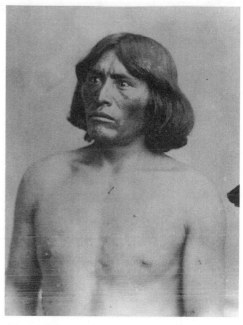

A less well-known photograph of Victorio, which seems to validate the authenticity of his widely published photograph, undated. (Courtesy of the Arizona Historical Society, Tucson, #19748)

Who was to blame for these onslaughts of one race against another? Victorio did not wait for judgment. Instead, he—perhaps understandably—acted in haste and immediately left the area. He and his people were on their way to Chihuahua, a Mexican province where the Mimbreños could mount raids against the much-despised Mexicans, as well as periodically venture into the southwestern United States. An angry and grieving Victorio could see no other solution; he could not watch his people starve to death and die of illness on ill-supplied reservations. Had he remained in the Pinos Altos area, however, he would have discovered that some Anglos supported the Indians. For example, Steck's assistant, Acting Agent Pinckney R. Tully, reported that the attack was "unprovoked" and "without the least cause of justification." He added that even the settlers in the Mimbres Valley thought the Apaches "were not the guilty ones." Still, the event was serious enough to cause a number of settlers to leave the area. One, Mima Wright of Tularosa, on her way to California with her family, wrote, "Pa altered his mind of staying on the ranch for another year" because "he thought the Indians were becoming worse."

Surely the part of Victorio that hoped for peace had misgivings about his pugnacious attitude, but two outrages occurred in 1861 that hardened his position. Early in the year, the *Mesilla Times* of February 7 reported that "the Overland Stage from the West was fired into some two miles the other side of Apache Pass by a large body of Indians." At subsequent peace talks, American soldiers seized the Chiricahua Apache leader Cochise, along with some of his kin, with the intention of holding them hostage until Anglo demands were met. Through a hole cut in the wall of his tent-prison, Cochise escaped. In retaliation, soldiers killed at least one of Cochise's relatives. Cochise gave support to Victorio and his Mimbreños by proclaiming open rebellion against Anglos. The second atrocity involved Mangas Coloradas. Anglos in Pinos Altos seized Mangas, tied him to a tree, and beat him severely with ox goads until his back was broken and bloody. After being released, the great man was left to stagger to his horse, which carried him to a place near Ojo Caliente where he could recover. Although Victorio knew about Mangas Coloradas's ordeal, he said nothing, allowing the older man to retain whatever dignity he had left.

In the meantime, the U.S. Civil War began, diverting soldiers and attention from the Indian problems in the West. When the soldiers withdrew, the Overland Stage stopped running and issues of government rations ceased. Victorio and other Apache leaders were surprised to find themselves largely in control of the Mimbres Valley. Victorio again acted in haste and anger. He and his followers became audacious, turning to settlers for food, horses, and other goods, taking what they needed and leaving death behind them as revenge for past wrongs. In 1862, however, the Apaches' short-lived dominance was shattered when Lt. Col. John R. Baylor, a Texan in charge of Confederate forces and the self-proclaimed governor of "Arizona," decided to "reconquer" the Apaches. In March, he ordered volunteer rangers to lure Indians into Indian agencies and settled areas "for the purpose of making peace." Further, he ordered them to "kill all the grown Indians and take the children prisoners and sell them" into slavery. Although Confederate president Jefferson Davis removed Baylor from his post late in 1862, the colonel continued to maintain that it was absolutely necessary to exterminate what he called "the hostile and treacherous tribes."

At the same time, Victorio and other leaders discovered that another threat to their newfound dominance was approaching New Mexico Territory. Eighteen hundred soldiers known as the California Column marched eastward to capture the Southwest for the Union and enforce white control of the area. In June 1866, the Apache leaders Mangas Coloradas, Victorio, Cochise, and Geronimo led their men against advance parties of the Column at Apache Pass. In requital, the Union leader, Brig. Gen. James Henry Carleton, issued an order to kill all Indian men wherever they might be found. This directive led to the death of Mangas Coloradas who, in January 1863, found himself a prisoner at Fort McLane. Because the commanding officer, Joseph R. West, inferred that he wanted Mangas shot, the leader was dead by morning. Victorio's scouts reported to him that soldiers had buried Mangas only to dig the body up, cut off the head, and boil the skull clean. For Victorio, this mutilation was an unspeakable affront because Apaches believed that a person's body went through the afterworld in the condition it was in at the time of death.

By the end of 1863, Victorio readied himself to fill the breach left by Mangas Coloradas. The young and hopeful Victorio had matured into a leader whose optimism was tempered by bitter memories and disillusionment with Anglos. Still, when Dr. Michael Steck, now superintendent of Indian Affairs in the area, advanced his own solution to the unremitting "Indian question," Victorio was guardedly hopeful. Steck recommended that related groups of Indians—such as the Mimbres and Mescaleros—be assigned to reasonably satisfactory lands near forts where military personnel could protect them from "the encroachments of settlers and the consequent evils that always result from a free intercourse with the white population."

What Victorio could not know was that although Steck was pro-Indian, he too harbored underlying racialist and colonialist attitudes. In one of Steck's reports, for example, he argued for the destruction of "absurd" Indian customs, which among the Mimbreños included burning the property of a dead person and holding a four-day ceremony when a girl reached puberty. According to Steck, at puberty rituals, tribespeople danced and made the "night hideous with their songs from five to ten days." In place of such "barbarous" practices, Steck recommended that Indians, like Anglos, learn to "accumulate & retain property," land they would learn to farm. Steck also argued that it was far too expensive to exterminate Indians, which he thought would cost three billion dollars annually, when they could be sustained on reservations for about one-twentieth of that cost.

Victorio could only watch as the seemingly tireless Steck put forth his reservation plan again and again. Unfortunately, Steck had a powerful opponent in Brig. Gen. James Henry Carleton, who came to New Mexico Territory with the California Column and first fought Apaches at Apache Pass. Because he was a military leader, Carleton was in a different relationship to the Apaches than was Steck. As superintendent of Indian Affairs, Steck hoped to establish what he believed were humanitarian policies, whereas Carleton wanted Apaches to behave in an orderly fashion and obey Anglo law. The general made clear that Indians who refused to cooperate with what he called his "plan" would be eliminated, including women and children. The rest were to be sent to the Bosque Redondo Reservation, some 12,000 acres of bleakness, sand, and wind near Fort Sumner, established in 1862 expressly to accommodate Indians.

In 1863, under duress, between 400 and 500 Mescaleros arrived at the Bosque Redondo. Only a few Mimbres Apaches joined them. Although Victorio reportedly met with one of Carleton's representatives in Pinos Altos, saying he and his people were tired of war and wanted "to make peace, a lasting peace," he never led his Mimbreños to the Bosque. Victorio appeared two-faced to Anglos, but his actions were soon justified. In 1864, Navajo Indians who survived the "long walk" from Arizona began strag-gling in. By mid-1865, Navajos at the Bosque Redondo numbered around 8,000. Land that could not support the Mescaleros was totally inadequate for so many additional people. In addition, Navajos, who were traditional ene-mies of Apaches, took the opportunity to harass the relatively few Apaches, especially by stealing their stock. Apache folklore had it that when smallpox hit the Navajos, so many died that Anglo authorities ordered them to dump their dead in the Pecos River, which was the Mescaleros' source of water. Two young Mescalero women recalled their horror at finding a partly decomposed corpse full of maggots as they dipped their water jars into the river. According to legend, that very night, November 3, 1865, the Mescaleros deserted the Bosque Redondo to return to their former camp on the Bonito River north of Fort Stanton.

Meanwhile, Victorio's Mimbreños had to exist. Leaving young, old, and infirm family members behind in safe havens, as in the San Mateo Mountains, Victorio's men raided settlers' stock. They also went on cam-paigns seeking revenge—an important element of Apache culture—for dead Apaches. Sometimes, able-bodied women supplemented men's num-bers. In the Apache cultures, women had their own sphere of influence. Also, women with ability and strength served as "head women," who organ-ized other women for such tasks as foodgathering and who spoke to war parties the day before they left on a mission. Given the position of Apache women, it was not surprising that a number of married women accompa-nied their husbands on hunting and military expeditions. Rather than living with their husbands, women performed the tedious work of setting up camps, making meals, and providing medical care. Moreover, they dug rifle pits, built stone breastworks, and stood guard. When fighting began, such women as Siki and Gouyan among the Mimbres Apaches who carried knives, pistols, and other weapons, fought beside their husbands.

During the mid-1860s, Victorio's followers executed more forays than ever. From the Anglo perspective, Apaches heedlessly took their animals,

killed people who happened to be in the way, and imposed terror throughout the area. Victorio's adept troops even seized military herds. In spite of
what he viewed as successes, he understood that things were about to
change. During late 1864 and early 1865, he heard from his scouts and from
traders and travelers that the war the Anglos fought among themselves was
nearing an uneasy end. With apprehension Victorio watched grizzled war
veterans, Confederate and Union, fill places in the Indian-fighting army of
the Southwest. He was right to fear these veterans. One soldier who went
west in 1868 thought that Apaches were "savages in all that the word
implies." Victorio also heard that the citizens of Pinos Altos and surrounding towns raised such a cry that it was heard in the territorial capital, Santa
Fe. In 1866, outraged citizens sent petitions to the Santa Fe New Mexican
imploring officials to establish a reservation for the Mimbreños in their
homeland of Ojo Caliente "to give peace to this section of the territory."
Instead, the territorial legislature extended to Indian-fighters the right to
form volunteer companies, hunt Indians, and take for their pay any plunder
they found, even keeping Indian captives as slaves.

At this point in his life, Victorio did not have much faith in the ability
of Anglo leaders to agree on anything, much less select a good site and con-
struct a feasible agency. In his view, which had become increasingly
jaundiced over the years, Anglos had no intention of leaving Indians in their
homelands. Rather, they wanted to make Indians dependent and unable to
feed or protect themselves, looking to the U.S. government for direction. In
fact, in 1874 the secretary of the Interior told members of Congress, "I
regard the destruction of such game as Indians subsist upon as facilitating
the policy of the Government, of destroying their hunting habits, coercing
them on reservations, and compelling them to begin to adopt the habit of
[white] civilization."

Adding to Victorio's pessimism was confusion resulting from the rapid
succession of military officers, government officials, Indian agents, and missionaries who arrived in New Mexico. A few of the newcomers, including
Territorial Governor Robert B. Mitchell, continued to pronounce Indians
"outlaws" and to call for their extermination. Those who were sympathetic
to the Apaches often departed in disgust or despair. Even the good Dr. Steck
gave up; in 1866 he resigned his post to try his hand at a commercial venture.

Compounding the problem, the Bosque Redondo reservation experiment began to collapse in 1866. Because of the controversy he had caused,
General Carleton's superiors ordered him to leave New Mexico Territory
and rejoin his regiment in San Antonio. The Bosque Redondo reservation,
with eight Apaches and more than 7,000 Navajos, struggled on until 1868,

when Gen. William Tecumseh Sherman visited the reservation. In horror at the abject conditions he found there, Sherman ended the experiment and eventually agreed to allow the Navajo to return to their homeland.

Part of the dilemma was that the U.S. government lacked a clear Indian policy. On the one hand, it acted forcefully by scattering handfuls of forts and soldiers over the West; on the other, it turned into a benevolent "father," luring Indians into forts for peace talks with food and gifts. Also, during the late 1860s, federal officials had to cope with post–Civil War problems, especially Reconstruction, and were thus unable or unwilling to give the time and attention Indian resettlement demanded in the West. Complicating matters even more were newspaper editors who, now deprived of Civil War news, happily set about sensationalizing reports from the West.

In 1869, however, new hope blossomed when the "peace policy" of the "Great Father," President Ulysses S. Grant, began to influence New Mexico. Fortunately for Victorio and his Mimbreños, the new program resulted in the appointment of 1st Lt. Charles E. Drew as agent to the Apaches. Drew was determined to make contact with leaders of Apache bands who had been at war for almost eight years. Drew spoke with the Mimbres Apache leader Loco who said he wanted "a good peace," but Victorio, now wary and distrustful of Anglos, remained in the mountains. Not until that fall did Drew meet with the highly skeptical Victorio. In October 1869, and again on January 1, 1870, Victorio reluctantly agreed to do whatever was necessary for peace between Anglos and Apaches.

Victorio had numerous misgivings. He was no longer certain that peaceful coexistence was possible. In addition, he and his followers resented giving up their free and roving way of life. Yet Victorio realized the cost of raiding, especially in lives lost. When a small appropriation for supplies came from the Indian Office, he gradually settled his people near Cañada Alamosa, a Mexican town in the vicinity of Ojo Caliente. The Mimbreños had long favored this area, partly because it was a holy place where the deity White-painted Woman had appeared to them and partly because it offered good hunting and gathering. Victorio was pleased with Agent Drew, whom he judged one of the best the Apaches ever had. Unfortunately, on June 5, 1870, Drew died trying to apprehend cattle rustlers.

The first years of the 1870s were more chaotic than ever for Victorio and his impoverished Mimbreños. Agent 1st Lt. Argalus Garey Hennisee and U.S. Special Agent William Arny met with Apache leaders, ranging from Victorio to the feared Cochise, to find a location where the Apaches would be free of illegal traders in whiskey and ammunition as well as from corrupt or agitated Anglos. Finally, a site was chosen on the Tularosa River, approximately eighty miles west of Socorro. Victorio and others were to have no choice; they would move to the new reservations or be hunted as "hostiles." Despite this threat, Victorio and several Mimbreño lieutenants, including Loco and Nana, refused to move to the Tularosa area. Because Indians around Cañada Alamosa numbered in the hundreds, officials granted the truculent Apaches a limited reprieve.

In March 1871, the proposed move to the Tularosa area was again in the works. Fearful of more fighting and loss of lives, Victorio agreed to move his band to the Tularosa site. After much delay, Victorio, along with Loco, rode into Tularosa on May 24, 1871. Soon, the half-built agency, a bumbling agent, and inadequate rations alienated Victorio and others who again saw their followers

Chief Nana, who led the Warm Springs Apache after Victorio's death and is best known for "Nana's Raid," 1885. (Courtesy of the Arizona Historical Society, Tucson, #12563)

hungry and ill. During the fall of 1872, Victorio met with Brig. Gen. O. O. Howard, sent west by President Grant as a special Indian commissioner. Afterward, Victorio declared his intention to march his people back to Ojo Caliente, where Howard had "promised" to build a fort. Howard agreed that he had indeed promised to establish a fort provided that all Apache leaders, including Cochise, brought their people in. Although Victorio arranged a meeting between the two men, Howard could not persuade Cochise to relocate near Ojo Caliente.

Without his consent, Victorio was assigned to the new Tularosa agency, which never lived up to hopes for it. Again disgruntled with poor conditions and the lack of adequate supplies, a number of Mimbreños resumed raids in the Tularosa neighborhood and as far away as Old Mexico. Although Victorio himself was usually present at Tularosa, his men—for the first time since the mid-1860s—outwardly rebelled against the U.S. Thus, even though Victorio appeared to be at peace, his reputation as a war leader grew and the number of his followers increased. When Tularosa closed, Victorio moved back to the Ojo Caliente site, where talk began about "concentrating"

Indians on the San Carlos Reservation northeast of Globe (founded 1876), Arizona. At Ojo Caliente, Victorio and Loco maintained a dour silence. It soon became apparent that more Apaches were off reservation lands than on. Apache bands made short stays at reservations, hunting and raiding in between times. Others stayed hidden in the mountains, sometimes coming in for rations, especially during the winter. As a result, agents noted the appearance and disappearance of Indians unknown to them.

To deal with what Anglos saw as an impending crisis, troops were sent to the New Mexico Territory, notably the African American Ninth and Tenth Cavalries and the Twenty-fourth Infantry, also known as buffalo soldiers because Indians thought the black men's hair resembled that of the bison. Thus were members of two aggrieved races pitted against each other. Black soldiers were, however, on a different trajectory than that of the Apaches. Rather than being confined to reservations, beginning in 1869, African American men were offered the opportunity to serve as Indian fighters in the West. Yet the buffalo soldiers, arriving in companies in New Mexico Territory in late 1875 and early 1876, also felt the sting of racial prejudice. Called "darkies" and "niggers," they were blamed for all manner of problems. One irate white officer declared that he wished that "every God damned nigger was in hell and that the Indians would kill every God damned one of them." Although the buffalo soldiers encountered the difficulties posed by a cultural triangle composed of red, white, and black, they soon proved themselves, also mastering Indian-style guerilla warfare.

In April 1876, the expected crisis began to take shape. When the Ninth Cavalry traveled from Santa Fe to Ojo Caliente, they found Victorio's Mimbres, as well as other Apaches, milling around, disgruntled, and well armed. The men had newer rifles, carbines, and revolvers, whereas the women and boys carried lesser-quality arms. To the soldiers, Victorio, Loco, and Nana announced their intention to make peace with the Mexican state of Sonora and to raid U.S. territories from there. Victorio grimly declared that he would do better at war with the United States than at peace. He said he could no longer restrain his young men, who could sell purloined mules and horses to Mexicans for everything they needed, including excellent arms and ample ammunition.

Even though numerous observers, including Col. Edward Hatch of the Ninth Cavalry, pointed out that this tumult could be stopped by the appearance of adequate rations, the needed supplies were not forthcoming. Because of Anglo arguments, inefficiency, and corruption, the Apaches were stronger than they had ever been. As a result, Anglos everywhere were in an uproar, demanding that the government "do something." An increasing number of Anglos spoke on behalf of Native Americans. Back east, where an Indian reform movement was taking shape, its members, including former abolitionists, criticized everyone from the president to Indian agents. In the West, some people thought the philosophy of Manifest Destiny was at fault. In 1868, for example, army wife Margaret Carrington declared that colonialism—popularly called Manifest Destiny—gave American Indians few alternatives: "abandon his home, fight himself to death, or yield to the white man's mercy."

In this growing protest against ill treatment of Indians, the military received the sharpest censure of all. During the early 1870s, white Nebraska settler Caroline Winne expressed her frustration by wrongly accusing Gen. Philip H. Sheridan of being "drunk all the time in Chicago in his fine house." She also alleged that Gen. William T. Sherman had never fought an Indian and "knew nothing about them." Perhaps statements by Sheridan in the late 1860s and early 1870s that "Indians required to be soundly whipped, and the ringleaders ... hung, their ponies killed, and such destruction of their property as will make them very poor" and by Sherman in 1871 that "Indians are of a mischievous nature; semi-hostile, and would be converted into hostile the very moment troops are withdrawn" brought such ire down upon them.

In New Mexico, Anglos also indicted other Anglos. In Las Vegas in the late 1870s, the *Daily Optic* suggested that "the government would gain a chip or two by discharging [Col. Edward] Hatch and hiring Victorio to command the troops in New Mexico. Anything for economy." But a military man, Capt. John G. Bourke, who rode with General Crook saw the situation as being created by civilians. He maintained that "deceit by whites caused rebellion, leading in turn to defeat or exhaustion resulting in surrender, followed by false promises and/or illegal whiskey-selling by the whites, which aroused fresh rebellion."

In the meantime, Victorio found his immediate situation growing ever more perilous. Personally, Victorio was responsible for an extended family of fifteen people: his wife, five children, and four other dependents, as well as his son Washington, his wife, and three other dependents. In addition, Victorio headed a village of twenty-seven households, which could be attacked without warning. Indeed, on September 8, a company of the Ninth Cavalry hit Victorio's settlement, burning the dwellings along with outlying cornfields. Some of Victorio's followers fled to the mountains. One month later, those remaining fought off an assault by a local group. Meanwhile, even though newspapers in Silver City, Mesilla, and Las Cruces called black soldiers "cowards," companies of the Ninth Cavalry risked their lives scouting the rugged mountains and deep valleys for mutinous Apaches.

The one hope of Anglos was that John P. Clum, who in August 1874 had become the "boy agent" at San Carlos, could work a miracle—which he almost did. In his early twenties and ambitious, Clum hoped to "concentrate" five agencies of Apaches at San Carlos under his leadership. With the help of his San Carlos Apache Indian police force, Clum, who had received discretionary powers to implement the concentration program, transferred more than 3,000 Apaches to San Carlos. In 1877, Victorio succumbed, but stashed arms and other supplies near Ojo Caliente before leading his people to San Carlos. Although Clum wisely incorporated Victorio into the San Carlos establishment by appointing him a judge of the Apache Court, Victorio hated San Carlos with its poor soil, malaria, the usual inefficient system of rationing, and the presence of old enemies—the Coyotero Apaches. Also, Agent Clum was soon distracted by arguments between himself and several army officers. When a charge of mismanagement sent him reeling, he resigned from the Indian service as of July 1. Clum later wrote that "at high noon on July 1, 1877, I mounted my favorite horse and hit the trail for Tucson. ... Thirty-five years elapsed before I again returned to San Carlos."

The September after Clum's departure, a dissatisfied Victorio gathered some 300 of his followers, seized military horses, and fled into the mountains with Indian police, local volunteers, and various military commands hard behind. Victorio split his Mimbreños into small groups, the members of which disappeared into the mountains like so many ghosts. Some Mimbreños eventually reappeared near Ojo Caliente where they set up camps. Others materialized at Fort Wingate, wanting to talk peace. Within a few days, Victorio, Loco, and more than a hundred Mimbres Apaches joined them at Wingate. Victorio and Loco made it clear that although Fort Wingate was adequate, they would prefer Ojo Caliente and would not return to San Carlos.

Anglo officials gave in, at least temporarily. By the end of 1877, Victorio and many Mimbres Apaches were back at Ojo Caliente. During the hard winter months, more Apaches arrived. A few relatives, but none of Victorio's, were brought from San Carlos. During the spring of 1878, Victorio learned that the Mimbres were to return to San Carlos. He went in to Fort Wingate, arguing that everything from the bad water at San Carlos to the abusive Coyoteros mitigated against his going there. His arguments were useless, however. The Ninth Cavalry soldiers assigned to escort Victorio and the Mimbreños from New Mexico to Arizona spent a few days scouting the mountains for Mimbreños who had suddenly disappeared, and then set out with fewer than 170 Indians. On the way to San Carlos, rain, snow, and mud mired wagons and travelers alike, yet the Ninth brought in nearly 170 people.

Victorio was not among them. Evidently, he had once again lost hope and, with his forces, was engaged in raiding the entire Rio Grande valley. Although a few Mimbreños had gone to the agency near Fort Stanton where they lived with the Mescaleros, many others traveled with Victorio. Their onslaughts resulted in lives lost, both Anglo and Mimbreño. The diminishing number of Mimbres Apaches so demoralized Victorio that in the summer of 1879, he stopped raiding and went to the Mescalero agency. To Anglo officials Victorio said that he wanted "peace and quiet" and assurance that he would "not be sent to San Carlos." But in August, he learned that "a paper was out against him," meaning that three indictments stood against him in Grant County for horse stealing and murder. Although no record exists of Victorio ever killing an Anglo, he feared a white court.

Victorio's flight in 1879 was his final one. Exhausted by his attempts to negotiate peace and provide sustenance for his followers, Victorio decided to go down fighting. Victorio's War, as it is called, began in New Mexico's Black Range, where Victorio, Nana, their fighting men and women, and families initiated one last attempt to save what remained of their race, their culture, their lands, and, perhaps most important, their self-respect.

Mescaleros who fought with Victorio reported that his sister, Lozen, rode at his side. Although Lozen is a controversial historical figure in that some scholars hold that she was more myth than reality, others support her existence. Certainly, Mescalero Apaches believe that Lozen was a real person. According to them, she had all-important abilities in many areas. Along with other Apache girls, Lozen had been trained in hunting, fighting, and the handling of horses. Even in her youth, she showed great promise as a hunter, raider, and fighter. She was so competent in handling horses that some people credited her with having power over them. Having special power was very important to the Apaches, and those who had it often took leadership roles. Apaches generally believe that Lozen also had power to help people heal but, most importantly, she could divine the whereabouts of the enemy. She stood in an open space, held out her arms, turned slowly, and prayed: "Ussen, Great One above, this I pray. Not for myself but for my people. Grant that they may be protected from the enemy by knowing its position." Lozen's hands would tingle and turn purplish in color when she pointed toward the enemy; the sensations intensified when the foe was close to Victorio's camp. Because of her military skills and her power, Lozen was a "ceremonial woman" who sat in council with the men, offering advice to Victorio when he asked. Although unmarried, she also rode with the men.

Toos-Day-Zay, daughter of Chief Mangas Coloradas, wife of Chief Cochise, and mother of Apache leader Naiche, 1885. (Courtesy of the Arizona Historical Society, Tucson, #19740)

After all, it was a time of crisis when gifted, spiritually motivated people were needed—irrespective of marital status. To Victorio, she was essential to his success. He once said of her: "Lozen is my right hand. Strong as a man, braver than most, and cunning in strategy, Lozen is a shield to her people."

Mescaleros maintain that Lozen's presence and power to locate the enemy help explain Victorio's continuous victories in 1879, when he and his forces wreaked more destruction and led more U.S. troops astray than anyone would have predicted possible. Even the first-rate buffalo soldiers of the Ninth Cavalry had difficulty finding Victorio and his elusive Mimbres Apaches. Victorio seemed to have the knack of making himself and his followers invisible. On more than one occasion, his soldiers foiled enemies by holding in front of them uprooted bushes they moved surreptitiously or by wrapping their horses' hooves with buckskin to muffle sound. Some U.S. soldiers complained that chasing Victorio was like trying to scent out a puff of smoke, whereas official records put it more formally: "the campaign resolved itself into a chase of the hostiles from one range of mountains to another, with frequent skirmishes, but no decisive fights, until the Indians again escaped into old Mexico, the Mexican Government declining to allow further pursuit on their territory."

As a war leader, Victorio drew on everything he had learned during his difficult life, especially a range of military techniques and strategies. For instance, as a master hunter, raider, and combatant, he understood the importance of surprise. After leaving the Mescalero Reservation in mid-1879, he almost immediately launched an unexpected foray that killed eight black guards and ran off the Ninth Cavalry's horses. A few days later, Victorio's men took additional military horses from McEver's ranch south of the mining town of Hillsboro, and killed ten American soldiers and wounded several more in a five-hour fight.

Victorio was also unrelenting in his use of the ambush. In early November 1879, a party of eighteen Mexicans from the town of Carrizal pursued Victorio into the Candelaria Mountains south of El Paso, where Apache women and children had erected a *ranchería*, or camp, for the men. Of course, Victorio's scouts spotted the Mexicans and gave warning. With eerie quiet—only in Hollywood films did Apaches use nerve-shattering war cries to let enemies know they were coming—Victorio's men took places behind high rock peaks on each side of a pass. As the Mexicans rode through below, the silent Apaches on the north side suddenly opened fire on them, driving the Mexicans against rocks on the south side. Other of Victorio's men, who had waited above the spot, killed all the Mexicans. Knowing that more Mexicans would come to investigate when the first group failed to return, Victorio waited. Thirty-five more men rode into the pass, falling into the same trap. By the time U.S. soldiers and Texas Rangers arrived, Mimbreño women had packed up the encampment, and the entire group was gone from the spot, known thereafter known as Tinaja de Victorio.

In the following months, Victorio's intelligence and ingenuity led to many successes for the Apaches. For example, as he and his people traveled, he cached supplies along the way and returned to them unerringly in this land that he had once roamed. When they stopped, Victorio had his people build stone breastworks—just in case. Many nights, he ordered his men to sleep fully dressed, with knives concealed in their knee-high moccasins and emergency food bags tied to their bodies or to their already bridled and saddled horses. On some occasions, American soldiers reported that Victorio even sang "good medicine" chants during a fight, taunted soldiers to attack him, or goaded Indian scouts to join him and his people.

Over time, white and black soldiers began to believe Victorio was an apparition, an eerie shadow they could not find, much less capture. His followers could travel incredible distances, even with women and children. Unaccompanied Mimbreño men moved faster yet, covering as much as seventy-five miles a day. In a fight, Victorio's men could mount horses with a leap and zigzag through enemy fire while shooting and reloading their own rifles. And, even though U.S. troops, including the African American Ninth Infantry, patrolled the border between the United States and Mexico, Victorio's people slipped back and forth to escape either Mexican or U.S. troops who were not permitted to cross the border in pursuit of Victorio.

Yet, as Victorio knew it would, a turning point finally arrived. Three circumstances wore him down. First, he did not have a supply depot as U.S. troops did. In addition to frequent fighting, his men had to raid constantly for horses, weapons, ammunition, and food, sometimes from settlers and sometimes from the U.S. military. Second, Victorio commanded a finite number of hunters and fighters rather than a standing, professional army. Although a number of Mescaleros, and at times Juh's and Geronimo's Chiricahua Apaches, joined Victorio, he could not rely on recruitment and the draft as did the United States. Finally, U.S. military employed Apache scouts, mostly from Arizona, who were able to read Indian sign and were expert trackers. The scouts made it possible for soldiers sometimes to follow Victorio's trail and even occasionally find his camp.

These handicaps began to hurt him in 1880. In early April, a stunned Victorio watched thirsty and exhausted soldiers of the black Ninth Cavalry, along with twenty-one Apache scouts, straggle into the Mimbreños' haven in Hembrillo Canyon. Victorio's people, reinforced by some 250 recently arrived Mescaleros, opened fire. After Anglo reinforcements arrived, an eighteen-hour battle forced the Mimbreños and Mescaleros to flee the canyon. A month later near the Palomas River, Victorio suffered his first real defeat and lost some of his best fighters. Early in June, his son Washington, who had played a major role in earlier campaigns, was killed by soldiers of the Ninth Cavalry at a battle in Cook's Canyon. Victorio and his band soon escaped to Mexico, leaving stymied American troops sitting at the border. To supply themselves and their families, his troops raided in Chihuahua, trading their booty mostly at the town of Gallego.

With the guidance of Mescaleros who knew the country, Victorio and his forces also moved northward into west Texas. After engaging with Col. Benjamin H. Grierson and his Tenth Cavalry, Victorio bolted back to Old Mexico. Then, returning to the United States, he fell into a trap set for him at Rattlesnake Springs, Texas, by Grierson and his troops. When a fully loaded military supply train appeared, Victorio's men attacked it only to see black soldiers of the Twenty-fourth Infantry leap from the wagons and fire into their midst. Although Victorio's men got away, an official report showed that Anglo soldiers had captured his supply camp, including "twenty-five head of cattle" and "a large quantity of beef and other provisions on pack animals." Clearly, American buffalo soldiers chased Victorio into Mexico in a weak and demoralized condition.

Victorio's escape to Old Mexico would be his last. In Chihuahua, citizens fed up with Apache raids organized for their own defense. Led by scout and Indian fighter Joaquín Terrazas, a party of men set out in September 1880 to find Victorio. More men, including Lieutenant Baylor and thirteen Texas Rangers, joined along the way until Terrazas commanded 350 fighters. By October 8, Terrazas had weeded out ninety men he judged "worthless." After many false starts, his scouts trailed Victorio to

Tres Castillos, three stark out-crops of rock on a bleak plain. During the first night of the battle, Victorio's troops hastily erected stone breastworks, which were overrun the next day by Terrazas's force. The fight ended with one-on-one struggles; men literally wrestled for their lives.

Sometime during the conflict on October 16, the nearly sixty-year-old Victorio met his end. A Mexican soldier, Mauricio Corredor, claimed to have shot him, a boast generally accepted as true by Anglo historians of the battle. But James Kaywaykla, a four-year-old Mescalero boy present at Tres Castillo who escaped with his mother, later recounted that Victorio and three others had chosen "to fall on their own knives" rather than be shot down by Mexicans. The Apaches who went to Tres Castillo to tend to the bodies confirm this story.

From right to left: an unidentified runaway slave who became a scout and two unnamed Apache scouts who rode with Capt. Jack Crawford when he pursued Chief Victorio into Mexico. Photograph taken at Fort Wingate, New Mexico, undated. (Courtesy of the Arizona Historical Society, Tucson, #50140)

Terrazas, however, grabbed the major credit for freeing Americans and Mexicans of Victorio. Terrazas and his men marched around the city of Chihuahua carrying poles on which swung not just the scalps but the entire heads of the defeated Apaches. A *Chicago Times* correspondent claimed that Victorio's head was among them. According to the questionable and unverified report, Mauricio Corredo carried the head, its long black hair streaked with gray.

This macabre end to Victorio's life brought to conclusion the Victorio "war" of 1879–1880, but not the Indian wars in the Southwest. Hundreds of Apaches continued to believe that they might yet wrest a measure of justice from their adversaries. Others preferred, like Victorio, to die fighting rather than from malnutrition or disease. Victorio's successor, Nana, who had been away hunting horses during the battle at Tres Castillo, was one of the latter. According to James Kaywaykla, the Mimbres Apaches now looked upon themselves as Indeh, or dead people, yet the aged and lame Nana organized an offensive against settlers to avenge the deaths of Victorio and others. According to military records, in July, Nana "reentered New Mexico" and "whirled through the territory, plundering and killing a number of people." On August 27, the *Silver City New Southwest and Grant County Herald* lamented that eight days earlier in Ruidoso's Gavilan Canyon, an entire company of the Ninth Cavalry "marched into a deadly ambush" set by Nana and his fighters. The report added that the "red devils" killed three and wounded eight, and seized about thirty horses and one hundred rounds of ammunition.

Like Nana, Victorio's sister Lozen was a hold out. At the time of the Tres Castillo battle, Lozen was escorting a pregnant woman back to the Mescalero Reservation in New Mexico. The Apaches believe that if Lozen had been with Victorio, she would have warned him about the proximity of Terrazas's forces. After Victorio's death, Lozen fought with Nana and later with Geronimo until she was captured and sent in 1886, along with another woman fighter, Tah-des-te, to a Florida prison. A photograph of the prisoners substantiates the women's presence. The following year, Lozen's captors moved her to Mount Vernon Barracks in Alabama, where she died of tuberculosis. Her date of death is unknown and, because the Apaches buried her secretly according to their custom, her grave site is unmarked.

In the meantime, during the late nineteenth century the vanquished Victorio assumed legendary status in the Mimbres Valley. Anglo settlers in the area could forget neither his courage nor his bold and daring strategies. In the mid-1880s, a newly built hotel in the mining town of Hillsboro became the Victorio Hotel. In Silver City about the same time, the Victorio Mining Company operated. Later, during the mid-1890s, James and Sadie Orchard, owners of the Mountain Pride Stage Line based in Kingston, painted a portrait of Victorio on the doors of the company's premier coach. It is unclear whether these actions were in tribute to Victorio or in triumph over the defeat of such a daring foe. A snippet from a mid-1880s report of the Military Division of the Missouri suggests the latter: "the vast section over which the wild and irresponsible tribes once wandered," it read, has been "redeemed from idle waste to become a home for millions of progressive people."

Unsurprisingly, Victorio's people interpret differently the events of his era. Then and now, they celebrate the heroism of Victorio, Lozen, and the other Apaches who rode with them. According to a present-day Mescalero living on the reservation in southeastern New Mexico, Victorio was a hero who sacrificed his life for the good of his followers. A growing number of

Anglos also hold this view. In 1974, the journalist Dan L. Thrapp concluded his study, *Victorio and the Mimbres Apaches*, by stating that Victorio was "the greatest of Apaches of his time perhaps—and he would have been a bulwark of peace had he been dealt with fairly." In Thrapp's view, "The record is not one in which other Americans should take pride."

Clearly, Victorio's reputation lives on. Although he receives far less attention than Cochise or Geronimo, he is remembered and appreciated among Apaches as well as among empathetic Anglos.

CHIEF JOSEPH OF THE NEZ PERCE

A Western Tragedy

RICHARD W. ETULAIN

On the night of September 30, 1877, snow fell quietly and continuously, blanketing the northern Montana plains with a fresh, white cover. The new coating, disarmingly pristine and pure, masked a night of grievous suffering for the Nez Perce Indians. After a surprise attack earlier that day by the Seventh Calvary and hours of murderous fighting, the Indians were pinned down and under siege. Although freedom north into Canada loomed only forty miles away, escape for the brave Nez Perce looked impossible. Their valiant, courageous journey seemed at an end.

For several more days the Nez Perce tried to hold off their pursuers, hoping that aid would come from Sitting Bull's Sioux two or three days distant across the Canadian line. Meanwhile, wounds to many warriors, women, and children, and the freezing cold, took their toll. In the late afternoon of October 5, Chief Joseph rode somberly out of the Nez Perce camp and slowly up the hill to where Gen. O. O. Howard and Col. Nelson Miles were gathered with a small staff. The chief handed over his gun to military leaders, and several other Nez Perce followed suit. Just before his final surrender, Chief Joseph is rumored to have said: "Tell General Howard I know his heart. What he told me before I have it in my heart. I am tired of fighting. ... Hear me, my chiefs. I am tired; my heart is sick and sad. From where the sun now stands I will fight no more forever."

After outwitting the military for more than three months in their 1,400-mile retreat toward freedom, the Nez Perce were forced to surrender to their pursuers. Nonetheless, in those final, torturous days in the Bear's Paw Mountains of Montana, the Nez Perce and their leader Chief Joseph gained a notable place in the history of frontier conflicts between Native Americans and the U.S. military. In one respect, the events of 1877 are a story of tragedy; in another, a heroic struggle to maintain the freedom of a valiant, courageous people.

Chief Joseph at the time of the 1877 war and retreat. (Courtesy of Washington State University Libraries, Pullman, #79-027)

The earliest history of the Nez Perce contained none of the conflict and violence that marked the lives of so many tribal members in that tragic summer of 1877. From the earliest times, the varied bands of the Nez Perce or Nee-Me-Poo (also Nimipu), resided in the Wallowa Mountains and the nearby canyons of the Clearwater, Salmon, Snake, and Imnaha Rivers. In the converging corners of modern-day northeastern Oregon, western Idaho, and southeastern Washington, the Nez Perces (pierced noses) lived for hundreds of years before any white visitors came to their lands. The creation of these forested and canyon lands was a central part of the Nez Perce story of origins. According to this narrative, Coyote, that omnipresent figure in many Indian stories, played a shaping role in the creation of the Nez Perce. In one Nee-Me-Poo version, Coyote fights with a huge, malevolent monster that devours animals. By his wiles, Coyote succeeds in getting into the beast's belly with several sharp knives. Once inside, he slices a hole in the behemoth's side, frees the captured animals, and then quickly kills the beast by cutting lose his heart. Coyote then carves up the monster's gigantic body, scattering pieces around the region. Wherever a chunk lands, predecessors of modern Indian tribes spring up, including the Yakima (now Yakama), Spokans, Flatheads, Cayuse, and several other groups. When Coyote sees that the place where the three modern states converge is empty, he sprinkles drops of the beast's blood there. From these red drops on this beautiful land arose the Nee-Me-Poo, "The Real People."

In these homelands, the Nez Perce established their sociocultural traditions. Most of the men and women resided in small villages of approximately fifty people. Living on kouse (or cows) roots, camas bulbs, small animals, and an occasional buffalo, and especially on the yearly run of salmon, the Nee-Me-Poo were closely tied to their natural surroundings. For them the natural and the human were linked, with vibrating spirits emanating from animals, trees, grasses, and humans. The youngest to the oldest Nez Perce took cognizance of these *wayakins*, or special spirits, in their search for life's meanings.

For the most part, the Nee-Me-Poo remained a holistic, stable society until other peoples began to invade their homeland. In September 1805, an advance group of the Lewis and Clark Expedition stumbled into a Nez Perce camp. At first the Nee-Me-Poo were uncertain how to respond. Later, when the larger group of explorers arrived, they brought even more mysteries: the first black man (York) the Nez Perce had encountered, a young Shoshone woman (Sacagawea) and her child, and the largest dog the Indians had ever seen. Should the Nez Perce attack these white, bearded newcomers, or should they provide the requested food and supplies? After a few discussions, they decided to aid the expedition. They furnished dried salmon, camas root cakes (sometimes bringing on violent attacks of flatulence), and directions to the Pacific Ocean. When the explorers returned to the Clearwater country the next spring, they stayed several weeks with the Nee-Me-Poo, waiting for the snow-clogged mountain passes to clear. During these two visits, the Nez Perce and members of the expedition exchanged medical information and horses and competed in several races.

These early, friendly contacts in 1805–1806 paved the way for later accommodations between Americans and the Nez Perce. A half dozen years later, eleven men, hungry, searching for the best path west, and in need of horses, showed up in one of the Nez Perce camps. This new group was part of John Jacob Astor's overland trading contingent bound for the Oregon coast to join with another group of Astor's men coming around by the cape, aiming for a meeting at the mouth of the Columbia River. There the two groups were to reconnoiter and establish a trading post at Astoria. On their way west, Astor's men received valuable aid from the Nez Perce, but when they returned east, without apparent reason, they argued with and sometimes maltreated the Nee-Me-Poo. In the next few years, growing competition between the Americans and the British, during the War of 1812 and on into the 1820s and 1830s, especially for control of the fur trade domain, colored white-Nez Perce relations.

In other ways, the two races discovered common interests. First hearing about Christianity from American visitors and British traders, the Nez Perce became curious about God or, as they said, the Master of Life. Roman Catholic priests also spoke about a Supreme Being. In addition, excitement rose to higher pitch after two young Indians of the Spokan and Kutenai tribes traveled to the Red River region in Canada to study and returned in 1829 with rudimentary skills in reading, writing, and speaking English. They also had with them copies of *The Book* (Bible). Here were stimulating new possibilities for the Nee-Me-Poo that they did not want to overlook. Were they intrigued with the Christian teachings the English-speaking people mentioned, or were they primarily interested in any religion that provided them "medicine" (power) in their daily competitions with nature and other peoples? As historians have argued, quite possibly both; they wanted the spiritual power and magic they had heard about from several sources.

In 1831, spurred on by these happenings, four Nez Perce and three Flathead Indians traveled to St. Louis to find out about white medicine. The Flathead men turned back, and three of the Nez Perce died either in St. Louis or on the return trip. Yet notice of their quest spread to the East Coast. Perhaps it was the famed explorer William Clark, a visitor among the Nee-Mee-Poo in 1805–1806, who sent on their story. At any rate, it was published in church journals in the East in 1833 and helped attract the first group of Protestant missionaries to the Pacific Northwest in 1834. Two years later, Marcus and Narcissa Whitman came to Waiilatpu (near Walla Walla) to be among the Cayuse, and Henry and Eliza Spalding came to Lapwai, to minister to the Nez Perce.

In the next decade or so, the Spaldings became important figures among the Nee-Me-Poo, but not in the way they had planned. To convert the "heathen" Indians to Christianity, Henry Spalding worked indefatigably to build a church, school, and home at Lapwai even as he encouraged the Nez Perce to become farmers. Fiercely stubborn, frequently temperamental, and sometimes violent in his reactions to his charges, Spalding nevertheless modeled eastern, white versions of hard work, diligence, and commitment for the Indians. Eliza Spalding was more appreciated because her gentle, empathetic teaching appealed to the Nee-Me-Poo. Yet, in the long run, the Spaldings sowed more seeds of division than of unity among the Indians. As we shall see, a major cause of the developing factionalism among the Nez Perce derived from the Christian teachings of missionary Spalding.

One of the first of Spalding's converts and a leading figure in Nee-Me-Poo history from 1840 until his death in 1871 was Tuekakas (Old Chief Joseph). Perhaps contacts with the explorers and overlanders, but certainly later connections with the Spaldings, were important shaping influences on the life of Tuekakas. In turn, he became the most influential figure in the life of his son, Young Chief Joseph. Tuekakas, the son of a Cayuse chief and a Nez Perce mother, grew up with his mother's people after she returned home and married a second husband, a chief of the Kallapoon (Nez Perce) band. When Old Joseph was seventeen, his mother died, so he went to live with his Cayuse father. But the pull of the Wallowas in Nee-Me-Poo country was too great. He returned there and never left that cherished homeland.

Of all the whites Old Joseph encountered, Henry Spalding had the largest impact. Three years after Spalding established his mission station at Lapwai, Joseph was baptized in November 1839 into the First Presbyterian Church in Oregon. Over the next few years, Tuekakas became, in the missionary's eyes, an ideal Indian convert to Christianity. Each year, Joseph spent time at the mission station. His sons Joseph (born in 1840) and Ollokot (born in 1844) lived several months at Lapwai each year during their boyhoods. But after the Cayuse murdered the Whitmans in 1847, Spalding left the mission. At the same time, Old Joseph had a falling-out with some of his fellow Nee-Me-Poo. These events helped drive him back to his homeland in the Wallowas. Still, Tuekakas remained friendly with missionaries and territorial political leaders, for example helping Washington territorial governor Isaac Stevens set up a Nez Perce reservation in 1855.

The dramatic change for Old Joseph came in 1863. Reverberations from that pivotal year reshaped the rest of his life. When American treaty makers tried to force Tuekakas to give up his Wallowa country and move near Lapwai, he exploded in anger. As one historian has written, Old Joseph "denounced the Americans, renounced his church membership, destroyed his New Testament and his American flag, and segregated his group from the settlers as much as possible." Refusing to agree to the treaty and cede his homelands, Old Joseph returned to his Native beliefs and held to them until his death. Young Joseph, now in his early twenties, watched his father make these momentous decisions. Their impact undoubtedly later shaped the son's own decisions in the 1860s and 1870s.

Young Joseph, as the whites would later call him, was born in the spring or summer of 1840 in a cave near Joseph Creek. Missionary Spalding evidently baptized the newborn son as Ephraim, although Joseph would be the name by which he became known. Later, perhaps at the time of his coming-of-age ceremony when he was ten or eleven, he was given the Indian name Hin-mah-too-yah-let-kekht (Thunder Traveling to Loftier Mountain Heights). During his boyhood years, Joseph visited the Lawpai mission, possibly learned some English, and was taught Christian concepts. But he also lived among the Wallowas and may have accompanied his father and family on camas-gathering and buffalo-hunting trips over the Rockies to Montana and down into southeastern Idaho.

Young Joseph's life shifted direction after 1847. After the Whitman martyrdom, factionalism broke out among the Nez Perce. Some Nee-Me-Poo wished to follow closely the teachings of Spalding, others were less inclined in that direction, and still others chose to remain aloof from Christianity. Old Joseph tended to follow the second path, meaning that

Young Joseph and Ollokot now learned primarily from tribal elders and shamans. Gradually, the two sons became Dreamers, following the revivalistic and dream-driven teachings of the Columbia River prophet Smoholla. By the 1850s and 1860s, many of Old Joseph's band were considered Dreamers because of their growing alienation from Christianity, their separation from the mission of Nez Perce, their increasing discontent with government-sponsored treaties, and their telltale long hair brushed into a roll above their foreheads. The Dreamers also taught that no Nee-Me-Poo should become a farmer because turning over the sod meant tearing open their mother's bosom.

Much later, in the year following the Nez Perce War of 1877, Chief Joseph helped prepare an essay for an eastern magazine that summarized his views of that war and events leading up to the conflict. Even though the article passed through a translator and probably an editor or two on its way to publication, and not all the words may be Joseph's, it nonetheless reveals much about his father's influence on his son. Most of all, Young Joseph viewed his father as a man whose hands never spilled white blood. Yet his father was, Joseph said, "the first to see through the schemes of the white man and he warned his tribe to be careful about trading with them." Of even more importance to Joseph, Tuekakas refused to sign the Treaty of 1863 giving up the Wallowa homelands. Another Nee-Me-Poo leader, Lawyer, "was a great talker [and] ... sold nearly all the Nez Perce's country," Joseph continued, but his father held tenaciously to his beautiful Wallowas. The father's implacable opposition to giving up any of his land became the son's lifelong stance.

As Old Joseph grew older in the late 1860s, he remained aloof from the increasing numbers of whites invading the Nez Perce country as miners and settlers. Although Tuekakas seemed to accept the Treaty of 1855, which set up the boundaries of the Nee-Me-Poo Reservation, he and other leaders of the Nee-Me-Poo resented what they considered the supercilious attitudes of Governor Stevens in his treatment of them. In the following months, when Stevens and others failed to fulfill some of their treaty promises and broke other agreements, Nez Perce discontent mounted. Then, when gold discoveries on Nee-Me-Poo reservation lands in 1860–1861 attracted hundreds of prospectors and settlers, Old Joseph and Nez Perce leaders knew that a new, much more dramatic controversy loomed ahead.

In the early 1860s, the U.S. government pressured the Nez Perce to give up most of their lands to make way for the whites flooding into the region. In 1863, as government officials arrived to make a new treaty, Tuekakas stoutly opposed all these moves. He knew that a treaty, if signed, meant that he and his followers would lose all their land in the Wallowas; they would have to give up their annual hunting trips and would be forced onto a much smaller area with all the other pro-treaty Nez Perce. Old Joseph would not sign this new treaty, refusing to budge from the Wallowas. Young Joseph took the same unyielding position. The two became known as nontreaty Nez Perce; they had never signed the treaty, they had not given up their lands, and they would not move.

After 1863, times grew only worse for the nontreaty bands of Old Joseph. Hundreds of prospectors and settlers pushed into their domain. These white invasions took place particularly during the summer months, when the Nez Perce migrated east to gather camas bulbs and used the cooler, greener mountain pastures for their livestock. As Old Joseph was dying in 1871, he swore his son to remember—to "think of our country. ... Always remember that your father never sold his country ... and to "never sell the bones of your father and mother." The son never forgot those words. For more than thirty years he spoke and wrote about his promises to his father to never abandon the Wallowas. As Joseph said later, "A man who would not love his father's grave is worse than a wild animal."

After his father's death, Young Joseph became the major spokesman but not the military commander for most of the nontreaty Nez Perce. He was a caretaker, a camp and diplomatic leader—and a warrior—but not a military chief. From 1871 to 1876, Joseph met with several peace commissioners and military officials to help resolve the growing tensions between the nontreaty Nee-Me-Poo and white settlers. One commissioner who worked with him provided a revealing though rather idealistic profile of the Indian leader in 1876: "He is in full vigor of his manhood, six feet tall, straight, well formed and muscular; his forehead is broad, his perceptive faculties large, his head well formed, his voice musical and sympathetic, his expression usually calm and sedate, when animated marked and magnetic." This observer and others acquainted with Joseph often commented on his "remarkable" "alertness and dexterity in intellectual fencing."

Joseph resolutely held to his and his father's position: the nontreaty Nez Perce had not signed a treaty, they would not move to the reservation stipulated in the Treaty of 1863, and their lands must be protected from the avaricious whites moving illegally onto those lands. Meanwhile, military and governmental officials, under intense pressure from squatters and the State of Oregon, denied the claims of the two Josephs, even though the officials had accepted those claims in the 1860s and early 1870s. Now, said the commissioners in 1876, Joseph's people must give up the Wallowas and relocate to the smaller reservation that encompassed Lapwai and the Christian and treaty Indians. Other meetings continued throughout spring 1877, with the U.S. government putting increased pressure on the nontreaty Nez Perce to resettle within the boundary lines of the Treaty of 1863. When Joseph responded that he would never leave his homeland unless compelled to do so, General Howard moved troops to the area and told Joseph that he had one month to move his people, their livestock, and all their other goods to the reservation headquarters at Lapwai. Resentments among the Nee-Me-Poo, mounting over the past two decades, were nearing the boiling point.

The events that ignited the summer-long conflict occurred in mid-June 1877. As nontreaty bands moved reluctantly toward the reservation lands, they delayed for a brief respite. During the stopover, several young warriors grew increasingly restive and sullen about their forced move. Tempers flared. Then, on June 12, the horse of two young Nez Perce riding double accidentally stepped on a pile of kouse roots. Witnesssing the incident, an angry Nez Perce man yelled at the young riders: "Playing brave you ride over my woman's hand-worked food! If you are so brave, why don't you go kill the white man who killed your father?" He was taunting Wahlitits whose father, Eagle Robe, was murdered two years earlier by a white settler. The taunt quickly fanned smoldering resentments into flaming action.

The next day, Wahlitits and two of his friends set out to find the man who had killed his father. Unsuccessful, they went on "a mission," writes historian Alvin Josephy, "to slay white men who had mistreated Indians." Other members of Chief White Bird's band, including women and children, joined the assault on white settlers. With stolen whiskey fueling tempers, the killing frenzy mounted. Nearly twenty Nez Perce ravaged the settlers they met, killed men, mistreated women and children, and destroyed homes and animals. In the two or three days of the outbreak, about twenty white settlers were murdered and dozens of others chased from their homes. In these violent deeds, the young Nez Perce men fired the first shots of the Nez Perce War of 1877. Their outburst obviously built on nearly twenty years of gathering pressures and growing bad feelings between the Nee-Me-Poo and incoming settlers and miners.

Hearing of the assaults, General Howard reached a quick but mistaken conclusion. He assumed that Chief Joseph, whom he considered the leader of the nontreaty Nez Perce, had encouraged the attacks on the whites. But Joseph and his brother Ollokot were absent from the area. They were returning from a cattle-butchering trip when they heard of the outbreak. Counseling restraint and peace, the two brothers hoped Howard would send a few observers into the inflamed area to find out what had happened. If he should do so, they were convinced, war could still be avoided. Instead,

Howard decided the outbreak had to be put down quickly and decisively. Explaining the happenings two years later, Joseph wrote that Howard blamed "my young men and I blame the white men."

Moving speedily, Howard outfitted about one hundred men of Companies F and H, First Cavalry, and sent them under the command of Capt. David Perry toward the camps of the nontreaty Indians. Had Howard and Perry been more willing to investigate what occurred, war might have been averted. Under mounting pressure from nearby farmers and townspeople to confront the Nez Perce before they crossed the Salmon River and moved toward Montana, Perry went after the Indians—quickly but ineptly. Supporting his troops were about ten nonmilitary volunteers and, revealingly, a few treaty and Christian Nez Perce. Perry moved on the double, south and east from Lapwai, and made contact with the nontreaty Nee-Mee-Poo in White Bird Canyon, near the confluence of White Bird Creek and the Salmon River. After their forced march, the troops were tired—some nearly exhausted—as they moved toward conflict with the Indians.

Early on Sunday, June 17, Captain Perry, believing a direct attack would rout the enemy, went headlong against the Nez Perce. He was mistaken. The Nez Perce, numbering about sixty to seventy warriors, came up from their lodges to meet their foe. From the first shots to the end of Perry's retreat two and a half hours later, the Nez Perce dominated the battle. When the volunteers on the left end of the battle line fell back toward the center of the field and thereby disrupted Perry's other troops, they also allowed the Nez Perce to sweep around and up the left flank of Company F. When the left crumbled and other soldiers suffered the accurate killing fire of the Nee-Me-Poo sharpshooters, a chaotic retreat began. Once out of the line of fire, Perry and his officers surveyed their heavy casualties. Thirty-three soldiers and one officer had been killed and two other soldiers and two volunteers wounded. The Nez Perce suffered no deaths and only two or three wounded.

The brief but decisive battle at White Bird Canyon taught both sides important lessons. The U.S. military should have learned even more. Perry and his officers, as well as their commander, General Howard, in one day ascertained that their foes were quick, dexterous shooters. Yet the soldiers still seemed to think that, given another opportunity, they would surely defeat their "redskin" enemies. That misplaced self-assurance continued for too long before Howard and his charges learned how valiant and mobile the Nez Perce were. Concurrently, the Indians realized a corner had been turned. They could not return to their home country. Since Perry had refused the white flag of parley, the Nee-Me-Poo would have to fight the war that so many of the nontreaty Indians wanted to avoid.

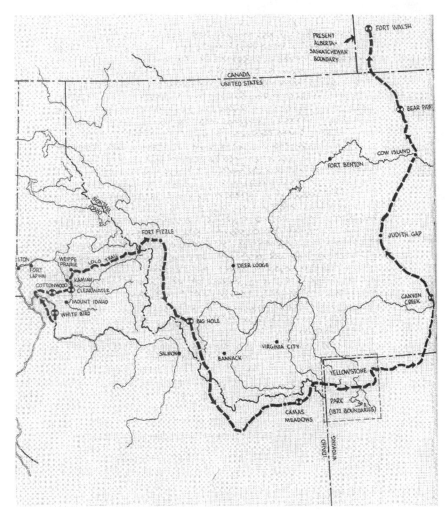

The Nez Perce retreat route and the battle sites of 1877. (Courtesy of the Idaho State Historical Society)

The battle at White Bird Canyon also helped define the primary role Chief Joseph played in the summer of 1877. White Bird, Ollokot, Two Moons, Toohoolhoolzote, and later Looking Glass and Lean Elk were the primary military leaders. From the beginning Joseph helped direct the camp movements, protect the families, and maintain the horse herd. Because all these important duties were paramount to the defense the Nez Perce mounted against Howard's men, Joseph's multiple roles as a nonmilitary leader became increasingly important. True, he was also a warrior and took part in all the major conflicts with the U.S. military, but in no way was he a "Red Napoleon" directing all the military efforts of the Nez Perce, even though later writers and popularizers elevated him to that mythic status.

For nearly a month after their defeat of Captain Perry at White Bird Canyon, the Nez Perce seemed undecided about what direction to follow. During these four weeks before the next important conflict at the Clearwater on July 11–12, the Nee-Me-Poo kept on the move, trying to avoid Howard's expanding forces but unwilling to leave their homeland. On two or three occasions the Indians caught up with their foes or the soldiers accidentally made contact. In these engagements the Nee-Me-Poo either wiped out small clusters of troops who unwisely attacked or kept Howard's men at bay, including three days of hit-and-miss conflict near Cottonwood Creek, south of Lapwai and north of Grangeville. In these skirmishes at Cottonwood, the Nez Perce suffered their first casualty, after nearly fifty soldiers had been killed.

The most far-reaching event of these weeks came on July 1 when some of Howard's forces attacked the camp of Chief Looking Glass. Howard sent Capt. Stephen Whipple to capture this nontreaty leader, who thus far had not joined the fighting Nez Perce. Unfortunately for the soldiers, Whipple miscalculated the distance to Looking Glass's camp, thereby weakening his own plan to carry out a daybreak surprise attack. Instead, later in the morning, when Whipple approached the Indian camp, nearly all the villagers escaped to the nearby woods. But the soldiers did capture the Indians' large pony herds. Even more significant in the long run, the attack on Looking Glass drove him from among the noncombatants into the camps of the warring Nez Perce. As a result, not only did Looking Glass add needed warriors, he also brought considerable experience as a war leader and knowledge of Montana, where he had hunted buffalo and negotiated with the Crow Indians. In several of the next battles with the military, Looking Glass played a notable role in planning strategy.

The decisive conflict that forced the Nez Perce to leave their homelands occurred on the Clearwater River on July 11–12. As military historian Jerome Greene writes, "the Battle of the Clearwater was indisputably a watershed in the army's campaign against the Nez Perces." The number of fighters on both sides expanded significantly just before the clash. On July 7, Looking Glass's people joined the other Nee-Me-Poo, enlarging their camp to about 740 men, women, and children, including about 250 warriors. On some occasions, the Nez Perce women also took up weapons against the soldiers. Meanwhile, Howard's numbers had mushroomed to more than 400 regulars, with another 100 volunteers, packers, and scouts swelling his total to about 500 men. During the two-day battle, the troops capitalized immensely on their superior numbers.

Howard clearly won an important victory on the South Fork of the Clearwater. He took advantage of his numerical superiority and abundant ammunition to defeat his Indian opponents. At times the fighting was close up and ferocious. The Nez Perce warrior Yellow Wolf, whose published reminiscences appeared sixty years later, provided a revealing description of the warfare at Clearwater: "Indians and soldiers—almost together. We could not count the soldiers. There must have been hundreds. Bullets came thicker and thicker." Pushed back by Howard's forces, their leaders unde-cided on what strategy to follow, the Nee-Me-Poo retreated and withdrew from the field. Although Howard's men suffered forty casualties (fifteen dead and twenty-five wounded), they captured the field and valuable sup-plies of the Nez Perce, who lost only four men.

The battle at Clearwater meant something very different for each side. Howard, taking the victory as a large breakthrough in his campaign, cabled his superiors—even contacting President Rutherford B. Hayes—about his win. Yet in his euphoria, Howard underestimated the resiliency and tenacity of his opponents, as he learned in the coming weeks. For the Nez Perce, the outcome at Clearwater forced them to face several large questions: Should they give up and agree to live on the reservation? (This was and remained Chief Joseph's position early in the war.) Should they stay where they were and try to wear down the will of Howard and his forces? Or should they abandon their homelands, head east, and hope to join with friendly tribes there? After considerable discussion and obvious differences of opinion, the Indians, following the leadership of Looking Glass, retreated east. It must have been a momentous, emotional decision for Chief Joseph and his people. Leaving their homeland at this time was traumatic enough. But Joseph, along with many of his followers, could not have known that they would never again come home to their beloved Wallowas.

In the next two weeks, the Nez Perce moved east over the difficult terrain of the Lolo Trail into western Montana. Although the band now included about 200 men and as many as 500 women and children, riding and packing horses for each, and a herd of an additional 2,000 to 3,000 horses, they made good time through the brush and over steep hills and mountains. It was Chief Joseph's primary duty to take care of the planning and implementation of these group movements. Meanwhile, Howard sta-tioned troops at each end of the Lolo Pass to block whichever way the Nee-Me-Poo planned to move.

Howard's plans fell apart at the Montana end. There, a group of thirty soldiers and nearly 200 volunteers awaited the Nez Perce. When the Indians encountered these gathered forces, they told them that their conflict was

The site of the Big Hole battlefield. (Courtesy of Washington State University Libraries, Pullman)

solely with Howard, that they wished to move through the erected barrier (later dubbed Fort Fizzle), and that they promised no bloodshed. Most of the volunteers went home. Capt. Charles C. Rawn then withdrew and the Indians moved into council to decide their future.

The steps leading to the next decision reveal much about the Nee-Me-Poo and Chief Joseph. Chief White Bird and others wanted to go north, to travel through what is now Glacier National Park on their way to Canada. Others, including Chief Looking Glass, voted to go south through the Bitterroot Valley, swing even farther south through Yellowstone Park, turn east, and end up in eastern Montana with their friends the Crows. But Joseph, seemingly alone among the chiefs, wished to return to the Wallowas. He favored making the best treaty possible with Howard so that the Nez Perce could go home. When Looking Glass remonstrated with the other chiefs about his being elected to serve as their military leader, Joseph reportedly said: "You are right, Looking Glass. We did elect you head man of the camp. Go ahead and do the best."

So to the south went the Nee-Me-Poo, through the Bitterroot Valley running just west of the Rocky Mountains. After nearly two weeks of sustained travel, the Indians, at the suggestion of Looking Glass, decided to rest their families and horses before setting out again. They were now in the Big

Hole country, just over the Continental Divide to the east. This fateful decision to stop shaped the events of the next few days—and those of the later
summer. As Howard tagged along behind the Indians, Col. John Gibbon
gathered forces from Fort Shaw and Fort Benton located to the northeast of
the retreating Nez Perce. With troops and volunteers totaling about 200,
Gibbon hurried down the Bitterroot Valley, covering nearly thirty miles a
day, before sneaking up on the Indians.

Early on August 9, at a place called Big Hole, Gibbon's men rushed in
upon the Nez Perce, surprising them in a deadly attack. Caught almost
entirely unprepared for battle, the warriors scrambled to protect their families, secure their weapons, and save their horses. In the first waves of firing,
dozens of Nez Perce men, women, and children were killed. At first it
looked as if the Indians would be driven from the field. Then, surging back
on the eastern flank of Gibbon's forces after the troop leader there was
killed, the Nee-Me-Poo, through their murderous fire, pushed back the
colonel's men to a defensive position on a nearby knoll. After two or three
hours of frantic battle, Gibbon was in a bad way, with nearly thirty men
killed and another forty, including himself, wounded.

Once the soldiers were driven from the battlefield, the Nez Perce dealt
with their own losses. Between sixty and ninety were dead, mostly women
and children, but also several prominent warriors. Nearly every Nee-Me-
Poo family suffered a casualty, and more than a few other wounded died in
the next days of travel. In spite of the large number of casualties, perhaps as
much as one-seventh of their entire group, the Indians gathered their families and horses and hobbled off farther south, hoping to keep ahead of the
soldiers. In rescuing the families and rounding up the horses, Joseph played
his familiar role as a leading camp chief.

The battle at Big Hole was devastating for both sides. Gibbon's forces
were in such bad shape that he could not mount an attack on the weakened
and retreating Nez Perce. Even when Howard arrived on August 11, after
the Indians had left the scene, the general realized he must help Gibbon's
ravaged troops before taking up the pursuit. The embattled Nee-Me-Poo,
besides their numerous losses, had to travel with their wounded. Later,
Yellow Wolf described the pathetic scene: "Wounded children, screaming
with passion; women and children crying, waiting for their ... dead! The
air was heavy with sorrow. I would not want to hear, I would not want to
see again."

Moving south over the next ten days, the Nez Perce swung back across
the Continental Divide into Idaho. On their retreat southward, they ransacked homes and ranches, stole horses, and even killed settlers. Although

The scene of the Bear's Paw battle at the end of the 1877 war and retreat. (Courtesy of the Washington State University Libraries, Pullman)

Indian leaders criticized young warriors for these acts, the Nez Perce seemed to feel that after the Big Hole battle all military forces and most settlers were now their enemies. They placed their families in front of their retreat, allowing warriors to protect their rear and to avoid a surprise attack. On August 20, when Howard drew too near for comfort, several warriors stole into his camp at Camas Meadows and ran off his mule herd and some of his horses. For the moment, the Nez Perce had gained a bit more time for their retreat.

In the next three weeks, the Nee-Me-Poo pushed directly east through Yellowstone Park and then turned abruptly north. To Howard's chagrin, national and local newspapers were now criticizing and satirizing what they considered his inept campaign against the courageous Indians. Defending themselves against these darts of criticism, army administrators added to Howard's support by sending soldiers from the east to head off the Nez Perce from that direction. Howard was also urged to speed up his pursuit from the rear.

When it looked as if they might be cornered, the Nee-Me-Poo initiated another remarkable maneuver. After Col. Samuel D. Sturgis, with more than 350 men from the Seventh Cavalry, marched into the Clark Fork River area, the Indians fooled him about their intentions. Once Sturgis headed south to head them off, the Nez Perce swung north. Embarrassed, Sturgis found himself now behind both the Indians and the pursuing Howard. Recovering quickly, however, Sturgis caught up with the Nez Perce at the entrance of Canyon Creek on August 13, but the swift reactions of the Indians and the difficult, narrow terrain kept his forces from winning a battle. Although once again escaping the military, the Nez Perce were now forced to realize that the Crow, from whom they wanted aid, were their enemies too. The Crows had participated in several skirmishes against the Nez Perce on their way north.

When Howard and Sturgis realized they might not catch the fleeing Nez Perce before they escaped into Canada, the commanders sent couriers to Col. Nelson Miles. Stationed on the Tongue River in eastern Montana, Miles was asked to hurry in a northwest direction to cut off the Indians. He set out immediately. It was Miles and his quickly advancing troops who charged into the Nez Perce camp on Snake Creek in the Bear's Paw Mountains on the morning of September 30. Miles sent his forces galloping against the Nez Perce, catching many of them by surprise.

Speedy reactions by the Indian warriors kept Miles's troops from over-running the Indians and ensuring their immediate defeat. After the initial, intense, close-up fighting on the first day, the battle at Bear's Paw settled into a siege, with Miles and later Howard surrounding the Indians. Some of the Nez Perce, including Chief White Bird and as many as one hundred others chose not to surrender and slipped through the soldiers' lines to make their way to Canada. But after four days of negotiations and promises from Miles and Howard that if he and the other Nez Perce gave up, they would be allowed to return home to the reservation, Chief Joseph surrendered on October 5. A bit after noon, Joseph slowly rode up to Howard and Miles. As he handed over his rifle to Miles, he told the colonel, "My people needed rest—we wanted peace."

Perhaps that day—or the day before, as accounts differ—Joseph spoke at more length. Despite the problems of translation and faulty memories, most historians and biographers agree that Joseph, at the least, uttered words similar to the often-cited poetic phrases:

> Tell General Howard I know his heart. What he told me
> before, I have it in my heart. I am tired of fighting. Our
> chiefs are killed. ... Hear me, my chiefs. ... My heart is
> sick and sad. From where the sun now stands I will fight
> no more forever.

The Nez Perce Indians camped on the Colville Reservation after returning to the Pacific Northwest in 1885. (Courtesy of the Idaho State Historical Society, #77-177.3)

These lyrical words and their dramatic uses have become the foundation stones for the huge legends that have grown up around Chief Joseph and the Nee-Me-Poo.

Less poetic realities soon faced the Nez Perce. Indeed, their tragedies mounted in the next months. Stories of Chief Joseph often emphasize his pre-1877 life and enlarge on his role during the Nez Perce War of 1877, but his leadership during the next quarter century of disappointments is equally revealing about his life and character.

Chief Joseph and his Nee-Me-Poo followers faced nearly a decade of frustrations and broken promises before they returned to the Pacific Northwest. Even then, when the 268 or so survivors of the original 417 men, women, and children who surrendered in 1877 were sent back to the Northwest in 1885, only half returned to the Lapwai Reservation. The remaining half, including Joseph, were relocated to Nespelum on the Colville Reservation in north-central Washington. Chief Joseph resided there until his death nearly twenty years later.

If the promises Joseph and his Nez Perce thought they heard at the Bear's Paw surrender in October 1877 were exactly those Colonel Miles and General Howard gave, none was kept. "Miles had promised," Joseph wrote in 1878–1879, "that we might return to our country with what stock we had left. ... I believed General [sic] Miles, or I never would have surrendered." It is unlikely, however, that Howard promised a return to the Wallowas, since his goal before fighting broke out was to remove Joseph and his band to the Lapwai Reservation.

Joseph thought that he and his people would be detained through the winter in Montana, or nearby, and then returned to the Idaho-Oregon border area the next year. It was not to be. Transferred first to Bismarck, North Dakota, the Nez Perce were removed again to Fort Leavenworth, Kansas, by late November 1877. Joseph immediately began his petitions to be returned to the Northwest, if not to the Wallowas, and urged government officials to move soon when alarming numbers of his band, especially children, began to die in the unhealthy climate. Although relocated to the Quapaw Reservation in Kansas by mid-1878 and then to a section of the Ponca Reservation in Indian Territory (Oklahoma) in June 1879, the Nez Perce continued to suffer. As many as one hundred, particularly infants (including one of Joseph's daughters), died by the end of 1879.

Joseph's continuing petitions, the support of Miles and Howard, and the worsening health conditions of the Nez Perce finally gained the attention and sympathy of policy makers. The Nee-Me-Poo were relocated to the Pacific Northwest by the end of 1885. When white residents now living in the Wallowas and even some of the treaty Nez Perce opposed Joseph's return there, he was sent to Nespelum among other Indian tribes in the territory of Washington. Resentments erupted immediately. Military support was needed before the Nez Perce could settle on the reservation. In the 1890s, the lands they and other tribes controlled were greatly reduced when, following allotments of land to individual Indians, the remainder of the area was thrown open to homesteaders.

Gradually, during the years following the battle at Bear's Paw Mountains, Joseph's stature as an Indian leader took on mythic status. Although Joseph was but one of the half dozen or so leaders among the Nez Perce and not a military chieftain, General Howard usually referred to Joseph as *the* Nez Perce leader in his reports. Then, one by one, the other leaders were killed. In the final confrontation in Montana, these were Ollokot, Toohoolhoolzote, Lean Elk, and Looking Glass, the last warrior killed. When White Bird decided not to surrender and escaped to Canada to join Sitting Bull, Joseph was the remaining leader of the nontreaty Nee-Me-Poo. Thus, when subsequent writers wished to present a sympathetic portrait of the final, unsuccessful retreat of the Nez Perce toward Canada, they usually focused on Chief Joseph as the sole military chief of the Nez Perce. But he was no Red Napoleon.

What was it about Chief Joseph and the Nee-Me-Poo that attracted so much positive attention if not adoration? For some, Joseph's reaction to being displaced from his home seemed much less negative and violent when compared with the actions of Sitting Bull, Crazy Horse, and Geronimo, for example. For others, Nez Perce conduct toward opponents and captives was remarkably fair and humane when contrasted with that of the Sioux, Apache, and Blackfeet. For still others, Chief Joseph seemed more human through his concern for his wives and children. From the beginning of the conflict in 1877, during the summer of war, and on through the post-1877 period, many of Joseph's military opponents as well as newspapermen covering the Nez Perce portrayed him not as a "savage red man" opposing civilization but as a man of another culture trying to hold on to his land, family, and society.

Besides General Howard, Colonel Miles, and several journalists, one other person did much to transform Chief Joseph into a legendary figure. Charles Erskine Scott Wood, a young second lieutenant, an aide to General Howard, and an aspiring author, was present at the Bear's Paw settlement. Indeed, some think Wood may have crafted much of Chief Joseph's surrender speech. Even if the words are not all Wood's, he, more than any other person, was responsible for the wide circulation and popularizing of the speech. For many close to Joseph and for several of the white military leaders, Wood provided words and revised phrases that put the Nez Perce and especially Joseph in a positive, humane light. Wood and Joseph eventually became good friends, leading Wood to send his young son Erskine to stay several months with Joseph at the Colville Reservation in the 1890s.

Conversely, for others Joseph's stubbornness cut him and his followers off from something rightfully theirs. In 1889, when allotments on the Lapwai Reservation were proffered to Joseph and his band, they refused. Some think he rejected the offer because he was not given land in the Wallowas. Perhaps he thought that accepting land at Lapwai would forever close the door to his returning to his homeland. From 1877 onward, Joseph never gave up hope for that return, nor did he abandon other vestiges of his culture. At Nespelum, he chose to remain in his tipi rather than live in a cabin built for him. He also held to his Dreamer beliefs rather than support a day school opened to teach Nez Perce children English and American values. The Colville Reservation agent, who disliked Chief Joseph, libeled him as un-Christian and uncooperative because Joseph had two wives (and perhaps also married two of Looking Glass's widows), as did many Indians, and refused to follow other reservation guidelines.

In other ways, Joseph seemed to mellow in his last years. Besides inviting young Erskine Wood to stay with him at Nespelum, in 1900 Joseph encouraged a youthful historian at the University of Washington, Edmond Meany, to visit. "A long time ago we were not friends to the white people," Joseph wrote to Professor Meany, "but we are friends now." In speeches given in 1903 and 1904, Joseph persisted in his calls for a Nez Perce return to the Wallowas. Yet he also seemed to realize that this would not happen so long as white settlers there told the government they would never give up the lands they resided on, lands that before 1877 belonged to Joseph's band.

After 1900, when Joseph turned sixty, his health began to fail. Although he remained adamant about regaining his homeland, he seemed, in other ways, to accommodate to changing times. He continued to travel, give speeches, and write (through interpreters) to those who contacted him, but remained separate from white ways. Remarkably, he seems not to have despaired or to be greatly saddened by the many broken or delayed promises he had experienced. On September 21, 1904, Joseph died while sitting near the entrance of his tipi. Some thought his death resulted not so much from a heart attack, as some medics indicated, but from sorrow and a broken heart. A year later, Professor Meany and others helped erect a monument near his grave in the Nespelum Valley. At the dedication of the monument, Joseph's longtime friend Yellow Bull, wearing Joseph's headdress, said: "This monument will stand for many many years. Joseph's words will stand as long as this monument."

Yellow Bull was right. The monument continues to stand, and Chief Joseph's life and words remain tragic reminders of events that, although representing the rising power of one society, also illustrate that culture's mistreatment of another society. Perhaps, in the end, the defeated rather than the victors are better models of virtue and charity. If so, Chief Joseph of the Nez Perce is an enduring symbol of courage and humanity, worthy of emulation.

O. O. HOWARD

The Christian General

RICHARD N. ELLIS

On September 1, 1874, Brig. Gen. Oliver Otis Howard assumed command of the Military Department of the Columbia. That appointment would involve the forty-four-year-old officer in complex issues with the Nez Perce tribe and bring him into conflict with Chief Joseph, the best known of the leaders of the nontreaty Nez Perce. The Nez Perce campaign of 1877, the result of failed diplomacy, brought national attention to Howard and his Indian adversaries and made Joseph a figure of national significance. It did less for Howard's reputation. The general's actions during the campaign became the subject of controversy in 1877 and the years that immediately followed. His role in the diplomatic events that preceded the campaign also have been the subject of scholarly analysis, particularly in recent years. Today Howard receives much of the blame for a costly and perhaps needless conflict.

Born in Maine in 1830, Howard graduated from Bowdoin College and then attended the U.S. Military Academy at West Point, graduating near the top of his class. Then followed an undistinguished military career until the outbreak of the Civil War. Howard, who was politically well connected and could count on the support of Maine politicians such as Anson Morrill and James G. Blaine, rose quickly in rank during the war. He became a brigadier general after the first battle at Bull Run and was a brigade commander at Fair Oaks where he lost his right arm. His role at Chancellorsville and Gettysburg, however, brought criticism and reassignment to the West where he commanded the Army of the Tennessee and marched with Gen. William T. Sherman through Georgia. By war's end he was known for his empty right sleeve and for the Bible he clutched in his left hand. Howard had found Christ before the war and was noted for his expression of Christian sentiments, his piety and morality, and his support for Christian causes, earning the sobriquet "the Christian General."

O. O. Howard. (Courtesy of the U.S. National Archives, public domain)

A competent military record, political support, and religiosity led to an appointment to head the Freedmen's Bureau, placing Howard in the middle of Reconstruction and virtually guaranteeing that he and his bureau would be at the center of controversy. Surrounded by northern radicals and unrepentant southerners and lacking the support of President Andrew Johnson, the bureau was accused of both doing too little and doing too much. That controversy continues today with scholars such as William McFeely criticizing Howard and the Freedmen's Bureau and Howard's biographer, John Carpenter, defending him. It was a controversy that bothered Howard and remained as a source of worry even after his arrival in the Pacific Northwest in 1874. Despite such criticism, he could be justifiably proud of some achievements. He was a strong supporter of education and a founder of Howard University in the nation's capital and of Lincoln University in Tennessee. He also would serve as superintendent of the military academy at West Point.

Howard added to his reputation as a Christian general in 1872 when he was dispatched to the Southwest to try to solve problems with the Chiricahua Apaches. Conflict with various Apache groups had existed for decades, and in 1871, Arizonans focused attention on Apache relations by killing some eighty-five, mostly women and children, in the Camp Grant massacre. A failed peace mission by a member of the Board of Indian Commissioners led the secretary of the Interior to ask President Ulysses S. Grant for the services of O. O. Howard. Clothed with broad powers, Howard arrived in Arizona in 1872 to meet with Gen. George Crook, who resented Howard's disruption of his plans for a military campaign. Crook recalled in his autobiography that Howard "thought the Creator had placed him on earth to be the Moses to the Negro. Having accomplished that mission, he felt satisfied his next mission was with the Indian."

After escorting an Indian delegation to Washington, D.C., Howard returned to Arizona later in the year to find and negotiate with Cochise, the noted Chiricahua Apache leader. The story of his journey is replete with drama and color. Howard located Thomas Jeffords, who was acquainted with Cochise, and convinced Jeffords of his sincerity, and Jeffords recruited Chie and Ponce, Chiricahuas related to Cochise by blood and marriage. In the autumn Howard, his aide, Jeffords, Chie, and Ponce entered Chiricahua country and made contact with Cochise. In October a peace was made that brought an end to conflict and created a reservation for Cochise's branch of the Chiricahuas in southeastern Arizona. No less a critic of the army than Governor Anson Safford congratulated Howard: "No one can but admire the energy and persistence on your part in finding him and getting him on a reservation and whether it proves lasting or not you have done your duty nobly." Howard wrote, "By the Divine help something was done," and the wildest Apaches were "conquered, without arms, by Gods [sic] help." Although the peace collapsed after the death of Cochise, the picture of Howard, two white men, and two Apaches riding into hostile country to find the wildest Apaches did nothing to tarnish his reputation.

As marvelous as this story of courage and determination may be, it also contains insights into Howard's personality and his attitudes toward Native Americans. Historian Edwin Sweeney, who edited the journal of Capt. Joseph Sladen, Howard's aide, finds that even though the facts are essentially the same, there are telling differences in Howard's and Sladen's accounts of these events. Sladen was open-minded and came to admire the Chiricahuas and aspects of their culture. "Unlike Sladen," concludes Sweeney, "Howard was unable to appreciate the culture of Cochise's people as something unique and admirable. He felt that the Apaches' religious beliefs disagreed with his profound faith in Christianity and his personal relationship with God. Howard's self-righteous and condescending attitude prevented him from expressing admiration for a society that condoned raiding and killing in order to preserve its way of life." This flaw would become evident again when he dealt with the nontreaty Nez Perce several years later.

The roots of the problem that Howard would encounter can be traced to the arrival of increasing numbers of white settlers in the Pacific Northwest in the 1840s, which caused the government to seek land cessions from tribes throughout the region. Isaac I. Stevens, governor of Washington Territory, arrived to carry out government wishes and soon conducted a whirlwind of treaty conferences with tribes on both sides of the Cascades. In 1855 the energetic and pushy Stevens secured treaties from the Nez Perce and other tribes in the region. Led by Lawyer, whom the government treated as head chief, the Nez Perce headmen signed a treaty that ceded some of their eastern and southern lands but retained the core of their territory in a large reservation. The discontent of many Nez Perce over the treaty was exacerbated by the failure of Congress to ratify it until some four years later, and by the failure of the United States to fulfill its treaty obligations. Even the tractable Lawyer later complained, "we have no church as promised: no school house as promised: no doctor as promised." More serious was the discovery of gold in tribal territory in 1860 and the arrival of thousands of miners and the creation of towns such as Lewiston on the reservation. Acting as it did in other comparable situations, the government decided not to eject trespassers from Indian land but to seek the purchase of the mining regions that whites illegally occupied. Before that was accomplished, however, miners seized or destroyed Nez Perce property in blithe disregard for the treaty.

The 1863 treaty sharply reduced the size of the reservation and sharply divided the Nez Perce as the United States ignored the tribe's band structure, which placed political leadership in band headmen empowered to make decisions only for their own group. Because the non-Christian bands refused to participate in the negotiations or sign the treaty, federal officials secured the signature of Lawyer and other like-minded headmen and then considered the treaty binding on the entire tribe. The new reservation encompassed the land of the Christian bands who signed the treaty, but not the land of the non-Christian bands who did not sign the treaty. The result was a significant division of the Nez Perce into the so-called treaty and nontreaty groups. Among the nontreaty leaders were Looking Glass, Toohoolhoolzote, White Bird, and a leader known as Old Joseph, who came from the Wallowa Valley in Oregon and who had two able sons named Joseph, or Young Joseph, and Ollokot. So distressed by the treaty was the old chief that he renounced Christianity and told his sons never to sell that land.

The nontreaty bands continued to live on their traditional lands off the reservation. Soon after Old Joseph died in 1871, however, white settlers began to encroach on the Wallowa Valley, bringing to the fore the issues caused by the 1863 treaty. Disputes over land between Joseph and the settlers brought Nez Perce agent John Montieth to the valley, who, convinced by Joseph's logic, suggested to the commissioner of Indian Affairs that a way should be found to save the valley for the Indians. Subsequent meetings led Montieth and the superintendent of Indian Affairs for Oregon to question the legitimacy of government title to the valley. They concluded that the 1863 treaty was not binding on the nontreaty bands and that the Wallowa Valley was still part of the reservation. Their recommendation worked its way up through channels, and in 1873 President Grant issued an executive order setting aside part of the valley and adjacent land as a Nez Perce reservation. That order did little to remove settlers from the valley or prevent additional encroachment, and it caused loud demands from Oregon officials for the removal of the Nez Perce from the state. With settlers talking of war, the government made no effort to enforce the executive order, and President Grant ultimately bowed to political pressure. In 1875, he rescinded the 1873 order and returned the disputed land to the public domain. This was the situation when Oliver Otis Howard arrived in 1874 to command the Department of the Columbia.

In the spring of 1875, shortly before the president abolished the executive order reservation, Howard and Joseph met for the first time. Howard later reported that Joseph had looked him in the eye: "I thought he was trying to open the windows of his heart to me. ... I think Joseph and I became then quite good friends." By the time of this meeting, Howard certainly was aware of the political pressure that Oregon officials directed at the executive branch, and that it had caused Montieth to abandon his support for Nez Perce ownership of the Wallowa country. His predecessor had informed him of the situation, warning him that the nontreaty bands were upset because of the encroachment of settlers on their lands, while settlers complained that the Indians were talking "very saucily" to them. Howard, who would learn to distrust the settlers, had, at the request of Montieth, sent troops into the valley to preserve order. He learned more direct information about the situation from the troop commander, who was sympathetic to Joseph's cause and who concluded that the valley was of little economic value to whites because of its elevation. Howard thus concluded in his annual report for 1875 that justice lay on the side of Joseph's Nez Perce: "I think it a great mistake to take from Joseph and his band of Nez Perce Indians that valley. ... Possibly congress can be induced to let these really peaceable Indians have this poor valley for their own."

The situation continued unabated over the ensuing months until settlers fabricated a scare to lure troops to the area so they could profit from sales. That changed with the killing of a Nez Perce, which Montieth called a "willful, deliberate murder." This was just the latest of a series of outrages committed by whites. Historian Lucullus V. McWhorter listed twenty-seven such murders and concluded that only one individual had been convicted of the crime and there was no record that his sentence was ever carried out. This led Montieth to conclude that it was almost impossible "to get testimony that will satisfy the jury to convict a White man." In this most recent case, Howard urged local officials to act justly, but charges against two settlers were eventually dropped.

Howard also dispatched his adjutant, Maj. H. Clay Wood, whom Howard called "the best adjutant I ever had," to prepare a detailed report on the Nez Perce situation. Wood conducted a remarkable research project, reviewing federal court decisions and government correspondence and gathering information from Montieth and Joseph. The result was an equally remarkable forty-nine-page document that provided Howard with a thorough history of the situation and which was thought important enough to be published by his military department. It must also have been the subject of thorough discussion between the adjutant and his commanding officer.

Wood reviewed the history of federal law as it pertained to Indian land and also chronicled the history of Nez Perce treaties, identifying a four-year delay in the ratification of the 1855 and 1863 treaties. He then reviewed Nez Perce relations with whites, noting their kindness and assistance to Lewis and Clark and many others. They were, he noted, conspicuous in "their warm friendship and unshaken fidelity to the pale-faces" and had aided the military during conflict with other tribes. With one probable exception "it is a fact, without precedent in American Indian history, that no Nez-Perce of the full blood ever killed a white man."

The reverse was not the case, Wood added. The discovery of gold brought "a mass of the very worst whites" to the reservation in disregard of treaty provisions. The Nez Perce were "constantly abused by unprincipled white men." "I could fill page after page in portraying the number and nature of the outrages the Indians and their families were subjected to," reported Wood. "Their land was overrun and taken from them; stock was turned into their gardens, and their fences were taken or destroyed." It was enough, he noted, "to make us blush with shame." Whites considered the reservation to be too valuable for a group of "savages," and local newspapers incited settlers to seize reservation land in disregard for treaties. Worse yet, the government "had with criminal neglect disregarded its obligations"; in fact one army officer noted in 1862 that after seven years he could "find but few evidences of fulfillment of the treaty" and "few of their annuities have ever reached them."

After reviewing treaty documents, Wood concluded that there was strong opposition to both treaties and that the approval of Old Joseph and Looking Glass for the 1855 treaty "was forced." He also noted that the non-treaty headmen who rejected the 1863 treaty consistently repudiated it and denied the authority of others to speak for the tribe. Wood also reviewed the conclusions of the meeting that Montieth and the Indian superintendent had held with Joseph in 1873. Those officials noted that Lawyer was head chief because Isaac Stevens had appointed him and that less than half of the tribe ever recognized him as chief. Old Joseph not only refused to sign the 1863 treaty but also protested against the sale of his lands without his consent. As a result, the two officials concluded that the treaty was not binding on Joseph and that the Wallowa Valley still was part of the reservation. Subsequently the president issued the 1873 executive order upon the recommendation of the secretary of the Interior. On the revocation of the order, Wood stated emphatically, "If *not* a crime, it *was* a blunder. In intercourse with the Indian, it is not wise to speak with a forked tongue." Wood concluded, however, that the valley was owned by all Nez Perce and that Joseph had "no rightful, exclusive ownership," basing this conclusion on a letter from Montieth that he was "deceived" by Joseph regarding rightful ownership of the valley. The accuracy of Montieth's statement will forever remain elusive, but we must remember that he was under intense political pressure and had become the target of personal attacks by Oregon politicians. Nonetheless, Wood concluded that "the non-treaty Nez-Perces cannot in law be regarded as bound by the treaty of 1863" and that the Wallowa Valley was held in common by the tribe. He then highlighted twenty points to support his conclusion.

So interested had Wood become in the Nez Perce that he continued his research and arranged a meeting with Joseph and others to discuss the recent murder of a tribal member in the Wallowa Valley. Joseph complained that whites in the valley were encouraged by authorities to assault and injure Indians, and explained that chiefs were held responsible for the acts of their people and therefore white authorities were responsible for the recent murder. Wood also received an earful from Reuben, who had replaced Lawyer as head chief, and from other reservation leaders who complained about the failure of the United States to protect the reservation or to pay the annuities promised in the 1863 treaty. Wood was impressed with Joseph and his determination to retain the Wallowa Valley and concluded in a lengthy report to Howard that Joseph could "prove a powerful agent for peace and friendship" between whites and Indians. Wood also had informed Joseph that Howard had proposed a commission to meet with Joseph to "hear all they had to say" and attempt to effect a settlement of their differences with the government.

The idea for a commission to settle the Nez Perce problem undoubtedly came from A. L. Lindsley, a prominent Presbyterian minister in Portland, who wrote to Howard in 1876. Here was a man to whom Howard might listen. Lindsley identified bad treatment by whites and failures by the government and also stated that Nez Perce title to the Wallowa Valley "has never been rightfully extinguished." He believed that the 1863 treaty had been adopted by only a portion of the tribe. His solution was to have a commission of "well qualified men" negotiate with the Indians for the fair purchase of their lands and then persuade them to move to the reservation but with permission to hunt outside the reservation. Although this was an unrealistic proposal because Joseph would not consider the sale of the Wallowa area, Howard forwarded it with a strong endorsement and a list of five names that he suggested for the commission. The secretary of the Interior approved this proposal but ignored Howard's nominees and appointed businessmen D. H. Jerome of Michigan and A. C. Barstow of Rhode Island, William Stickney of the Board of Indian Commissioners, Howard, and Major Wood to secure the permanent settlement of the Nez Perce on the reservation. One observer noted that the easterners had "not a speck of Indian sense, experience, or knowledge."

In his wonderful history of the Nez Perce, historian Alvin Josephy argues that by the time the commission was authorized, Howard's views regarding the nontreaty Nez Perce had crystallized and that he had abandoned his earlier belief that it had been wrong to take the Wallowa Valley from the Nez Perce. "Now," writes Josephy, "he would take it, by negotiation and payment if possible, but by force if necessary." Whatever the merits of Joseph's claim to the valley, it had been opened to settlers, and Joseph's people would have to move to the reservation. "The hope of a peaceful solution disappeared," writes Josephy. If Howard's position had not hardened during the summer of 1876, it certainly did during the meetings of the commission at Lapwai in November. The general had lobbied for the commission, which he would dominate, and he increasingly inserted himself into Nez Perce policy matters. The dispute became focused on Howard and the nontreaty leaders as Howard controlled negotiations and Indian Office officials were pushed into the background. Howard's intransigence became evident in the November meeting, and thereafter he never wavered. It is here, too, that he began to focus on the Dreamer faith as the source of Nez Perce resistance. Howard had learned of the Dreamers from Indian agents in the Northwest who blamed them for hindering efforts to Christianize and civilize Indians. The agents suggested the existence of a conspiracy of Dreamer leaders from several tribes who caused discontent among tribal members in the region and identified Joseph and other nontreaty leaders as followers of Smohalla, the Dreamer prophet, who called for a return to traditional ways and recalled the connection between Indians and Mother Earth. To the Christian general and for Indian agents such teachings were an anathema.

One important observer of the proceedings was Emily FitzGerald, wife of the post surgeon at Lapwai, who attended some of the meetings and provided housing for one of the commissioners. She was a careful observer whose forthright letters to relatives describe some of the tension that existed during the meetings as well as her fear of trouble. In letters before the conference she noted, "Everybody wants to prevent bloodshed, for this lot of settlers in the Wallowa are an awful set of men and have made all the trouble for themselves." Fearful that all the whites would be massacred, she nonetheless attended some of the discussions and left colorful descriptions of the Nez Perce, including the women, "all gathered around outside in their best, brightest clothes, with lots of babies on their mothers' back," never realizing that the Nez Perce would not perpetrate violence with their women and children present.

The council was held in the church at Lapwai and began after days of delay caused by Joseph's slow progress to the agency, which gave Howard ample time to educate fellow commissioners. If Joseph expected frank discussion and fair negotiation, he quickly learned otherwise. The commissioners, though impressed with Joseph and his "alertness and dexterity in intellectual fencing," quickly informed him that he must move to the reservation because the Wallow Valley was no longer his. Their explanations, described by Josephy as "specious reasons," indicate how the commission had made its recommendations. Clearly the deck was stacked. Joseph was informed that the 1863 treaty was binding and that the Wallowa Valley had been sold to the government. It now belonged to Oregon, and state law existed there so that the federal government could not protect the Indians if trouble with settlers occurred. Also, Joseph was told, the valley was too cold for the Indians, and white settlers already were living there. "In a spirit of generosity," however, the commission would "treat for an adjustment of present difficulties." Joseph's defense of Nez Perce ownership fell on deaf ears. Emily FitzGerald, who heard reports from the commissioners, wrote that Joseph would accept "no boundary to his lands but those he chooses to make himself," an interpretation held by General Howard. "I wish somebody would kill him before he kills any of us," she wrote.

As the conference continued at an impasse, tensions increased. FitzGerald wrote, "The Indian Commissioners departed on Wednesday without Joseph coming to any terms. They all got indignant at him at last and threatened him." They told him what had happened to the Modocs, Seminoles, and Sioux. General Howard told her, "the Indians were just unwilling to admit the government's authority or any authority but their own, and he believed if the Commissioners had said to Joseph that he should have Wallowa Valley, he would not have accepted it from them or admitted their right to give it to him." Howard also told her that if trouble again occurred in the valley, he would "send out two men to Joseph's one—no matter how many he raises—and whip him into submission." Howard clearly was no longer sympathetic to the Nez Perce cause and had abandoned all thought of compromise. He wrote later that Joseph seemed ready to compromise but the Dreamers persuaded him to do otherwise. Justifying his actions at this later date, Howard argued that Joseph set up an absolute title to the lands and claimed an independent sovereignty so that any adjustment the commission could have effected "would have been … simply temporary." In a later publication Howard complained, "Indian Joseph and his malcontents denied the jurisdiction of the United States over them. They were offered everything they wanted, if they would simply submit to the authority and government of the United States agents," although that explanation clearly stretched the truth.

After the commissioners scattered, their report was written at Howard's headquarters and seemed to reflect Howard's views, particularly his dislike for the Dreamer faith. The report claimed that the Dreamers, "among other pernicious doctrines," believed that the Earth was created perfectly by God and should not be disturbed by man and that cultivation of the soil was wrong. "This fanaticism" was kept alive by the "superstition" of the Dreamers, who taught that "if they continue steadfast in their present belief, a leader will be raised up in the East who will restore all dead Indians to life, who will unite with them in expelling the whites from their country, when they will again enter upon and repossess the lands of their ancestors." (Lucullus McWhorter challenges the accuracy of this claim.) After accusing Joseph of refusing to enter into any negotiations, the commissioners recommended that leaders of the Dreamer faith be required to go to their agencies and that they should be immediately transported to Indian Territory if they refused. If Joseph's people returned to the Wallowa Valley again, troops should be sent to maintain order, and unless they agreed to settle on the reservation within a reasonable time, they "should be placed by force" there. If they "overrun land belonging to the whites and commit depredations upon their property, disturb the peace by threats or otherwise, or commit any other overt act of hostility, we recommend the employment of sufficient force to bring them into subjection. … "

Remarkable as it may seem, Major Wood disagreed with his commanding officer and refused to sign the report, sending instead his own minority report to the commissioner of Indian Affairs. A careful and thorough man, Wood reviewed the instructions to the commission to "effect a *just and amicable* settlement," to examine the status of Joseph's claim to the valley, "to devise means whereby his title thereto (if any be found to exist) may be extinguished," and to "select some suitable locality for his permanent home." Wood referred the commissioner to the lengthy study he had prepared for Howard earlier in the year and stated further his belief that Joseph and his people "*must* be excluded from the Wallowa Valley and the State of Oregon, and permanently settled elsewhere, with just compensation," because the valley was settled by whites and because Indians could not receive legal protection from state courts and local officials. Ultimately they should be placed on an existing reservation or on a new reservation, "but until Joseph commits some overt act of hostility," Wood concluded, "force [should] not to be used to put him upon any reservation." He continued, "I recognize the fact that the Indian *must* yield to the white man; the inferior to the superior race; barbarism to civilization; but power is not justice, force is not law. The American Republic cannot afford to consummate a wrong, even toward an Indian, especially the Nez-Perce Indian." Although no bleeding heart, Major Wood had a stronger sense of right and wrong and of justice and honor than did his commanding officer, the Christian general.

Historians have discovered additional incongruities in the work of the commission. Alvin Josephy contrasts the hard line taken by the commission with its discovery that the United States had failed to honor its treaty obligations to the tribe, had failed to remove whites who occupied reservation land, and had not yet paid Nez Perce men who had aided the government during the 1856 Indian conflict. Historian Mark Brown notes the recommendation stemming from a visit by Howard and Jerome to the Umatilla Reservation that part of that reservation be sold because a "whole tract of valuable land [is] ... occupied by a mere handful of Indians who are incapable of developing its rich treasures, all ready to reward the industry and skill of the farmer."

The report of the commission and its speedy approval by the secretary of the Interior set in motion the chain of events that led to the outbreak of violence. Previously the situation had been fluid. Settlers had moved into the valley, and tensions erupted each summer when Joseph's people returned to the valley, causing troops to be dispatched there to maintain order. But no outbreak had occurred and there was room for compromise and negotiation, especially as there is evidence that settlers were willing to be bought out by the government because the high elevation and short growing season limited the economic value of the area. Whether some compromise was possible in light of political pressure, typical government inertia, and the willingness of people in nearby communities and the local press to incite hostility toward the Nez Perce is unknown, but once General Howard adopted his hard-line position and the commission formally recommended it to the secretary, room for maneuver was lost. Despite words of caution from Major Wood, Howard seemed intent on forcing a crisis in the belief that Joseph would back down to avoid conflict. Joseph's determined and articulate defense of his position clearly frustrated the general. At the same time, Howard's focus on Joseph and the Wallowa Valley obscured the fact that the issues were more complex and also involved Looking Glass, Toohoolhoolzote, White Bird, and other nontreaty headmen. Events that followed would test the credulity of the Christian general and severely damage his reputation, for the Nez Perce conflict would become the defining event of his military career.

On January 6, 1877, the commissioner of Indian Affairs instructed Montieth to carry out the commission's recommendations and send a tribal member from the reservation to urge Joseph to come in. Urging caution, the commissioner wrote, "You will give them a reasonable time to consider and determine this question." While Montieth was informed that the cooperation of the army had been requested, he also was told, "It is to be understood, however, that should violent measures become necessary for effecting the end desired, that report thereof must be submitted to this office for consideration of the department, when more definite instructions will be issued." Montieth decided to act quickly and decisively rather than cautiously and sent a delegation of reservation residents that included relatives of Joseph, plus Reuben, head chief and brother-in-law, to persuade Joseph and his band to go to the reservation. They returned with the message from Joseph, "I have been talking to the whites many years about the land in question, and it is strange they cannot understand me; the country they claim belonged to my father, and when he died, it was given to me and my people, and I will not leave it until I am compelled to."

Montieth suggested that they be offered the privilege of spending four to six weeks annually in the Imnaha Valley to hunt and fish as an inducement to get them on the reservation. The commissioner approved this proposal, and Montieth also acted swiftly. According to his February 8 letter, he had given Joseph until April 1 to move to the reservation, surely not what most would consider "a reasonable time" in light of conditions in the mountainous parts of the Northwest at that time of year and the large herds of horses and cattle they owned. Montieth further recommended that the army be asked to tell Joseph that if he did not move, the soldiers would drive him to the reservation.

The request for troops to assist "in the execution of some efficient plan for their peaceful removal to the Nez Perce Agency" worked its way through channels. Ultimately, War Department approval reached Maj. Gen. Irvin McDowell, commander of the Military Division of the Pacific and

Howard's immediate superior. Since the secretary of war had warned his counterpart in Interior that the task of troops was merely to aid and protect Indian officials in the execution of their duties, McDowell moved cautiously. Howard was informed that the Indian Office expected resistance, so "It is therefore of paramount importance that none of the responsibility of any step which may lead to hostilities shall be initiated by the Military Authorities. You are to occupy Wallowa Valley *in the interest of peace*." He was instructed to act "to the extent only of merely protecting and aiding them" as they carried out their duties. "As this question of the removal of Joseph's band is a very delicate and important one, the Division Commander directs that it be done under your personal direction if practicable."

Although the Nez Perce had not been notified of the recommendations of the commission, the message delivered by Reuben alerted them about government policy. They discussed this in council in February, and when Ollokot visited Lapwai some weeks later, Montieth questioned him about the meeting. Ollokot responded that a great many lies had been told about the council, and people said that he wanted to fight, "which is not true." He continued, "I have a wife, children, cattle and horses. I have eyes and a heart, and can see and understand for myself that if we fight, we would have to leave all and go into the mountains. I love my wife and children and could not leave them. I have always been a friend of the whites and I will not fight them." Meanwhile Howard had ordered two cavalry companies with Gatling guns to the vicinity of the Wallowa Valley. Based on the number of Joseph's band and on their past actions, this was overkill. As Josephy writes, "It was Howard, not Joseph, who was threatening conflict." Searching for a solution, Joseph talked with the Umatilla agent and indicated that he wished to speak with Howard, who sent a junior officer to meet with the Nez Perce. The meeting between Lt. William Boyle and Ollokot on April 1, Montieth's deadline, accomplished little. Boyle told Ollokot that Howard had ordered them to the reservation and that they "get ready to move at once." After a moment, Ollokot rose with his first and index fingers spread, indicative, noted McWhorter, of a serpent's tongue, and said, "liar," demanding to know why Howard was not there. "He promised to come to this council. I came, a chief to talk to a chief! ... Where is General Howard? General Howard talks with forked tongue! He has lied to the Nez Perces! Was he ashamed to meet men to whom he has talked two ways?"

As Ollokot indicated that Joseph wanted to meet with Howard personally, Howard agreed to meet at Walla Walla on April 20. It seems that Howard lacked interest in these meetings. For the first he sent a junior officer; for the second he reported that the Nez Perce spoke for four hours, but he provided only a very brief summary of what they said. Because Joseph was ill, Ollokot represented his brother at the April 20 meeting. Howard simply noted that they wanted to choose between the Umatilla and Nez Perce Reservations if they were forced to move and that they did not want to fight. Ollokot repeatedly stated their peaceful intentions. Howard did inform Ollokot that he would visit the agency at Lapwai in May and would be willing to meet with Joseph at that time. Although the general did not think it was important enough to provide any detail on Ollokot's conversation, Duncan McDonald, trader at the Flathead Agency, collected Nez Perce testimony after the war and wrote a series of articles for a Deer Lodge, Montana, newspaper. According to McDonald's sources, Howard repeated the refrain that they must move to the reservation while Ollokot tried to reason with the general, pointing out that his band was self-sufficient and asked nothing from the government "but protection in our rights," and that the reservation was too small to support their herds. "You say your people are too well settled to be disturbed, and I say the Indians are too well settled to be disturbed. So it is better to leave the Indians alone," Ollokot told Howard. "Why are you so determined to remove them? This is where we were born and raised. It is our native country. It is impossible for us to leave. We have never sold our country. Here we have all we possess, and here we wish to remain."

The May meetings at Lapwai were tumultuous. If the purpose was to have free and open discussion, General Howard's behavior was shameful, and his explanation, which changed over the years in an apparent attempt to justify his actions, indicates a guilty conscience. Before the gathering took place, Howard met with Montieth. The time had come, he told the agent, "to concert measures of cooperation," and he instructed him to ready his letter requesting the military to enforce the agent's orders to the nontreaty bands. The two also agreed that if the nontreaty bands moved to the reservation, it would be necessary to remove whites who illegally resided on the reservation, a problem that had existed for some time and had vexed Montieth mightily but about which the government had done nothing. Howard also moved troops to the Wallowas and to Lewiston and reinforced Fort Walla Walla. Still living at Fort Lapwai, Emily FitzGerald noted on the very eve of the council that Joseph was "to have his last day of grace" and that Howard was gathering troops "to drive him on or kill him" if he did not promise to go to the reservation immediately.

The council opened on May 3 when Joseph, Ollokot, and others rode in single file and circled the post three times before they stopped, stacked their arms, and entered the big tent that had been pitched on the parade ground.

Emily FitzGerald reported, "I felt very glad of the precautions the General saw fit to take. ... He says that he has made it a rule all his life to be prepared. ... The guards were doubled this morning and both companies are armed in their quarters." After an opening prayer, Howard began by stating that he was there to hear what the Nez Perce had to say, but he seemed in a hurry as if the proceedings were just a formality. The other nontreaty bands had not yet arrived, and Joseph indicated that there was no reason to rush because they would arrive tomorrow. Howard quickly interjected, "Mr. Montieth's instructions and mine are directly to YOUR people. ... We will not wait for White Bird; instructions to him are the same; he can take his turn." At that point one of the elders, described by Howard as an old Dreamer, urged the interpreter to be accurate, and another, "with a somewhat querulous spirit," said that they wanted to talk at length about their land. Howard responded that he would listen to whatever they had to say but they must know they were there to obey the orders of the government.

The Indians must have been stunned at the tenor of the proceedings, but they sat quietly as Montieth read his instructions from the Indian Office and told them that they must move to the reservation. Howard followed by telling them that if they did not do so, soldiers would be used to bring them there. Howard's determination became more evident when "two old Dreamers" became "very saucy and quarrelsome in their manner." The general told them "with as much severity of manner as I could command" that if they did not give good advice, he would have them arrested and punished and that if they persisted, he would send them to Indian Territory. Such was the nature of Howard's "negotiations."

The meeting adjourned on that happy note and reconvened in the morning with White Bird and other nontreaty leaders now in attendance. After Montieth again read his instructions, the Nez Perce put forth Toohoolhoolzote, who had been selected to speak for the nontreaty bands. He spoke directly to the issues, quickly irritating Howard, who called him "a large, thick-necked, ugly, obstinate savage of the worst type." In 1881, Howard added that Toohoolhoolzote "betrayed in every word a strong and settled hatred of all Caucasians" and that "he always counseled war." Toohoolhoolzote's only crime was that he was direct and not particularly diplomatic. Howard was too impatient to listen to words about the law of the Earth and told the gathering that the Treaty of 1863 was binding on the nontreaty bands.

Howard took an opportunity to adjourn the meeting and told the Indians that they would meet again on Monday, three days hence, which gave him time to move troops into position. Emily FitzGerald, the careful observer, reported that a courier had been sent with spare horses so that he could ride day and night to have troops near the agency by Monday night. Fearing trouble, she wrote, "Oh, how I hate them. I wish they could be exterminated, but without bloodshed among our poor soldiers." She also noted that Howard "was promenading the porch quoting scriptures. Indeed, I think he is real good, but he is awfully queer about it."

When talks resumed on Monday, Joseph was aware that troops were in the Wallowa Valley where his women and children had been left unprotected. Toohoolhoolzote, "a cross-grained growler," according to Howard, began where he left off, and "his manner was loud, harsh, and impudent." Howard told him, "I don't want to offend your religion, but you must talk about practicable things; twenty times over I hear that the earth is your mother and about chieftainship from the earth. I want to hear it no more, but come to business at once." He "became more impudent than ever," Howard recorded. Clearly irritated and uninterested in such talk, Howard interrupted and told him that the government had set aside a reservation and the Indians must go to it. When Toohoolhoolzote asked "who pretended to divide the land and put him on it," Howard sharply responded, "I am that man. I stand here for the President, and there is no spirit, good or bad, that will hinder me. My orders are plain, and will be executed." When Looking Glass and White Bird endorsed Toohoolhoolzote's statements, Howard told them they needed to understand that the question was "will the Indians come peaceably on the reservation, or do they want me to put them there by force"?

Howard's position could not be any plainer, and the general reinforced the message when Toohoolhoolzote continued to protest by telling him that Toohoolhoolzote had given the Indians bad advice and for that reason he would be taken to Indian Territory. "I will send you there if it takes years and years." Having lost his temper, Howard ordered the arrest of Toohoolhoolzote, and Howard and Captain Perry took him to the guardhouse.

The conference was in a shambles as the Nez Perce sat stunned. Soon thereafter, Howard reported, the Indians changed their demeanor and agreed to accompany him to look for sites for them to live on the reservation. Howard's anger had surfaced, and he violated normal council procedures. As Yellow Wolf later recalled, "Howard showed us the rifle." The general must have thought better of his actions. His official report of the meeting gives no evidence of hostile Nez Perce reactions. However, by the time he published his first book on the subject, he claimed that there was evidence "of anger and bad blood," that the Indians "were trying to see how saucy they could be" through this Dreamer. Howard "noticed that some of them had weapons" and feared a repeat of the Modoc massacre, in which the Modocs had killed General Canby. Howard would make this charge more dramatically in subsequent writings.

As far as General Howard was concerned, his arrest of Toohoolhoolzote had the desired effect because the worried and humbled Nez Perce did act in a more friendly manner. As Alvin Josephy wrote, "They had come to the meeting as free men, to talk as equals with Howard, to try to persuade the military man of the injustice of what he was demanding of them. They left in humiliation, with their last illusion of fair treatment by the Americans totally shattered." For his part, Howard had exceeded his orders and had dominated this phase of relations with the nontreaty Nez Perce.

In the days that followed, Howard toured parts of the reservation with the nontreaty headmen to choose locations where they would live. Howard later reported that they were happy and laughed a lot with the escort. He was pleased, too, that they did not select the property of several whites, who occupied some of the best land on the reservation and whom the government still had not removed from Indian land. Nez Perce testimony collected by Duncan McDonald contradicts the picture of camaraderie between soldiers and Indians. He was told that Howard gave the Indians ten days to move to the reservation and said to them, "I shall move the Indians with bullets or bayonets." When they responded that ten days was inadequate, Howard said, "I don't want any humbugging. Do as I tell you to do—move immediately to the reserve." When Howard answered the question of what made him a chief by saying that he had fought bravely in big battles, the Nez Perce interpreted it to mean that he was anxious for war, a not so unlikely conclusion in light of his behavior at the council.

Confident that the nontreaty bands would proceed to the reservation as promised, Howard called the headmen together on May 14 and informed them that they had thirty days to do so. Shocked once again, they protested that they would need more time to move their people and gather their large herds of livestock, especially as the rivers were full with spring runoff. Joseph later recalled that Howard told them that if they took one day longer, the soldiers would be there to drive them to the reservation and whites would confiscate any livestock they found outside of the reservation. That Howard knew the validity of their objection is clear because the day before, one of his couriers had crossed the Grande Ronde. "It was with much peril, for the river is here wide, full, and torrent-like, with water very cold," he noted. Once the campaign started, Howard would find that the inability of his soldiers to cross the rivers inhibited his ability to maneuver.

The Nez Perce would have to move a population of all ages, and Joseph's band would need to cross the Snake, the largest river in the region. Howard also erred by reading to them a letter from settlers along the Salmon River who complained of the continued presence of "unruly" Nez Perce in their area. He believed it showed the need for haste and that it would strengthen their determination to come to the reservation, but it only served to increase their resentment against those settlers who had forced them to lose their land. And so Howard departed. "Having now secured the object named, by persuasion, constraint and such a gradual encircling of the Indians by troops as would render resistance evidently futile, I thought my instructions fulfilled," he reported. He had pressed and threatened them and arrested their spokesman; he had cut them short and had little interest in what they had to say; he acted with haste and gave them insufficient time to move their families and livestock; and he was oblivious of the tension he had created. Above all, by taking over "negotiations" with the Nez Perce, he had violated General McDowell's instructions.

In the days that followed, the Nez Perce gathered what livestock they could, came together, and prepared to move to the reservation. It was a time of stress, disagreement, and acrimony, and some of the young men vented their frustration and killed settlers, leading Howard to dispatch troops to the scene. For Howard the Nez Perce campaign consumed some four difficult months from July to October 1877. Military involvement began with the defeat of Capt. David Perry's command at White Bird Canyon on June 17, and ended with public criticism of Howard and an acrimonious dispute with Col. Nelson Miles following the surrender of Joseph near the Montana Bear's Paw Mountains on October 5. It was a grueling campaign for all involved as Howard personally took command of troops in the field and pursued the Nez Perce over Lolo Pass and the rugged backbone of the Rockies, up the Bitterroot Valley, through Yellowstone National Park, and then northward across the sere plains of Montana.

From July 30, when the army began pursuit of the Nez Perce, to the surrender in October, the army and attached civilians had 113 killed and 144 wounded, and the cost of the campaign, excluding loss of civilian property, totaled $1,873,410, which translates to $22,405,989, according to historian Jerome Green. At least 120 Nez Perce were killed, and their loss of livestock is incalculable.

Howard was on the trail of the fleeing Nez Perce for more than 1,700 miles and soon came under criticism for his failure to catch and defeat them. Far from supply depots and constantly on the march, his men soon were worn out, causing Gen. William Sherman to suggest that he turn over the chase to a younger officer, earning an angry if defensive retort from Howard: "I never flag." Other officers did little better. Col. John Gibbon, who marched from Fort Shaw in Montana and surprised the Nez Perce on the Big Hole, had his command severely mauled as the Indians escaped. Col. Samuel D. Sturgis failed to block the exit of the Nez Perce from Yellowstone National Park, and after skirmishing with the warriors, wore out his command and had to abandon the chase. Howard continued on the trail and at the surrender joined Colonel Miles, who had marched from his base at Tongue River to cut off the Indians at the Bear's Paw Mountains.

Nelson Miles. (Courtesy of the Montana Historical Society, #943-884)

Although Howard's performance as military commander during the Nez Perce campaign was adequate, the public credited Colonel Miles with the victory, and Howard suffered further from an acrimonious debate with the colonel. He suffered, too, from growing public admiration for the Nez Perce, admiration that existed even among troopers in Sturgis's command. Citizens of Bismarck, Dakota Territory, home base for George Custer's regiment before his defeat a year earlier at the Little Bighorn, lionized Joseph when the Indians stopped there on their way to Fort Leavenworth.

Dispute over the treatment of the nontreaty Nez Perce only added to the controversy. The government chose to ignore the surrender terms and Howard's decision that the surrendered Indians would be returned to the Pacific Northwest the following year. Instead they were sent to Fort Leavenworth and ultimately were located on the Quapaw Reservation in Indian Territory where they suffered from the climate and from disease. It is to Miles's credit that this ambitious, self-promoting master of army politics pushed as hard as he dared to remedy this wrong. Howard, meanwhile, was content to accept the violation of surrender terms and the harsh treatment of his former adversaries.

Finding himself on the defensive, Howard, a career army officer, chose the written word to defend his actions and wrote *Nez Perce Joseph* (1881),

My Life and Experiences Among our Hostile Indians (1907), and *Famous Indian Chiefs I Have Known* (1908). In July 1879, he also responded to published statements by Joseph three months earlier in the *North American Review* by contributing an article to the same periodical, which later was reprinted in *Northwestern Fights and Fighters* (1907). These publications demonstrate that with passing years Howard became increasingly strident in his criticism of the nontreaty Nez Perce. For modern readers this written record does little to enhance the reputation of the Christian general.

Although Howard's first published comments in 1879 generally agree with his official correspondence from 1876 and 1877, he interpreted events to support his actions and demonstrated an ability to stretch the truth. He suggested that trouble could have been averted by giving the Wallowa Valley to the Nez Perce but that Indian management belonged to the Indian Office. He also suggested that when officials proposed "to give this land to the tribe as a *home*, the offer was refused" because the Indians wanted it to satisfy their roaming disposition, not as a home. For the first time he raised the specter of possible violence at the May conference by stating that the Indians were armed only with a few tomahawk pipes but "could penetrate the skull-bone of an enemy." He also claimed that White Bird and others who escaped following the surrender had broken and voided the terms of the surrender.

By the time Howard penned *Nez Perce Joseph*, he was willing to stoop to the ridiculous. Joseph and Ollokot now were discredited and dangerous because their father had "married a wife among the fierce and treacherous Cayuses," a tribe that "capped the climax of their diabolism by the 'Whitman Massacre.'" Thus Joseph shared the "treacherous slyness of his mother's people" although he also was "influenced by Indian dreamings and superstition." As a result, Joseph and Ollokot had a "tendency to evil" and "it was hate and destruction in every form." According to Howard, they plotted and planned for war as early as January 1877 and when Ollokot met with Lieutenant Boyle in April, it was for the opportunity to spy on the military.

By 1907, Howard claimed that at the May conference the Nez Perce "were fully armed with modern weapons. They put war paint on their faces and their manner was insolent, defiant, and hostile." Moreover, during Sunday church services, the warriors in Joseph's camp "went through with a weird dance, accompanied by the incessant beating of tom-toms, and other ceremonies characteristic of their heathen worship." Howard explained that he arrested Toohoolhoolzote to prevent an outbreak because every Indian had "some weapon ready at hand for use." He also noted that the Imnaha, Wallowa, and Grande Ronde valleys, which were excluded from the reservation by the 1863 Treaty were occupied by "several thriving cities." If one excludes La Grande, which is outside the area claimed by Joseph, the largest town has a population of some 2,000 people, and towns are few and far between in northeastern Oregon. And so General Howard defended his record during the thirty years following the Nez Perce campaign. Interestingly, he never mentioned Major Wood's report in these publications.

Although O. O. Howard's military career did not seem to suffer—he retired as a major general—he has not fared so well with scholars. True, Howard was a humanitarian whose life was guided by Christian principles, yet it was he who forced a crisis with the non-treaty Nez Perce and who seemed unable to view them with Christian kindness after 1877. His initial proposal for a land adjustment to satisfy Joseph's band seems wise and fair, but he changed his position because of intense pressure from Oregonians, perhaps because he believed that the Nez Perce truly wished to avoid violence and that they would ultimately accede to his demands. Montieth, too, underwent a similar transformation, and both acted outside the scope of their orders. Howard was instructed to avoid any action that might lead to hostilities, and Montieth was told that he should seek additional instructions if the danger of violence arose. Neither was prepared for the persistence of the Indians in their belief that right was on their side. Howard, despite his disclaimers, became angry and issued threats and finally arrested Toohoolhoolzote, the nontreaty spokesman. Anyone familiar with mountain country in the West knows that the thirty-day period allowed for moving to the reservation was inadequate during spring runoff, but Joseph's claim that trouble would have been avoided had they been given more time remains unsubstantiated. Nonetheless, Howard and Montieth precipitated the crisis. Howard's judgment was clouded, too, by his attitude toward the Dreamers and his ethnocentric view of Indians.

If Howard's actions prior to the outbreak deserve criticism, so, too, does

Maj. Henry Clay Wood. (Courtesy of the Officers of the Army and Navy ... Who Served in the Civil War. *Philadelphia: L. R. Hamersly & Co., 1894, public domain)*

his behavior after the surrender. His silent acquiescence to the violation of the terms of surrender stands in marked contrast to the behavior of Nelson Miles. Even less appealing is his effort at guilt by association through claims that Joseph inherited evil Cayuse traits from his mother and that the Nez Perce at the May conference were fully armed and prepared to kill him. There is no evidence to support that position. The cost in lives and property and the cost of the military campaign also must be considered in evaluating Howard's relations with the Nez Perce. Influenced by political pressure from Oregon and by his own ethnocentric views, General Howard had concluded that the Nez Perce would accept his demands and move to the reservation and thus he had threatened them to achieve his goal. In so doing, he brought on a conflict that probably could have, and certainly should have, been avoided.

GERONIMO

The "Last Renegade"

L. G. MOSES

About an hour before dawn that winter morning on the southern plains, news of the old man's death spread to the Chiricahua settlements throughout Fort Sill, Oklahoma. The bloodthirsty savage, as some Americans thought of him, had finally died coughing up blood. His mortal wound came not from the business end of a Winchester carbine or a 1903 Springfield rifle, as a number of southwesterners would have wished, but rather from the pneumonia that had overwhelmed his lungs. In the late afternoon of the following day, February 18, 1909, with his surviving son and daughter from separate marriages brought down from Chilocco Indian School near the Kansas border, Geronimo's friends and relations buried him in the Fort Sill cemetery set aside exclusively for Apache prisoners of war. Many of the band had already been planted there, among them a few of Geronimo's children and grandchildren who had been born in captivity.

Naiche (Natchez), confederate and friend, son of the revered Cochise, and a hereditary chief, spoke at the graveside. He had years before disowned the Mountain Spirits, the boon bringers, and in their place substituted Christianity. He recalled many of the fights in the Sierra Madres with the Mexican and U.S. cavalries, of Geronimo's authority and skill as a war leader, and of how he had truly kept the peace since his surrender in 1886; but, except for a minor flirtation with the religion, he had stubbornly refused the exclusivity of Christ's saving grace. He therefore failed himself and his people. The Rev. Leonard L. Legters of the Reformed Church in America (descendent of the Dutch Reformed Church), missionary to the Fort Sill Apaches, ornamented Naiche's theme. He took as his text the parable of the wise and foolish virgins. Let the Apaches prepare for their summons that would surely come. Geronimo, the reverend observed, had doubtless been the greatest war leader American Indians had ever known. Yet, as all unregenerate sinners do, he had failed to subdue the temptations of the flesh. His mourners and witnesses might never achieve status as great leaders. They could, however, humble themselves, put their feet firmly on the Jesus road, and, unlike Geronimo, walk resolutely to their salvation. As attendants shoveled dirt upon the coffin, some of the elderly women began to drone, "Everybody hated you: white men hated you, Mexicans hated you, Apaches hated you; all of them hated you. You been good to us. We love you, we hate to see you go."

In time, river stones anchored in cement covered the grave. One of the last of Geronimo's soldiers quipped that the army had capped it so that the old chief's bones could not escape and ride the mountain ridges astride a spirit horse back to Arizona. Those bones still haunted the tribal memories of Arizona's majority legislators who, as recently as the 1990s, continued to spurn Apache efforts to repatriate Geronimo's remains. Yet for all that residue of hatred, more evenhanded images have emerged in the years since his interment.

Some American paratroopers during World War II shouted his name as they bravely hurled themselves into space from the relative safety of a C-47's interior. Contributing to that tradition since the Good War, generations of American children have learned to shout "Geronimo!" as they jumped off swings or out of trees. Workers in China have delicately painted six-inch-high statues of the Apache warrior, "Trap-Door" Springfield rifled musket in hand, memorializing his pose at one of his surrenders in the Cañon de los Embudos (Canyon of the Tricksters), just south of the Arizona border in Sonora. The Parris Manufacturing Company of Tennessee markets col-lectible action figures to be sold in such stores as those of the Gene Autry Museum of Western Heritage, Los Angeles, and the National Cowboy and Western Heritage Museum, Oklahoma City.

Two theatrical films and two documentaries produced during the 1980s and 1990s tell his story as both legend and fact. All largely concentrate on the theme of resistance. It is that very resistance, years of defending against the loss of home and a way of life, that created the image of Geronimo, "the last renegade." He is remembered not so much for bending to the inevitable and accepting defeat but for resisting so long and so hard. His story still challenges those of other people, stories likewise born in the unforgiving landscape of the American Southwest. The legends of those hardy and fear-less—and ultimately victorious—"white" pioneers, especially in places where the desert is made to bloom with their non-native plants, have clashed most readily with the legends of those "red" or even "brown" people found inconveniently burdening an otherwise "unsettled" landscape. As esteemed western historian William T. Hagan once observed, one person's "hostile" or "renegade" can be another's champion or "freedom fighter." So, whether action figure or trophy, freedom fighter or renegade, Geronimo's life and leadership still bestride our memories.

His parents named Geronimo Goyahkla, meaning "Sleepy" or "One Who Yawns." Children among the Apaches, like so many others in Native America, shed their childhood names when significant events or visions shaped their lives. He was born near the upper Gila River somewhere in the mountains that straddle an imaginary line marking Arizona and New Mexico. It must have been in June, he reckoned, during the 1820s, but certainly no later than 1830. He belonged to the Bedonkohe group of the Chiricahuas who, along with their kin to the west and east, had been alternately fighting and trading with the Spanish for generations. When New Spain became Mexico in 1821, the names may have changed but the hostility and commerce continued.

One of a series of photographic studies arranged by William Edward Irwin of Chickasha, Indian Territory, at Fort Sill. Geronimo is dressed in anomalous garb, from split-tail eagle-feather war bonnet to Cheyenne-style fringed buckskin shirt. Geronimo and the photographer sold these photographs to the public. (Courtesy of the Archives and Manuscripts Division of the Oklahoma Historical Society, #14209)

The Apaches lived in an oval that encompassed the jagged mountains and deserts of Arizona, New Mexico, west Texas, and northern Chihuahua and Sonora. Their name could mean "enemy" if it came from the Zunis, or "men who fight" if it originated among the Yumans. To themselves they were always simply "The People." Although ethnologists have made careers of trying to discern all the divisions among them, it is generally believed that six different tribes made up the Apaches, and each of these in turn included separate, autonomous bands, further divided by village or family groups. According to their sacred origin stories, the Apaches emerged from an underworld into this world sometime in the distant past. Following their sacred origins, as some scholars explain, they migrated over centuries southward from the Northwest, perhaps close on the region of the Fraser River in British Columbia, arriving in *Apachería* (Apache homeland comprising parts of Arizona, New Mexico, Chihuahua, and Sonora) sometime in the sixteenth century (though certain sources put them on the Mogollon Rim of Arizona by 1400).

They traded with and raided among the Pueblo peoples and other nations already living in the Southwest. Some Apaches blended horticulture with their hunting economy, but most lived a migratory existence, moving from region to region during the year. This seminomadic lifestyle, as some scholars describe it, meant that, unlike the village nations of the Rio Grande Valley or the Hopis of northern Arizona, for example, they moved more frequently and fed themselves as best they could, hunting, gathering, and raiding.

Geronimo recalled an idyllic childhood, free of warfare with Mexicans or Americans. Usen, or the Life Giver, had given The People a warm and munificent world rich in plants and animals. They wanted for nothing. He remembered playing around his father's home with his "brothers" and "sisters," of whom all but one sister were actually cousins. They lived in a home with other dwellings gathered around the mother's kin (though this matrilocal system was never rigidly enforced). Apaches lived in these homes or in smaller family settlements. In the way that Apaches constructed their families, they made no distinction between cousins and siblings. All were brothers and sisters, and their children, nieces and nephews. These younger relations might also become brothers and sisters once they reached adulthood. Throughout adulthood, Geronimo kept his family close. His brothers and sisters became his most trusted allies and soldiers.

From his father, Taklishim, and especially from his "uncles" Geronimo learned to make bows and arrows, to hunt, and to ride horses. Working cooperatively on the hunt would prepare him for other supportive efforts, as in the protection of families. From his mother, Juana, and "aunts" he discerned how to work collectively in their fields and gardens. In times of peace the Apaches cultivated many plants, each family working about two acres of corn, beans, melons, and squash. Goyahkla discovered how to break the ground with a plowing stick, plant the corn in rows, and sow the beans among the cornstalks. They grew pumpkins and melons along the periphery of the fields, wherever the ground was easiest to cultivate. The children would help protect the gardens from foraging animals. In the ripening season known as Thick with Fruit, the late summer or early fall, men and women, young and old, would gather the harvest to their homes.

Goyahkla's youth ended abruptly with his father's death sometime in 1844. After bearing his body to the mountains, his family sealed it and his prized possessions in a cave. As in all deaths among The People, no one would ever again speak his name. Juana never remarried. Goyahkla took on many of the familial responsibilities of his deceased father. His true sister, Nahdoste, about this time married Nana, a prominent Warm Springs Apache leader. With two beloved members now absent from the home, Goyahkla and his mother went south into the Sierra Madres to visit their relations, including his favorite "sister," Ishton, among the Nednhi Apaches. She had married Juh (pronounced "who"), son of a prominent counselor, and himself a war leader.

During this sojourn in the Sierra Madres, Goyahkla participated in his first raid against Mexican settlements. He certainly knew about the reigning hostility between Apaches and Mexicans, but he had yet to experience its consequences directly. As an apprentice soldier or "warrior," he would have been trained in the discipline of survival: how to travel unobserved, find water, and even what kind—and how much—food to carry. Mastering all these skills and more, he could then join a raid. On the journey to the enemy settlement, he would have served his elders as a sort of squire, to fetch and carry, prepare the meals, and guard the horses. If he performed his duties well on at least four raids and showed bravery and presence of mind, he would be admitted to the council of warriors, a singular honor in the band. Goyahkla performed well, doing all he was asked and more. By his recollection he was admitted to the Nednhi military order at the age of seventeen (which, in the fluid organization of Apache groups, would have made him a member of the band). Through his prowess in battle he achieved leadership rank first among the band, and eventually among the Chiricahua. In time, his renown and notoriety—but under the adult name of Geronimo—would spread throughout Apacheria, Mexico, and the United States.

When Geronimo reached the age of marriage recognized by the warriors' council, he chose a young woman of the Nednhis named Alope. He, as a fatherless suitor, negotiated with her family. Goyahkla and Alope married without ceremony only when he had acquired the bride price of a large string of ponies. Yet, rather than join her family's settlement, he, Juana, and Alope went to live in his mountain home among the Bedonkohes. Not much is recorded about these years. In later life, Geronimo described what could be called his salad days. Alope bore three children and the family prospered. The Mexican-American War did not invade his mountains. The transfer of title to Apacheria also went largely unnoticed for a while.

The government of Chihuahua tried a newer tactic in fostering better relations with the Apaches. State administrators on the northern frontier

invited Indians to trade in the towns. Townspeople, on occasion, even provided rations for the eager traders. Such commerce had frequently taken
place between Indians and Chihuahuans or Sonorans with whom they had
developed mutually beneficial relations. Indians exchanged animal hides
and furs and other products for manufactured cloth, metal tools, and jewelry.
As often happened, to the exasperation of the Mexican government, Apaches
raided one settlement to be able to trade with another. Because the state of
Chihuahua had created a ready market, hoping to maintain the peace, the
Chiricahuas could trade their goods and animals snatched in Sonora.

General José María Carrasco, commander of the Mexican troops in
Sonora along the frontier, decided in the summer of 1850 to end the charade.
He crossed into Chihuahua, exceeding his jurisdiction, and attacked an
Apache camp outside Janos. The Bedonkohes under the leadership of Mangas
Coloradas had come south that season planning to trade at Casas Grandes.
Because it was a trading expedition, many in the party took their families
along. They paused to trade a little at Janos. When the men went into town,
they left the women and children behind. Only a few guards kept watch.

Late in the day on their return to camp, the Indian traders came upon a
few traumatized survivors. Mexican troops had attacked the camp, slaugh-
tering its inhabitants, burning its lodges, and making off with weapons,
goods, and the pony herd. Because they were deep in hostile territory and
numbered fewer than eighty souls, Mangas Coloradas ordered a retreat.
Few challenged him. Many had lost loved ones, Goyahkla most of all.
Carrasco's soldiers had butchered his mother, his wife, and his three children. His sorrow in time transformed itself into a dreadful hatred.

For two days and three nights the refugees ran for the border. Upon
reaching it, they rested. In a few more days of hard travel, they arrived at
their *ranchería*. Years later, Geronimo described his homecoming: "There
were the decorations that Alope had made—and there were the playthings
of our little ones," he remembered. "I burned them all, even our tepee. I also
burned my mother's tepee and destroyed her property." For the rest of his
life Geronimo knew little contentment. He vowed to repay the murder of
his family. "Whenever I saw anything to remind me of former happy days
my heart would ache for revenge upon Mexico." Decades later, as a prisoner
of war at Fort Sill, he said that were he still young, incurable hatred would
again lead him into Mexico. Mexican villagers came to think of him as the
devil sent to vex them. Eventually, many Americans thought the same way.

Geronimo's loss transformed him in other ways as well. As the Apaches
knew, all things in the universe, worldly or heavenly, had power. Religion
concerned itself with that power: getting it, using it, keeping it. Power's

manifestation in the corporeal realm could influence events. Humans, by approaching the earthly or comprehensible form of a thing, could attain for themselves a tiny portion of the power that belonged to its supernatural governor. When this happened, a person became a *diyin*, often described, for want of greater understanding, as a shaman, medicine man, or medicine woman. Age or gender had no bearing on achieving the status and power of a *diyin*.

Alone one day with his grief, Goyahkla received his power. It spoke his name four times. It told him, when he finally listened, that no gun could ever kill him. The power would render his enemies' bullets useless. Because he was a *diyin* blessed with this knowledge and power, his arrows would fly straight to their targets. Goyahkla needed just such insight. Although wounded many times in battle, no wound proved lethal.

In 1852, Mangas Coloradas organized a raid into Mexico to punish the perpetrators of the Janos massacre. Because of his devastating loss, Goyahkla had the moral authority to enlist the help of all the survivors' relations. He found sympathetic allies in Cochise and Juh, who brought with them many other avengers. They learned that the ravishers of their kin had returned to Arispe deeper in Sonora. The Apache army traveled south through the mountains and highlands and along the river courses. Learning of their approach, the Mexican cavalry and infantry advanced to meet them. Mangas Coloradas and his confederates met their enemies in a frontal assault, a rare tactic among the Apaches, and soon had the Mexican soldiers surrounded.

Again and again, Goyahkla dashed from cover, killed an opponent, claimed his weapon, and then scrambled to his place of concealment. The fighting lasted a few hours and grew more desperate as the shadows lengthened. Watching so many forays by this crazed warrior, the soldiers either shouted his name as warning, mispronouncing it, or called upon St. Jerome to protect them—perhaps it was his feast day (September 30). The time seems right. In any case, the name "Geronimo" stuck, even among his Apache compatriots, who that day turned a shouted warning or entreaty into a battle cry.

He became a *diyin* for war, a charismatic leader who inspired fierce loyalty among his devoted followers. Once, on a foraging mission, they even credited him with the ability to stop the sun's climb into morning. Geronimo wished to arrive at the objective in darkness, not wanting the enemy to see the Apaches' approach. So he sang the special song of power, delaying the dawn another two or three hours. The witnesses spread the news about his *indah keh-ho-ndi*, the "Against Enemies Power." Thus empowered, he could bless weapons and shields and fashion protective scapulars. Other powers came to him in time, but none could surpass his calling as a *diyin* for war.

For more than a decade after the fight at Arispe, Geronimo led one or two raids yearly against the citizens of Sonora and Chihuahua. Sometimes he collected great quantities of useful goods, from herds of livestock to barrels of cheese destined for the mining camps of California. For the first time his people tasted beef, and they liked it. His generosity increased his status in the tribe. Increasingly he and other Apaches took firearms from their enemies, adding greatly to their traditional weapons, spears and arrows. On other occasions the raids failed miserably. Geronimo would lead his men hundreds of miles and accomplish nothing. Worse were those invasions that garnered nothing except the death of his followers. He would say of these disasters, "Again I was blamed by our people, and again I had no reply." He nevertheless succeeded more often than he failed.

Also in the decade after the Janos massacre, Geronimo prospered enough to marry two women and begin new families. Cheehashkish, a young Bedonkohe woman, bore two children, Chappo, a son, and Dohnsay (Tozey), a daughter, both of whom would share his exile at the end of the Apache wars. His second Bedonkohe wife, named Nanathatith, bore a boy whose name is no longer remembered.

Geronimo had embraced a life of raiding and revenge and his extended family would share its consequences. After one raid, in perhaps 1860 or 1861, three companies of Mexican cavalry, pursuing Apaches north of the border, struck Geronimo's *ranchería*. Geronimo escaped, but Nanathatith and the young boy were not so lucky. The *federales* killed them along with another twenty or so Bedonkohes. Geronimo's rage grew exponentially.

During the 1850s, as the United States extended its administration to those territories seized from Mexico, Apaches deep in the mountain defiles of southern Arizona encountered "Americans" for the first time. In the beginning, both people strained to maintain good relations, but in a culture where land and its mineral wealth urge possession, clashes inevitably occur with those people who love the land in a different way. And were that not enough, the Americans began to fight one another. One region of the United States refused to accept the outcome of the election of 1860. The fighting spread even to Apacheria. One "Confederate" leader from Texas, Col. John Robert Baylor, endorsed an extermination order against "all hostile Indians" supposedly passed by the secessionist congress. Baylor proclaimed himself the territorial governor of Arizona. His version embraced the southern part of what is today Arizona and New Mexico. But nothing came of this, and by the summer of 1862, the bloody-minded Baylor scampered back to Texas. Unable to discern the differences among Americans of varying ethnicities or national origins, Apaches soon engaged them in an incessant conflict of raids and counterraids.

Blue-clad soldiers and uncivilized miners invaded Apacheria, and war without mercy engulfed the region. It led certain leaders among civilian Indian agents, army officers, and the Apaches to make peace. The inability of any overall Indian leader to compel his comrades to maintain the peace regardless of provocation led to what one historian has characterized as America's Thirty Years War, 1860 to 1890. One group of Indians would commit "depredations," and many others would likewise receive the blame. In the American Southwest, however, Geronimo's belligerency would dominate the first half of the 1880s.

Not until April 1870 did the commanding general of the army designate Arizona as a department in the larger Military Division of the Pacific. Troops no longer received orders from division headquarters in San Francisco, sometimes requiring, despite telegraphy, three months to reach isolated outposts in Arizona. Maj. Gen. George Stoneman, the department's first commander, tried forthrightly to implement the Peace Policy established by President Ulysses Grant early in his administration. It was an attempt to establish specific lines of authority between the army and civilians in the administration of federal Indian policy. Indians were to be concentrated on reservations where, it was hoped, they would adopt the culture of majority Americans. The focus of the policy included education in the English language, discovery of the benefits of private property, and agriculture after the fashion of other Americans. Kindness and rations would be distributed by honest agents recruited first from among the Society of Friends (the Quakers) but afterward from an expanded list of nominees from other Protestant denominations. Nationally, a Board of Indian Commissioners—philanthropists and honorable men appointed by the president—would oversee the distribution of annuities and the fulfillment of contracts. The Office of Indian Affairs would exert its authority on the reservation where peace would reign. Off the reservation, the army was in charge and could use lethal force to destroy the renegades or force them back to the preserve.

No reservations existed in Arizona Territory. Stoneman established "feeding stations" at some of the forts in his effort to initiate the Peace Policy. Peaceable Indians would take up residence around the army posts. He pleased almost no one with this program, least of all a group of nonnative settlers near Camp Grant. Despite the establishment of the stations, depredations continued. The Aravaipa and Pinal Apaches around Camp

Grant were blamed for either conducting the raids themselves or harboring those who had. Near sunrise on April 30, 1871, a group of Tucson citizens, organized as a militia but little more than an armed mob, attacked the *rancherías*. The Tucson marauders killed as many as 150 Apaches and enslaved twenty-nine surviving children. These they sold to Anglo- and Mexican American ranchers and farmers in Arizona and Mexico. No territorial court ever punished a member of the mob for his homicidal actions. Arizona editors, unyielding in their hatred of Indians, proclaimed victory. The Apaches dissented and directed their vengeance indiscriminately. President Grant, however, appalled by the actions of all concerned, considered declaring martial law. Instead he sent Vincent Colyer, secretary of the Board of Indian Commissioners, to Arizona in July 1871.

Colyer's mission was to make peace and establish temporary reservations. The following spring, the president delegated Gen. Oliver O. Howard, onetime head of the Freedmen's Bureau and then president of Howard University, to establish a reservation system. He built upon Colyer's labors. He placed Cochise's people on the Chiricahua Reservation near Fort Bowie. To San Carlos on the middle Gila River he sent the Aravaipas, Pinals, and part of the Coyoteros. Yavapais received two smaller reserves at Camp Verde and Camp Date Creek. Finally, to Tularosa in New Mexico Territory, he assigned the Warm Springs, Mimbres, and Mogollons. All began to draw rations, though many continued to raid. A few, like Geronimo and his followers, refused to come in. From September 1871 to September 1872, the Apaches killed at least forty-four people, wounded others, and stole many hundreds of horses, sheep, and cattle.

Grant also relieved Stoneman, appointing in his place Lt. Col. George Crook, who had been successful using unconventional tactics in his campaign against the Paiutes. Crook opened his operation to punish or kill the Apache raiders in November 1872. He had his troopers carry their provisions with them in sure-footed mule trains, assisted by a detachment of Apache and Yavapai scouts. By the fall of 1873 the soldiers and scouts had forced 6,000 Indians to enroll at the reservations. They promised to remain there at peace.

Depredations in Arizona and New Mexico declined. In Sonora and Chihuahua, however, the raiding went on as before. Demands for economy in administering Indian affairs in territorial Arizona led to an effort to reduce the number of reservations. The Indian Office ordered the concentration of tribes. All the Apache bands and tribes along with the Yavapais were to be consolidated on the San Carlos Reservation. On June 12, 1876, 325 Chiricahuas, less than half of the tribe as it turned out, started their trek to the Gila, prodded along the way by the entire Sixth Cavalry. The forced removal of so many bands and tribes triggered a resumption of hostilities in Arizona that soon spread to New Mexico. The remaining Chiricahuas, numbering around 400, retreated to the Sierra Madres. Led by Juh and Geronimo, they murdered and pillaged on both sides of the border.

The Chiricahuas began to use the Ojo Caliente Reservation in southwestern New Mexico as a place to replenish their ammunition and visit their relations. Some of the tribe had escaped removal to San Carlos by joining the Warm Springs Apaches (the Mimbres, Gila, and Mogollon groups), who had long been their close friends and allies. Realizing the aid and comfort accorded to Geronimo's band, military and civilian authorities agreed to close Ojo Caliente.

A detail of one of the photographs taken by Camillus S. Fly of Tombstone, Arizona Territory, at Geronimo's surrender to Gen. George Crook at the Cañon de los Embudos, March 25–27, 1886. Soon afterward, Geronimo fled to the mountains. (Courtesy of the Archives and Manuscripts Division of the Oklahoma Historical Society, #1763)

The inhabitants, about 400 in number, were to be transferred to San Carlos. When the agent arrived at the New Mexico reservation in April 1877 to begin the transfer, he found Geronimo and sixteen of his followers recuperating there. The agent, assisted by Indian police, shackled these sojourners, holding them in the reservation jail until companies of the Ninth Cavalry arrived. The War Department detailed a regiment of the buffalo soldiers, African American troopers led by white officers, to escort the Indians to San Carlos. Geronimo agreed to be repatriated. Victorio, who had succeeded to leadership following the death of Mangas Coloradas in January 1863, with more than 300 of his people and some Chiricahuas, fled San Carlos in September. Geronimo refused to join them; he remained at San Carlos for about a year and then joined Juh in Sonora to raid Mexican settlements. Harassed continually by Mexican soldiers, Geronimo, Juh, and about one hundred compatriots returned to the reservation on the Gila. Conditions there did not ease any of the pressure they felt.

San Carlos now confined Warm Springs, White Mountain (Coyotero), Chiricahua, Aravaipa, and Pinal Apaches with Apache-Yumas, Yavapais, and even a small contingent of Mojaves and Yumas. Factionalism among the tribes, as well as factionalism between civil and military authorities, encouraged some strange if temporary alliances. Where historic antagonisms did not exist, conditions at the reservation created new ones. Heat, hunger, boredom, and *tizwin*, an intoxicating drink fermented from corn, aggravated the problems. To make matters worse, the non-Indian population of Arizona doubled to 80,000 from 1880 to 1882. Pressed on every side, the inhabitants of San Carlos warmed to the revelations of an Apache holy man, Nakaidoklini, who preached an Indian resurrection and the disappearance of the whites. The killing of Nakaidoklini by federal authorities led to a battle between White Mountain Apaches and soldiers, but the army's suppression of one perceived rebellion touched off another.

With the people who surrendered early in 1880, Geronimo, Juh, Nana, and Loco inhabited the region around the Camp Goodwin subagency, fifteen miles up the Gila River from San Carlos. These Warm Springs and Chiricahua Apaches were among the most fiercely independent—incorrigible, according to detractors—of any Indians on the reservation. George Crook, who had earned his general's star in his first Apache campaign, dubbed them "tigers of the human race." "Renegade" Indians were regarded as those who, unlike their brothers and sisters, refused to behave. They were therefore, according to their American keepers, enemies of their own people. The renegades who fought the last of the "Apache wars" between 1881 and 1886 came from these bands. In another world, they might have been regarded as the resistance, fighting for the liberation of their homeland, but certainly not in the dominant culture of Arizona Territory—or anywhere else in the United States, for that matter. Geronimo, the most obdurate of the rebels, even to his own defeated people, was the last to surrender.

The concentration of troops on the reservation following the bungled arrest of Nakaidoklini troubled the settlers in the Camp Goodwin *rancherías*. They feared the soldiers would punish them for their previous raids into Mexico. On the evening of September 30, 1881, they fled the reservation. The warriors skirmished with the trailing cavalry at Cedar Springs as their families escaped across the border. Nana, who led the remainder of Victorio's band, welcomed the fugitives to his Sierra Madre stronghold. In a daring raid the following April, Geronimo, Juh, Naiche, Chihuahua, Chato, and their followers invaded San Carlos. At Camp Goodwin, they killed the police chief, then absconded with Loco and several hundred of the Warm Springs band. They retreated up the Gila valley then turned southeast along the Peloncillo Range. When they finally reached Sonora, they had left about fifty dead Arizonans in their wake. Many more people, Indian and non-Indian alike, would be consumed in the war throughout Apacheria.

The Apache "outbreak" brought General Crook back to Arizona and would eventually send him, disheartened if not disgraced, into retirement. His storied jousts with Geronimo, who surrendered twice more only to flee again to Mexico, are told elsewhere in this book. Unable to achieve a peace based on the terms he negotiated, Crook asked to be relieved. His replacement, Gen. Nelson A. Miles, repudiated Crook's use of Apache scouts, but was himself forced to adopt some of Crook's more unorthodox, if successful,

Another William Edward Irwin photograph of Geronimo, "the Last Renegade," wearing a ceremonial hat infused with spiritual power in place of the "war bonnet." (Courtesy of the Archives and Manuscripts Division of the Oklahoma Historical Society, #8908)

tactics. Unable to run the old trickster to earth, Miles had to turn to other Apaches to find Geronimo. And unlike Crook, Miles was willing to lie to fulfill his mission. He promised them that, after a brief imprisonment, Geronimo would be allowed to go home. Nevertheless, of Geronimo's leadership during this conflict, one of his most faithful soldiers recalled that he "seemed to be the most intelligent and resourceful as well as the most vigorous and farsighted. In times of danger he was a man to be relied upon." Even General Miles, who accepted his surrender in September 1886, found him to be "one of the brightest, most resolute, determined looking men that I have ever encountered." He thought his eyes the darkest and sharpest he had seen, except perhaps for those of General Sherman in his prime. By the time of his last surrender, Geronimo was at least fifty-six. His "every movement," Miles remembered, "indicated his power, energy and determination. In everything he did, he had a purpose." In praising Geronimo, of course, he also praised the man who had forced his capitulation.

Geronimo surrendered for the last time when he learned that all the Chiricahuas had been sent into confinement in Florida. All his people were gone. General Miles had promised an eventual return to Arizona, but had done so only to secure the *diyin*'s capitulation. The only thing Miles had done honorably in accomplishing the end of the Apache wars was to insist, even in defiance of the president's wishes, that Geronimo be saved from the summary "justice" awaiting him at the hands of Arizonans. Geronimo's life would be spared, but he would never be allowed to return to his mountain haunts.

In many ways, Geronimo's remaining years at peace are among the more compelling of his long life. Because of his determined resistance to U.S. authority, and the death and destruction visited upon the American Southwest, virtually no non-Indians in Arizona could ever imagine an Apache world at peace. Responding to citizen complaints and to their own impatience with what seemed to be violent seasonal outbreaks, President Cleveland and his generals accepted the necessity of exile far from the American Southwest. The president ordered that all the Chiricahuas be imprisoned in Florida, including Geronimo and his handful of warriors at Fort Pickens and the nearly 400 others at Fort Marion. Those men and women who had never joined the "hostiles," who instead had remained peaceful at San Carlos trying to tease a regular living out of the desert, were nevertheless counted among "the Geronimo Apaches." That term persisted officially for years. Even the Apache scouts, Chiricahuas and Warm Springs who had joined Crook and Miles in their campaigns against Geronimo— who had fought against their own people to restore the peace—accompanied him to that tedious and deadly place. All the surviving "Geronimo Apaches" remained prisoners of war for the next twenty-seven years. This was longer than even those sentences handed out to all but the worst Nazis whose crimes were judged against humanity. Of those miscreants not executed for war crimes, Rudolf Hess was the only Nazi to serve a prison sentence (life) longer than the Apache prisoners of war.

In 1887, after a number of the Chiricahuas and Warm Springs had sickened and died, the War Department gathered 352 prisoners at Mount Vernon Barracks, Alabama. It was thought to be a place that enjoyed a more salubrious, though almost equally humid, climate. It proved otherwise; the Indians continued to sicken and die. Over the first eight months of their confinement at Mount Vernon, two men, ten women, and nine children perished. The Indian Office sent thirty-four youngsters and adolescents to Carlisle Indian School in Pennsylvania for an education in the style of other Americans. Its environment proved equally lethal.

In 1894, the prisoners were relocated to Fort Sill, Oklahoma Territory, where they remained until 1913. When finally released, even taking into consideration the number of births and deaths within the band, just 264 remained. None were allowed to return to Arizona. One hundred sixty-three chose homes on the Mescalero Reservation in east-central New Mexico; the others remained at Fort Sill, their home for nearly twenty years. By then they called themselves the Fort Sill Apache, and are still known by that name today. Mildred Imach Cleghorn, the last of the captives, died in 1997. The Fort Sill Apache endure, and the Mountain Spirits still visit them.

Geronimo adjusted to his confinement. Indeed, he even spoke for the group when they were consulted about their transfer to Fort Sill. He told the officer in charge of the prisoners that he had done his best to assist the authorities, keep the peace, and maintain good order. He also managed to keep his quarters clean. "We want to see things growing around our houses, corn and flowers," he told Lieutenant Allyn Capron. "We want you to talk for us to General Miles in the same way you have talked to us. ... Every one of us have got children at school and we will behave ourselves on account of these children, we want them to learn." That he could say such things marked his transition from implacable warrior to elder statesman, though not necessarily one beloved by his people. There were too many graves scattered over northern Mexico and the southwestern United States. Others had since been dug in Florida, Alabama, Pennsylvania, and Oklahoma. Many of the People still blamed him for their sorrows, and believed that he, more than any other person, was responsible for their exile. Yet the graves of his wives and children also marked his journeys from Sonora to Fort Sill. He wanted desperately to go home, but his grave would likewise be dug at the prison that was Fort Sill.

Geronimo once told General Miles that he longed for the acorns of the Gambel oaks, the piñon nuts, the quail and the wild turkey, and the saguaros and palo verdes of his home in the Chiricahua Mountains. All these things "miss me," he explained to his captor, and "I miss them, too." It was Army Day at the Trans-Mississippi Exposition in Omaha, 1898. Miles answered that men and women who lived in Arizona truly did not miss him. Asleep at night, they had "no fear that Geronimo will come and kill them." The mountains would have to abide without him.

Geronimo had been brought to Omaha to participate in an Indian Congress. In the twelve years since his surrender and the four since his arrival at Fort Sill, his celebrity grew, and not just as the last great warrior-leader. Historians, ethnologists, artists, tourists, and biographers eager to tell his story began to visit him. He usually met them graciously.

At the Omaha fairgrounds, the other Indian delegates erected their lodges and Native habitations in a central village. The Apache prisoners

resided in a tent city guarded by soldiers. Ethnologist James Mooney super-
vised the installation of the Indian exhibits. He remarked to his superiors at
the Smithsonian Institution that the "exiles devoted their time to good
advantage, making baskets, canes and beaded work for sale, and found
much pleasure meeting their old friends," the White Mountain Apache delegates from Arizona. Geronimo also attended the Pan-American Exposition
in Buffalo, New York, in the summer of 1901, and later still the Louisiana
Purchase Exposition in St. Louis, in 1904. On both occasions he sold photographs and the bows and arrows he fashioned. The superintendent of the
model Indian school at St. Louis, Samuel M. McCowan, at first resented
Geronimo's insistence that he be paid a certain salary for his participation
because of his fame. McCowan balked, calling him a "blatant blackguard,
living on a false reputation." But when the old *diyin* agreed to attend the fair
without pay, the former superintendent at the Chilocco school reconsidered
his estimation of the man. He assigned Geronimo his own stall in the
impressive model Indian school. Geronimo did a spirited business selling
photographs, arrows, and even the buttons off his shirt. The superintendent
changed his mind about the former renegade. He now found him "an agreeable, amiable old man, and happy as a bird."

Although proprietors of Wild West shows sought Geronimo's employment, both the War Department and the Indian bureau continually turned
them down. For some time, commissioners of Indian Affairs had grudg-
ingly given permission to employ Indians in these wildly popular shows.
None, however, could be convinced that the murderous old warrior should
be exhibited for profit and the pleasure of paying crowds. Ethnological
exhibits were one thing; historical reenactment was quite another. Despite
significant protest, President Theodore Roosevelt allowed the famous prisoner to ride horseback, along with five other venerable headmen and chiefs,
in his March 1905 inaugural parade. Even on this occasion, however,
Geronimo's presence served a higher purpose. He and the five mounted
anachronisms were followed immediately by a sharply dressed and disciplined contingent from the Carlisle Indian School, renowned for its football
if not its academics. In that area alone, Carlisle presaged a scandalous tradition in American higher education.

In his adoptive home at Fort Sill, Geronimo found it easier to travel
largely unsupervised by the otherwise ubiquitous military guard. He rode in
annual civic celebrations and Fourth of July parades, and even participated
in an absurd promotion sponsored by the notorious Miller Brothers whose
ranching and mercantile enterprise covered the better part of four counties
in north-central Oklahoma. In June 1905, the brothers staged a genuine

Publicity photograph from the "Big Round-up" for the National Editorial Association Convention at the Miller Brothers 101 Ranch, June 11, 1905, Oklahoma Territory. Geronimo, at the wheel of a 1905 Locomobile owned by the Millers, sports a silk hat placed on his head for the occasion. (Courtesy of the Archives and Manuscripts Division of the Oklahoma Historical Society, #2659)

(Jen-You-Wine) roundup for the National Editorial Association. They brought Geronimo up from Fort Sill to take part in something touted as a last buffalo hunt. There is considerable dispute concerning the event: some stories suggest that Geronimo skillfully dispatched the *black horn* with either an arrow or a rifle shot, whereas others claim he simply wounded the unfortunate beast purchased for the occasion from a ranch in the Texas panhandle. Another hunter supposedly applied the coup de grâce, and all lunched on the doubtlessly chewy meat.

Geronimo married many times in his life. Most of his wives preceded him in death. Those not killed in the Apache wars were taken captive and disappeared from the record. Others shared his exile beyond the familiar mountains of Apacheria. Ziyeh, mother of Eva and Fenton (who died in 1897), died at Fort Sill in 1904. Eva, a beloved daughter, lived fewer than three years after her father's death. Itedda, a Mescalero imprisoned along with the Chiricahuas at Fort Marion before her husband surrendered, gave birth to Lenna who, like so many of Geronimo's children, died young. Because she had been swept up in the dragnet of Chiricahuas, she was allowed to return to the Mescalero Reservation in 1889. Geronimo insisted that she go. In New Mexico in August, Itedda gave birth to Robert, the only one of Geronimo's children to live to old age. It was only when he matriculated at Chilocco—and met his half-sister Eva—that he came to know his father more fully. Robert died in 1966. Following Ziyeh's death, Geronimo married, quickly divorced, and married again. His last wife, Azul, accepted removal to the Mescalero Reservation once the Apache prisoners won their freedom in 1913.

Geronimo, the last renegade, hated by his people but celebrated by the tourists, passed his declining years tending his garden and selling his written name. He had lived perhaps eighty years. Corn and flowers grew around his house at Fort Sill. On occasion when he drank too much whiskey, illegal but easy to obtain in the former Indian Territory, he slept it off in the bushes away from the social scolds and the federal liquor suppression agents. The last time he imbibed, he fell from his horse on his way home from Lawton and spent a frigid February night lying partially submerged in a creek. Taken to the Indian hospital in the morning, the severely injured elder lingered six more days, the last three in the tiny Apache hospital at the post, deliriously arguing on occasion with the spirits of former warriors who had traveled the Jesus Road. They encouraged him to make a profession of faith, but he demurred. Although he had many good things to say about Christianity, he never fully converted. Power was power, and what *diyin* would not welcome its increase? He had been unable to follow the exclusively Christian path in life and now it seemed too late. Why had they not come to him earlier, he asked the specters, when redemption could have been possible? They answered that missionaries had been there for a long time, but Geronimo, renegade to the last, had failed to surrender spiritually.

Memories of Geronimo, like the symbolism associated with his grave, conjure different things for different people. The stone and cement monument traps him in Oklahoma. Pioneer societies in Arizona might be hurled into paroxysms if the crypt were sundered and the exile's calcified remains were allowed reburial in the Chiricahua Mountains. Other pioneer hobbyists, with unintentional irony, can purchase at a champion price the Geronimo Tribute Revolver from rare gun collectors. It is one of the fifteen "closed issues" of America Remembers, a business that markets premium collectibles such as special-issue firearms, porcelain, and more. The Geronimo Tribute Revolver is a Colt Cowboy .45-caliber, single-action revolver, nickel finished, with artwork featured in 24 karat gold and a special blackened patina. Its recoil shield features the classic pose by the photographer A. Frank Randall of Geronimo kneeling and holding his rifle. According to advertising copy, Old West enthusiasts will immediately recognize the image, "which captures the stoic and determined face" of the legendary Apache, "arguably the most famous Indian leader of the 19th century." These full-metal clichés sell for thousands of dollars.

Another interesting tribute to Geronimo's bones is *At Geronimo's Grave* by Armand Garnet Ruffo, a poet and essayist strongly influenced by his Ojibway heritage. He describes it as a love letter to people who struggle to make their way in a world that has no place for them—people "trapped in the slow-moving vehicle of another culture that is taking them nowhere." Or consider the haiku by Linda Jeannette Ward, which received honorable mention from the Haiku Society of America at its 2000 competition:

> Geronimo's grave
> someone has left
> plastic flowers

Did she know that plastic flowers are the only blooms that can abide the heat and cold of Indian country's many western cemeteries? Cut flowers remain fresh just a little longer than it takes to read haiku. Or was Linda Ward just being enigmatic? Heat can do more than trick the eye looking across the ghost-carved landscape of basins, ranges, and plains. It can wither. It can kill.

Finally, and most bizarrely, charges emerged, and just as quickly faded during the 2000 presidential campaign, that George W. Bush's grandfather, while stationed at Fort Sill in 1918, plundered Geronimo's grave. He and a few companions confiscated the head, a buried stirrup from a favorite saddle, and a few odd bones. During the campaign, stories circulated, achieving incredible legs in the paranoid press and on the Web. The ugliest fraternity house at Yale, appropriately called The Tomb, secreted the *diyin*'s skull in its basement. The naughty ghouls of Skull and Bones used Geronimo's deracinated head in their nighttime frolics. If one were to look dispassionately at the controversy, it would be the only artifact that might actually lend a touch of class to the sorry enterprises associated with that unfortunate society. Geronimo, just as many of his real and ethnic descendants, might view the grave-robbing as typically barbarous. Claiming that it was only a hoax concocted by members of Skull and Bones back in the hungry thirties, a lawyer for the scamps on High Street insisted that Geronimo's bones remained entombed in Oklahoma. One could say, recalling his surrender at the Canyon of the Tricksters, that this is only the most recent example of the fear and loathing that occasion a break from the reservation by Geronimo.

Along with the women that chilly February afternoon at Fort Sill almost a century ago, Americans have variously chanted over the decades about his place in their imaginations: "Everybody hated you. ... You been good to us. We love you, we hate to see you go." To all but his extended family and loyal friends, his unremitting hatred for the killers of his wives and children created a world of enemies. The overwhelming majority of Chiricahuas wished only to be left in peace, even in such a severe place as the San Carlos Reservation. Geronimo's rebellion became theirs. Their punishment became his. And like his own people, Americans have come to admire his tenacity while perhaps secretly fearing his passions. Today, for many Americans who endorse "family values," their beliefs are expressed most passionately only on the rear bumpers of automobiles.

GEORGE CROOK

The Humanitarian General

DARLIS A. MILLER

On February 23, 1887, George Crook arrived in Boston, at the invitation of the Boston Indian Citizenship Committee, to share with local citizens his views of American Indians. At age fifty-eight, the mild-mannered, six-foot-tall general stood ramrod straight; when in uniform, he "looked the soldier to the very core." But since he rarely wore a uniform, having a profound dislike of military ostentation, he surely met his Boston hosts in civilian clothes. Earlier in his career, he had been called the greatest Indian fighter in the U.S. Army; now humanitarians also knew him as a defender of Indian rights. Before the Boston engagement, he had written in a private communication: "I wish to say most emphatically that the American Indian is the intellectual peer of most, if not all, the various nationalities we have assimilated to our laws, customs and language. He is fully able to protect himself, if the ballot be given, and the courts of law not closed against him."

Crook was ahead of his time, for few Americans, other than a small corps of reformers, shared his views. On this Boston trip, during which he averaged one speech a day, Crook appeared before friendly audiences, usually in church meeting halls. At Wellesley College, he addressed about 700 young women, "a very appreciative audience," Crook later wrote in his diary. Wherever he spoke, he conveyed the same message: "The Indian is a human being." The vast majority of American Indians were not citizens of the United States, yet Crook emphasized their right to be guaranteed justice and equal treatment under the laws of this country:

> One question today on whose settlement depends the
> honor of the United States is "How can we preserve
> [the Indian]?" My answer is, "First, take the government
> of the Indians out of politics; second let the laws of the
> Indians be the same as those of the whites; third, give the

Indian the ballot." But we must not try to drive the Indians too fast in effecting these changes. We must not try to force him to take civilization immediately in its complete form, but under just laws, guaranteeing to Indians equal civil laws, the Indian question, a source of such dishonor to our country, and of shame to true patriots, will soon be a thing of the past.

Crook continued to speak out for Indian rights during the last three years of his life. By the time he died, unexpectedly, in 1890, he had garnered the respect of former foes. Crook's longtime aide, John G. Bourke, writes in his classic, *On the Border with Crook* (1891), that when Indians near Fort Apache, Arizona, heard of Crook's death, they "sat down in a great circle, let down their hair, bent their heads forward on their bosoms, and wept and wailed like children." The Sioux leader Red Cloud also expressed the devastation felt by his people: "Then General Crook came; he, at least, had never lied to us. His words gave the people hope. He died. Their hope died again. Despair came again."

Probably no one had predicted that a farm boy from Ohio would have such an illustrious military career. Yet four factors help to explain Crook's

Lt. Col. George Crook in civilian clothes, circa 1870. (Courtesy of the U.S. Army Military History Institute, Carlisle Barracks, Pennsylvania)

success. First, he studied Indians intensely—their culture, environment, and tactics—so that (as an associate later recalled) "he knew the Indian better than the Indian did." Consequently, he bested them in battle and thereby won the praise of President Ulysses S. Grant, who called Crook "the best, wiliest Indian fighter in this country." Second, he championed Indian rights and advocated reform, devising one of the most enlightened Indian policies ever implemented in the West. Third, he mastered army politics, having learned early on that a favorable public image and the support of influential politicians led to advancement. Fourth, his wife, Mary, also proved an asset in Crook's rise to military prominence.

George Crook was born on September 8, 1828, on a farm near Taylorsville, Ohio, then considered part of the American West. Here, on the east bank of the Miami River, his parents, Thomas and Elizabeth Crook, raised their large family of three girls and seven boys. From all accounts, the senior Crook was a successful farmer; his land was fertile, and construction of the Miami and Erie Canal across his property greatly increased its value. Thomas Crook also became prominent in local affairs and for several years served as a justice of the peace.

Had it not been for the intervention of fate, young George probably would have followed in his father's footsteps. The story of Crook's appointment to West Point first came to light in an interview with former congressman Robert P. Schenck, published in the *Washington Chronicle* in 1883. Schenck recalled that in his attempt to fill a vacancy at West Point, he talked to his old friend and fellow Whig, Thomas Crook, to see if he had a son who might be suitable. The senior Crook sent George for an interview. "The boy was exceedingly non-communicative," Schenck remembered. "He hadn't a stupid look, but was quiet to reticence." In fact, young Crook already had developed the quiet and modest demeanor that would accompany him through life. When asked by Schenck if he thought he could master the military studies, Crook replied simply, "I'll try."

First, however, Crook supplemented his limited education by taking classes in nearby Dayton, under the direction of Milo C. Williams, an instructor of mathematics, natural philosophy, and natural science. Late in 1847, Williams informed the congressman that Crook's "application and improvement satisfies me that he has a mind which will sustain him honorably in the required course at West Point." A few months later, Schenck officially nominated George Crook for appointment to the military academy.

In July 1848, the nineteen-year-old Crook began his studies at West Point. For the next four years he struggled with the demanding curriculum. As the editor of Crook's memoir notes, "Cadet Crook did not offer a great deal of mental competition to his classmates." He would graduate thirty-eighth in a class of forty-three cadets. Despite his taciturn and retiring nature, Crook made friends with several other cadets, including August Kautz, who graduated thirty-fifth in Crook's class and remained a lifelong friend. But Crook's friendship with Philip H. Sheridan (who was suspended for one year for attacking another cadet) would end in bitterness and recrimination.

Soon after his graduation in 1852, Bvt. 2nd Lt. Crook sailed from New

York to join the Fourth Infantry on the Pacific Coast. Stationed first at Benicia Barracks, about thirty miles by water from San Francisco, he found the army unfavorable at first. Most officers became drunk at least once a day, he later recalled, and caroused and gambled through the night. Also, "most of the commanding officers were petty tyrants. ... They lost no opportunities to snub those under them, and prided themselves in saying disagreeable things."

Soon Crook's unit was ordered north to Humboldt Bay where, to avoid dealing with the tyrannical outbursts of the commanding officer, Crook spent as much time as possible hunting for game in the countryside. Upon promotion to second lieutenant in October 1853, Crook joined his new company, then stationed at Fort Jones near Yreka, California. Here again he spent much time hunting, a passion that turned into a military asset. On nearly every new assignment, when he hunted for game, he made a careful study of the local terrain and its inhabitants.

During Crook's tour of duty on the Pacific Coast (which lasted until the outbreak of the Civil War), he was involved in several clashes with the Rogue River and Pit River tribes in the rugged California-Oregon border region. In June 1857, while on the track of Pit River Indians, Crook received a severe wound in his right hip, struck by an arrow that apparently had been tainted with rattlesnake venom. Despite such dangerous encounters, the young officer quickly came to sympathize with the Northwest tribes in their confrontations with recently arrived white intruders. Most of the region's violence, he concluded, was caused by white people's greed for land and general lawlessness. He was to write: "It was of no unfrequent occurrence for an Indian to be shot down in cold blood, or a squaw to be raped by some brute. Such a thing as a white man being punished for outraging an Indian was unheard of." This inhumanity led to Indian wars, which officers like Crook would rather not fight. "The trouble with the army," Crook observed, "was that the Indians would confide in us as friends, and we had to witness this unjust treatment of them without the power to help them. Then when they were pushed beyond endurance and would go on the war path we had to fight when our sympathies were with the Indians."

When the Civil War broke out in 1861, Crook returned to the East Coast as a captain in the regular army. In September, however, he became colonel of the Thirty-sixth Ohio Volunteer Infantry Regiment, then stationed in West Virginia. Among his first assignments was to rid the area of "bushwhackers," local brigands who used the same hit-and-run tactics of western Indians to waylay unsuspecting travelers. "Being fresh from the Indian country where

I had more or less experience with that kind of warfare," Crook wrote in his memoirs, "I set to work organizing for the task." The patrols he sent out eventually killed the marauders or ran them out of the area.

In the spring of 1862, Crook's troops defeated a Confederate force at Lewisburg, West Virginia, and later engaged in the Battles of South Mountain and Antietam in Maryland. For most of 1863, Crook commanded forces in Tennessee, taking part in the Chickamauga Campaign and action at Farmington. In several of these engagements he won recognition for his conduct, including the brevet of colonel following his success at Farmington.

As 1864 unfolded, Crook's endurance and ingenuity were fully tested as casualties on both sides mounted. Yet amidst the horrors of combat, he forged a lifelong bond with Rutherford B. Hayes, future president of the United States, while his relationship with West Point friend Phil Sheridan began to sour. Hayes first served under Crook during the Virginia Campaign, when Crook was assigned the task of severing a Confederate railroad line near Dublin, Virginia. Crook quickly gained Hayes's admiration and respect. To his mother Hayes wrote, Crook is "a considerate, humane man; a thorough soldier and disciplinarian. ... We all feel great confidence in his skill and good judgment." During the ten months that Hayes served under Crook, Lucy Hayes and their three sons frequently visited Hayes in camp, and Crook came to know the family well. In time he would become "almost a second father" to young Webb Hayes, and the senior Hayes was to name his fourth son George Crook Hayes. In May 1864, on their approach to Dublin, Crook's forces encountered strong resistance near Cloyd's Mountain. In the fighting that ensued, Hayes led his men down the mountain and across a meadow under heavy fire; only later, to his astonishment, did he learn that Crook had accompanied the charge.

The Crook-Hayes bond deepened that fall during the Shenandoah Valley Campaign, the same campaign that had caused a rift in the Crook-Sheridan friendship. Sheridan commanded the Army of the Shenandoah, which included Crook's West Virginia forces. On the afternoon of September 19, during the first major battle of the campaign, Rutherford B. Hayes led his men into a withering fire, and again Crook was in the thick of the battle, "waving his sword wildly and urging [the men] across the creek." Two later battles, however, led to Crook's enmity with Sheridan. The first concerned Sheridan's victory at Fisher's Hill on September 22. Although Sheridan had proposed a flanking attack on the Confederate right, Crook argued so strongly for attacking on the left that Sheridan finally agreed. Yet in his official battle report, Sheridan failed to acknowledge Crook for devising the battle plan, a slight that Crook bitterly resented. Because of the

Fisher's Hill victory, Hayes singled out Crook as "the brains of this army."

The second battle occurred at Cedar Creek, when Confederate troops surprised and routed Crook's forces early on the morning of October 19. Sheridan, with a small escort, had spent the night at nearby Winchester. Upon his return to the battlefield, Union troops rallied and repulsed the enemy. Because of the Cedar Creek victory, Sheridan was commissioned a major general in the regular army. But after the battle, he acknowledged to Crook that he, Sheridan, would receive much more credit for the victory than he deserved, implying that Crook would have rallied the troops without his presence. Sheridan's cavalier treatment of Crook's accomplishments led the latter to write in his memoirs: "I learned too late that it was not what a person did, but it was what he got the credit of doing that gave him a reputation and at the close of the war gave him position." Crook never forgave Sheridan for failing to give him proper credit for the Fisher's Hill and Cedar Creek victories.

Following the Shenandoah Campaign, Crook returned to his headquarters in Cumberland, Maryland, still in command of the Army of Western Virginia. At about 3:00 A.M. on February 21, 1865, Confederate irregulars, known as McNeill's Rangers, slipped into town and captured Crook and another officer in their hotel rooms. Ironically, one of the rangers, James Dailey, would soon become Crook's brother-in-law. Within three weeks of his capture, Crook was paroled and then exchanged. But while being held in Richmond, he received a letter from a Bedford City, Virginia, resident, James Holcombe, the contents of which testified to Crook's gentlemanly nature. The previous summer, it seemed, Crook's troops had camped near Holcombe's residence, which was on a list of properties to be burned. Crook spared the structure, however, when he learned that Holcombe was away and only his wife, daughter, and a few other young women were at home. In gratitude, Holcombe now sent along a basket of provisions and offered other assistance to make Crook's stay more comfortable.

Shortly after his return to Union lines, Crook saw action near the Appomattox Court House in the closing days of the Civil War. He emerged from this conflict as a captain in the regular army, but also held the brevet rank of major general, a significant factor in his later controversial posting to command in Arizona.

Also important to Crook's future career was his marriage on August 22, 1865, to Mary T. Dailey, whose father owned the Revere House, where Crook lodged and had his headquarters at the time of his capture. From all accounts, Mary was an attractive, sociable young woman. Most likely the couple met at one of the social events Crook and his staff hosted at the hotel.

Not much is known about Mary's background, nor has much been written about her marriage. Although the couple remained childless, both seemingly enjoyed other people's children, becoming especially fond of the Hayes youngsters. Because of her social graces and a growing appreciation for military politics, Mary Crook became a valuable asset to her husband's career. She surely gave him a deeper satisfaction in his personal life than he had found as a bachelor. Years later, Hayes wrote in his diary (with his friend Crook very much in mind) that the final test of an ideal soldier was that he was "best loved" by a good woman.

Mary and George Crook, circa 1876 or 1877. (Courtesy of the U.S. Army Military History Institute, Carlisle Barracks, Pennsylvania)

In early November 1866, the recently promoted Lieutenant Colonel Crook left Mary in Baltimore and headed to Idaho Territory, where he would command the District of Boise, a region long plagued by Indian disturbances. Within days of his arrival in Boise, on December 11, he took to the field with his men. He later wrote of this expedition in his memoirs: "[I] left with one change of underclothes, toothbrush, etc., and went to investigate matters, intending to be gone a week. But I got interested after the Indians and did not return [to Boise] again for over two years." In fact, Crook so relentlessly campaigned against disaffected Paiutes, Klamaths, and related tribes that they eventually begged for peace. Over a twenty-month period, Crook led about a dozen scouts from the small military posts that dotted the region, and on six occasions personally led his men into combat.

During this time, he began to develop the techniques that would lead to his great success in Arizona. He employed Indians to scout against the warring tribes, for example, and used pack mules, instead of supply wagons, to enhance his mobility. And he campaigned in the dead of winter, when Indians usually hunkered down in villages close to their food supply. Crook endured the tough winter conditions along with his men. He recalled that on one winter scout, when the temperature fell below zero, the command spent the night in the open, unable to light fires for fear of alerting Indians.

Brig. Gen. George Crook, 1876. (Courtesy of the National Park Service, Fort Laramie National Historic Site, Burt Collection)

To keep from freezing, the men stamped their feet on the ground and pummeled their bodies with their own arms. "Our beards were one mass of ice," he remembered. When the Paiutes finally came into Camp Harney, Oregon, to ask for peace, Crook bluntly told them that if the "depredations" continued, his soldiers would hunt them down and kill them. This "hard-line diplomacy" would be typical of Crook's later negotiations with the tribes he confronted.

For part of the summer and fall campaigns of 1867, Crook had been joined by a newspaper correspondent, Joe Wasson, of the Idaho *Owyhee Avalanche*. During the Civil War, Crook had learned a valuable lesson: advancement depended in part on favorable public notice. Thereafter, whenever he went into the field, he seemed to welcome reporters, most of whom, including Wasson, came to respect the hard-driving commander. During the 1876 Sioux Campaign, John F. Finerty of the *Chicago Times* wrote admiringly of Crook. So did Charles F. Lummis of the *Los Angeles Times*, who met up with Crook during the last days of the Apache operation. In a dispatch datelined Fort Bowie, April 1, 1886, Lummis wrote: "I like the grim old General. There is that in him, which makes one want to take off one's hat."

In October 1867, Crook and Wasson rode together to Camp Harney, where Crook was to meet his wife and Wasson was to return to Idaho. Mary had traveled west with Gen. George H. Thomas and then spent about a month in San Francisco and Portland waiting for Crook's return from the field. The Crooks went on to Camp Warner, Oregon, where Mary experienced for the first time the frontier army's crude housing and the rigors of an Oregon winter. In his autobiography, Crook wrote: "Mrs. Crook and I lived through the winter in a log hut, with the cracks plastered with mud, no windows, and a tent fly for a covering. Our only light by day was through the roof." He also remembered that snow blanketed the area, with drifts measuring ten to fifteen feet in depth, and that temperatures often fell below zero. When the post became short of supplies, he supplemented the larder by killing jackrabbits.

Because of Crook's success in the Northwest, Gen. Henry W. Halleck, commander of the Military Division of the Pacific, chose him over officers of higher rank to temporarily command the Department of the Columbia, headquartered in Portland. At the start of this assignment, Crook made an excursion through southern Oregon and then attended to routine administrative chores. In his memoirs he made brief mention of this period: "Nothing of note occurred during these two years."

By the time the forty-two-year-old Crook left the Northwest in 1871, his associates recognized certain personality traits that defined his character. They knew him as a courteous man, modest, unselfish, and always accessible to both soldiers and citizens. He did not swear, use tobacco, or gamble, though he liked card games. He usually abstained from drinking alcohol but on occasion imbibed moderately. Although inherently reticent, he enjoyed good conversation, especially when he could listen to others hold forth. In pleasant surroundings he was known to laugh and joke. Constance W. Altshuler, in *Cavalry Yellow & Infantry Blue*, says of Crook: "Personally and professionally he inspired a high degree of affectionate respect. An extraordinary number of children were named for him, including Miss George Crook Thomas and Miss George Crook Furey."

Other traits and habits set Crook apart from most of his army contemporaries. In the field, he preferred rugged clothing made of corduroy or canvas rather than prescribed uniforms. He was an excellent marksman and an accomplished horseman, but preferred to ride a mule on campaign. His physical stamina was legendary. Newspaper correspondent John F. Finerty was to write: "General Crook seemed to be a man of iron. He endured heat, cold, marching and every species of discomfort with Indian-like stolidity. If he felt weariness, he never made anybody the wiser." One scholar has pointed out, however, that "Crook of course was not perfect. He could be stubborn, sanctimonious, and unfairly harsh in his criticism of others."

Lieutenant Colonel Crook's accomplishments in the Northwest led to his assignment in 1871 to command the Department of Arizona, where for years Apaches and whites had engaged in murderous conflict. On two earlier occasions, he had resisted this appointment, convinced that Indian fighting "only entailed hard work without any corresponding benefits" and fearful of the territory's reputed unhealthy climate. Although Secretary of War William W. Belknap and Gen. William T. Sherman, commanding general of the U.S. Army, opposed Crook's appointment because at least forty other officers outranked him, President Grant personally intervened and ordered Crook to take command anyway on his brevet rank of major general. "This assignment," Crook wrote in his memoirs, "had made me the innocent cause of a great deal of heartburning and jealousy."

Making his way from Portland to San Diego by steamer and then traveling overland by stagecoach and army transport, Crook reached Tucson on June 19. Within a month he and five companies of the Third Cavalry—a total of 204 men—started on a reconnaissance of Apache country. On this march of nearly 700 miles, they encountered only a few Apaches they deemed unfriendly, but picked up valuable information about the terrain. Crook suspended further expeditions, however, when he learned of the impending visit of Vincent Colyer, humanitarian and secretary of the Board of Indian Commissioners. Created by Congress in 1869, this board consisted of prominent citizens who were to advise the president and the secretary of the Interior on Indian policy. Colyer traveled to the Southwest with presidential authority to settle Indians on reservations through peaceful negotiations.

Crook predicted that Colyer's mission would fail, for he had no faith in negotiations, believing that peace would come only after the Apaches felt the full power of the military. Privately, he retained a sympathy for Indians, even though he believed they must change their traditional lifestyle. He expressed some of his views in September in a letter to the War Department. "I think the Apache is painted in darker colors than he really deserves," he wrote. "Living in a country the natural products of which will not support him, he has either to cultivate the soil or steal, and as our vacillating policy satisfies him we are afraid of him, he chooses the latter. ... I am satisfied that a sharp active campaign against him, would not only make him one of the best Indians in the country, but would save millions of dollars to the Treasury and the lives of many whites and Indians."

In fact, Indian raids continued after Colyer left the territory. For the second time, however, Crook's plans for chastising the offenders were interrupted when Gen. Oliver O. Howard, head of the Freedmen's Bureau, arrived in the spring of 1872 to carry on Colyer's work. Although Crook treated Howard with courtesy, he resented his interference, just as he had resented Colyer's. Still, Howard persevered with his work: he abolished or moved some reservations that Colyer had located and "negotiated a truce" with Cochise, leader of the Chiricahuas. But when the raids on white ranches and outposts continued, Crook started his long-delayed campaign against the bands he held responsible.

The Tonto Basin Campaign of 1872–1873, historian Robert Utley contends, "stands as one of the most brilliant and successful [offensives] ever mounted against Indians." For about five months, starting in November, units of the First and Fifth Cavalries, accompanied by Indian guides, went after Apaches in the rugged Mogollon country of south-central Arizona. Crook opted for a winter campaign, when the enemy's food supply would be most difficult to replenish. He was relentless in pursuit, admonishing his troops, "The trail must be stuck to and never lost." As casualties mounted among the bands, demoralization set in. By mid-April, groups of Apaches approached the military pleading for an end to hostilities. Crook's successful campaign brought peace to Arizona for several years and won him promotion to brigadier general in October 1873.

Crook's success in the Tonto Basin Campaign resulted from three major factors. First, during the delays caused by Colyer and Howard's visits, Crook came to thoroughly understand his department, both its personnel and terrain. Second, he made extensive use of pack mules, which added greatly to the mobility of his troops. Perfecting the use of pack trains had become another of Crook's passions, and he lavished care on the selection of mules, their civilian handlers, and the use of pack saddles. Third, he employed Indian scouts to lead troops to the enemy. Years later, Crook stated that he had felt sure of success at the start of the campaign because of the hours he had spent organizing and getting to know his scouts, "which I saw was to be my main dependence." Not only did Indians have superior knowledge of the countryside, but using them to fight their own people was a tremendous psychological blow to the latter. One Indian leader explained it this way: "They had never been afraid of the Americans alone, but now that their own people were fighting against them they did not know what to do."

With the campaign behind him, Crook began to implement a plan for turning Apaches into farmers and stock raisers. Like many other nineteenth century reformers, Crook believed that the survival of Indians depended on their becoming self-sufficient agriculturalists. At his urging, some Apaches used the pay they received as scouts to send off to California for horses and sheep. Other Apaches (both men and women) went to work constructing irrigation ditches, planting vegetables, and cutting hay and wood to sell to the quartermaster's department. To guarantee them a cash market, government supply advertisements soon carried the proviso "The right is reserved by the United States to purchase during the fiscal year such quantities of Forage and Fuel, as may be offered by, and accepted from Indians." Shortly after Crook left the territory in 1875, his successor estimated that the Apaches would sell to the army that year more than 100,000 pounds of corn and possibly 300,000 pounds of hay.

During Crook's first months in Arizona, Mary lived on the Crook estate in Oakland, Maryland, where she worked to advance his career. In September 1871, she wrote to Rutherford B. Hayes, then governor of Ohio, asking him to intercede with President Grant to secure her husband's promotion. Because officers in the nineteenth-century army often spent decades in one rank, wives sometimes sought the help of powerful people to speed their husbands' advancement. Crook's promotion to brigadier general, Mary knew, could be achieved only by presidential appointment. Although he had to wait two more years before reaching this rank, she continued to find ways to foster his success.

Early in 1872, Mary and her brother James, the former McNeill's Ranger, started west to join Crook at Fort Whipple, Arizona, site of his headquarters. In San Francisco, Mary and James met up with Gen. O. O. Howard, also en route to Arizona; together they journeyed down the coast on the steamer *Newbern*, and Mary charmed Howard with her singing and good spirits. She "added life and pleasure to our voyage," he later recalled. Upon Howard's arrival at Fort Whipple in April, the Crooks invited him to stay in their home. "The time passed pleasantly and swiftly," he wrote in his memoirs. "It was a delight to a fellow-officer to find himself at [Crook's] table, particularly when his genial wife presided at the head of it." Before long, Mary's sister Fanny Reade also joined the household.

Like other officers' wives, Mary Crook surely followed her husband west primarily "out of love and a sense of duty." Like them, she sought to establish a home where her husband would find comfort and relaxation. Moreover, as wife of the commanding officer, Mary assumed high rank among the wives, offering aid and comfort to the younger women. And as the official hostess of Fort Whipple, she handled her husband's social responsibilities with grace and enthusiasm, organizing dinners, receptions, and other entertainments, which helped to relieve the boredom of frontier military duty. In addition, these affairs brought officers' families together, contributing to harmonious relations, and helped smooth Crook's dealings with high-ranking officials.

Officers' wives appreciated the generosity of Mary Crook. Fanny Corbusier recalled with gratitude Mary's help in disposing of household goods when the Corbusiers changed stations during the summer of 1873, and Martha Summerhayes long remembered "the pleasant dinner" that Mary gave the following year while she and her husband were en route to a new assignment. John G. Bourke documents another of her contributions in *On the Border with Crook*: "Several of the springs in northern Arizona were planted with watercress by Mrs. Crook, the General's wife, who had followed him to Arizona, and remained there until his transfer to another field."

Mary had returned east, however, before Crook received his next assignment. The *Arizona Sentinel* of March 20, 1875, reported that Mrs. Crook recently had spent a few weeks in Washington, D.C. While promenading with President Grant at a social event, she asked that her husband be ordered away from Arizona because of his health. With some humor, the president replied that Crook was needed where he was and then added, "He serves his country so much better when his wife is with him that you will have to return."

At about the time this article appeared in the *Sentinel*, Crook received orders to take command of the Department of the Platte, headquartered in Omaha. Before he left Arizona, the citizens of Prescott tendered him a banquet and reception, at which his successor—and old West Point friend—Col. August Kautz wished him luck. When he arrived in Omaha, its citizens also welcomed him with a banquet and reception. Mary joined him at his new post, and together they attended General Sheridan's wedding in Chicago on June 3. Although they were outwardly still friends, the Crook-Sheridan relationship was to deteriorate further during the Sioux Campaign of 1876, and Crook's reputation as an Indian fighter would suffer as well.

Upon assuming his new command, he became caught up in the army's efforts to avert a major clash with the Lakotas, or Teton Sioux, over the issue of the Dakota Black Hills. The discovery of gold in the Black Hills, a part of the Sioux reservation, led to an invasion by white prospectors. In July 1875, Crook himself entered the region and ordered the trespassers to leave, but the army failed to stem the flood of gold seekers. Meanwhile, disgruntled Sioux hunting bands began raiding off the reservation, which led the government to order their return by January 31, 1876. When the Sioux failed to comply, the army prepared to wage war.

Gen. Phil Sheridan, who had overall command of the campaign, envisioned a three-pronged winter operation, with the columns converging on the hunting bands' territory. Crook's contingent was first into the field. Consisting of about 900 officers, enlisted men, and civilian employees, with five pack trains of eighty mules each and about eighty supply wagons, the column headed north from Fort Fetterman, Wyoming, on March 1, 1876. Within days, a cold, bitter snowstorm enveloped the troops; temperatures fell far below zero, the fierce north wind making it seem even colder. On March 17, a detachment of about 300 men under Col. Joseph J. Reynolds struck a Sioux-Cheyenne village along the Little Powder River in southeastern Montana. After initially fleeing their homes, the Indians staged a counterattack, forcing the troopers to withdraw in such haste that they left behind the bodies of two comrades. That night the Indians recaptured most of their pony herd, which the soldiers earlier had spirited away. Crook was furious when he learned of the outcome; later he would have Reynolds and two other officers court-martialed for "misbehavior before the enemy." For now, he abandoned the campaign and headed back to Fort Fetterman.

The severity of the weather, in fact, stymied Sheridan's plans to defeat the hunting bands by spring. Consequently, he would mount a summer campaign, again relying on a three-column advance: Crook to move north-ward from Fort Fetterman; Col. John Gibbon to push eastward from Fort Ellis, Montana; and a third column, eventually commanded by Brig. Gen. Alfred H. Terry, to march westward from Fort Abraham Lincoln, near present-day Bismarck, North Dakota. On May 29, Crook's contingent of 47 officers and 1,000 enlisted men started its trek toward the Bighorn-Yellowstone region of Montana. Unable to enlist scouts among the reservation Sioux (because of their anger over the Black Hills issue and their loyalty to other Sioux), he relied instead on the 176 Crows and 86 Shoshones who joined his column.

On June 17, as Crook's men stopped for coffee on the banks of the Rosebud, Sioux and Cheyenne warriors under Crazy Horse attacked. Crook's Indian auxiliaries took the brunt of the charge, giving the soldiers time to organize. After six hours of fierce fighting, the Sioux and Cheyennes withdrew. Although Crook would always claim the Battle of the Rosebud as a victory (because the army retained possession of the battlefield), many historians believe he had been "badly worsted." Still, in Crook's defense, they also point to an unusual set of factors that contributed to his difficul-ties: Indian warriors were massed in larger numbers than anyone had calculated and fought with "unexpected unity and tenacity" in terrain that favored the attacking force. Fearful of another ambush, Crook beat a hasty retreat to his base camp along Goose Creek in Wyoming to resupply and await reinforcements.

The Rosebud engagement badly damaged Crook's reputation; at most, his alleged victory was a stalemate. After Custer fell on the Little Bighorn on June 25, some critics held Crook partially to blame. Had he continued north, they reasoned, he might have drawn Indian warriors away from Custer, thereby increasing his chances for survival. Privately, both Generals Sherman and Sheridan expressed this view. The rest of the summer was no success for Crook either. When he finally received reinforcements, he left Goose Creek in early August with about 2,000 men. His only encounter with Indian adversaries on this expedition came about a month later on the so-called Horsemeat March. Short on supplies, drenched by unseasonable rains, and mired in tarlike mud, the command slogged forward for three weeks, finally subsisting on the meat of their exhausted animals. On September 9, en route to secure provisions in the Black Hills mining camps, soldiers stumbled upon and attacked a Sioux-Cheyenne village near rocky formations known as Slim Buttes. Crook's main force arrived in time to prevent a counterattack and thus ensure one small victory for Crook. For the remainder of the year, he kept his troops looking for Sioux. Finally he disbanded his column at Fort Fetterman in late December and then went on to Cheyenne, where a court-martial board was to convene for the trial of Colonel Reynolds. Undoubtedly anxious to see her husband, Mary Crook traveled from Omaha to join him in Cheyenne.

Crook's lackluster performance on the northern plains stands in marked contrast to his success in Arizona. John G. Bourke's observations, which he recorded in his diary at the start of the Sioux Campaign, help explain the difference: "We have not the same knowledge of [the] country which proved so invaluable in [the Apache] campaign, nor the same unerring Indian auxiliaries who led us into the dens and fastnesses of the enemy with clock-like accuracy." Crook himself blamed the lack of Sioux scouts for his military setbacks.

Still, by mid-1877 the Sioux war was over; the army's constant harassment had forced some Sioux to cross into Canada and others to surrender. Crook was kept busy during the first half of the year dealing with disaffected Sioux at the Indian agencies, and in September he accompanied Red Cloud, Spotted Tail, and other Sioux leaders to Washington, where they met with President Rutherford B. Hayes to discuss land issues.

Back in Omaha, Crook handled routine administrative chores and attended a variety of social events, which Mary may have enjoyed more than her husband. Still, the always polite general left a lasting impression on Elizabeth Burt, an officer's wife, who later recalled, "The winter [early 1877] passed pleasantly among so many agreeable people, including General and Mrs. Crook." The Crooks also entertained various traveling dignitaries, among them Ohio congressman (and future president of the United States) James A. Garfield and former president and Mrs. Ulysses S. Grant (on their return from a two-year tour around the world).

Meanwhile, during the Omaha period, Crook became increasingly outspoken in his support for Indians and sided with tribes enmeshed in struggles with white society. When the Bannocks of the Northwest waged war against white settlers in 1878, he sympathetically concluded that it was "*hunger. Nothing but hunger*" that drove them to violence. Furthermore, he told a reporter, "[the whites] have come and occupied about all the grounds the

Indians derived their living from. ... The disappearance of the game, which means starvation, may seem a small thing to us, but to them it is their all, and he must be a very contemptible being who would not fight for his life."

Crook's most significant public stand for Indian justice came during the Ponca Indian affair of 1879. Two years earlier, the government had forced the peaceful Poncas to leave their reservation along the Nebraska-Dakota border and relocate in Indian Territory (later Oklahoma). In this unfamiliar land, many of them sickened and died. After losing two daughters and then his only son, Chief Standing Bear set out for his homeland to give his son a proper burial. When he and about thirty of his people reached Nebraska, they were welcomed by the Omahas, a closely related tribe, who granted them land on which to settle and farm. Soon, however, Crook received orders to arrest the Poncas and return them to Indian Territory.

Distasteful as it was, Crook sent troops to make the arrests. Personally, he regarded this as another example of the government's injustice to Indians; he consequently sought the help of Omaha journalist Thomas Henry Tibbles, an advocate for Indian rights, to rectify this outrage. Tibbles in turn persuaded two lawyers to institute a habeas corpus case on behalf of the Poncas and wrote heated editorials to whip up public support for the beleaguered Indians. In the two-day trial of *Standing Bear vs. Crook*, which began on April 30, 1879, government lawyers argued that an Indian did not have legal standing as a "person" and therefore could not bring suit against the government. But in his landmark decision, U.S. District Judge Elmer S. Dundy ruled otherwise, stating that an Indian "is a *person* within the meaning of the [habeas corpus act]," and he ordered the Poncas to be released. Realizing that Crook's sympathy rested with Standing Bear, the judge also noted: "In what General Crook has done in the premises no fault can be imputed to him. He was simply obeying the orders of his superior officers as a good soldier ought to do." Later, on the recommendation of a special commission that Crook chaired, the Poncas were allowed to stay in Nebraska.

He continued to support Indian reform once the Standing Bear trial was over. In a long letter to Tibbles, dated June 19, 1879, Crook examined the shortcomings of federal Indian policy and suggested remedies. He decried the government's failure to fulfill treaty obligations, which caused Indians to lose confidence in the promises of federal officials. Likewise, he criticized a system that awarded more rations and supplies to defeated enemies (such as the Sioux) than to former allies (such as the Bannocks, some of whom had served as scouts for Crook in 1876). The solution to the "Indian problem," Crook believed, was for Indian people to become successful ranchers and farmers. For this transformation to occur, they had to be guaranteed protection of life and property as well as a market for their crops and animals. Clearly, this letter was intended for public consumption; Tibbles used portions of it in his speeches on behalf of Indian causes, and the *New York Tribune* published it in an October issue. Crook later repeated his message in letters sent to supporters of the Indian Rights movement.

While Crook handled military affairs in Nebraska, government officials in Arizona went about concentrating the scattered Apache bands onto the San Carlos Reservation, a stretch of barren desert on the upper Gila River. Tensions permeated this large reserve, the discontent caused by boredom, sickness, inadequate food, and factional wrangling both "within and between the white and Indian communities." Consequently, groups of Indians periodically left to raid on both sides of the U.S.-Mexican border. In light of his earlier success, Crook was ordered back to Arizona, where he assumed command at Fort Whipple on September 4, 1882. Almost immediately, he took to the field to try to quell unrest among the reservation Indians. He then prepared to hunt down the off-reservation Apaches, mainly Mimbreños, Mescaleros, and Chiricahuas, who had been raiding and killing in the United States and then taking refuge in Mexico's seemingly impenetrable Sierra Madre.

By late April 1883, Crook was ready to act. He had reorganized his pack train, recruited scouts, and stockpiled supplies and personnel at Willcox, a station on the Southern Pacific Railroad. He had also conferred with his counterpart in New Mexico and with Mexican officials in Sonora and Chihuahua. An agreement signed in 1882 by Mexico and the United States allowed troops from either country to cross the international boundary in pursuit of raiding Apaches. On May 1, Crook rode into Mexico with his column of about 45 cavalrymen, 193 Apache scouts, and a pack train of 350 mules. The scouts soon overran and destroyed an Apache camp, killing nine warriors in several hours of fierce fighting. Few captives were taken, but the fight thoroughly alarmed the Chiricahuas, for Crook not only had breached their stronghold but was hunting them down with other Apaches. Slowly the off-reservation Indians began drifting into Crook's camp to ask for peace. For about a week, he parleyed with Geronimo, Chato, and other leaders, treating them with his usual hard-line diplomacy. "They had been committing atrocities and depredations upon our people and the Mexicans," he told them, "[and] we had become tired of such a condition of affairs and intended to wipe them out."

Nonetheless, Crook allowed the Indians to surrender. Geronimo did so on his own terms; he would return to San Carlos but only after he had gathered more of his people. Short of rations, Crook had no other choice but to leave the Sierra Madre, recrossing the border on June 10 with his captives—52 men and 273 women and children—and Geronimo's promise to soon follow. Later that year, other Chiricahuas began their trek northward to San Carlos, but not until early March 1884, did Geronimo with eighty followers cross the border and surrender to Crook's forces.

By the middle of 1884, about 5,000 Apaches were on the San Carlos Reservation. Many had turned to farming, under the encouragement of Crook and his subordinates. They produced large amounts of barley, which they sold to the government, and also raised corn, beans, and melons and cut natural grass and wood to sell to the army. In his annual report for 1884, Crook asserted that even Geronimo and Chato, "who last year were our worst enemies," had taken up farming. Explaining his program to Indian Rights activist Herbert Welsh, Crook wrote, "No sermon that was ever preached on the 'Dignity of Labor' could print upon the savage mind the impression received when he sees that *work* means *money*, and that the exact measure of his industry is to be found in his pocket book."

With peace restored, Crook made an extended journey to the East Coast, where he addressed the graduating class at West Point on June 16, 1884. Since many cadets would serve in the West, he advised them to follow certain precepts that guided him in dealing with Indians: make no promises that cannot be kept, always tell the truth, and let them see that "you administer one law for the white-skinned and the red-skinned." In this way, he added, "you will gain [the Indian's] confidence because you have shown yourself worthy of it." Little did he realize that in attempting to abide by these rules, he soon would incur the displeasure of both President Grover Cleveland and Gen. Phil Sheridan, now commanding general of the U.S. Army.

Trouble, in fact, was brewing on the San Carlos Reservation, much of the discontent stemming from Crook's regulations banning wife abuse and the making of *tizwin* (an alcoholic drink made from corn or barley). On May 17, 1885, a group of malcontent Chiricahuas—forty-two men and ninety-two women and children—fled the reservation. Geronimo led his followers directly into Mexico, but another party raided through southeastern Arizona and southwestern New Mexico before crossing the border. Crook's immediate response was modeled on his earlier success; he would hunt down the runaways with his Apache scouts.

Crook sent two "highly mobile forces" into Mexico, each unit consisting of one troop of cavalry and ninety to one hundred scouts. Their first efforts to corral the fugitives proved fruitless. Nor did Crook's soldiers positioned along the border prevent Apaches from crossing into the United States in their quest for supplies and revenge. In October, he pulled his troops out of

Mexico to regroup and prepare for a second invasion. Meanwhile, officials in Washington nervously monitored the situation in the Southwest. At the behest of the War Department, General Sheridan traveled to Arizona in late November to discuss with Crook a possible solution to the Apache problem: the removal of all Chiricahua Apaches to a distant eastern location. Crook balked at the idea, because many of his newly recruited scouts were Chiricahuas, and he feared that removal of their families would adversely affect their performance. For the time being, Sheridan relented.

Brig. Gen. George Crook, 1885, mounted on his mule, Apache, near Fort Bowie, Arizona. (Courtesy of the Arizona Historical Society, Tucson, #25624)

Again, Crook sent two forces into Mexico. The one headed by Capt. Emmett Crawford consisted solely of Apache scouts (mainly Chiricahuas and Coyoteros) and two other officers. In January 1886, this unit—mistaken for "hostiles"—was attacked by Mexican troops, and Crawford was killed. Realizing that pursuers from both Mexico and the United States had breached their Sierra Madre sanctuary, Geronimo and other fugitive leaders now wanted to talk about surrendering, but they would do so only with General Crook. Consequently, on March 25, 1886, Crook and his staff met with the Apaches at Cañon de los Embudos, twelve miles south of the border.

Crook sought their unconditional surrender but finally agreed to terms: they were to spend not more than two years in confinement with their families in the East and then be allowed to return to the reservation. Without this compromise, he feared, the Apaches would lose themselves in the Sierra Madre and continue to raid. Leaving a trusted lieutenant to escort the Apaches, Crook rushed ahead to Fort Bowie, Arizona, to telegraph to Sheridan the news of Geronimo's surrender. President Cleveland, however, refused to accept the surrender terms, and Sheridan wired Crook to reenter negotiations: the Apaches must accept unconditional surrender or face annihilation.

Meanwhile, after getting drunk one night just south of the U.S.-Mexican line, Geronimo fled into the mountains with a small band of followers. Sheridan was furious when he received the news and held Crook responsible for Geronimo's escape. In an exchange of telegrams with Crook, Sheridan expressed his displeasure and seemed to question the loyalty of Crook's Apache scouts. Sheridan, in fact, had never approved of his reliance on Indian auxiliaries; especially now, he doubted their ability to "fight and kill their own people." Faced with Sheridan's implied censure and direct orders to disavow his agreement with the Chiricahuas, Crook wired Sheridan on April 1, 1886, the only response that an honorable man could make: "I believe that the plan upon which I have conducted operations is the one most likely to prove successful in the end. It may be, however, that I am too much wedded to my own views in this matter, and as I have spent nearly eight years of the hardest work of my life in this Department, I respectfully request that I may now be relieved from its command."

Sheridan agreed that it was time for a change. On April 2, he appointed Gen. Nelson A. Miles to command the Department of Arizona and reassigned Crook to the Department of the Platte. For the next several months, Miles's troops pursued the Chiricahua Apaches, unable to meet up with Geronimo. In the end, Miles was forced to use Crook's Apache scouts to make contact with the fugitives. Geronimo finally surrendered to Miles on September 4, 1886, thus ending the Sierra Madre operations. Despite Miles's success in apprehending Geronimo, "the real hero of the army's Apache campaigns," Robert Utley rightfully avows, "remains George Crook. He devised and carried out the only military techniques that ever seriously challenged Apaches in warfare."

The Apache wars dealt a final blow to the "long but stormy friendship" between Crook and Sheridan and led to a bitter feud between Crook and Miles. Crook never forgave either man for the unjust treatment accorded his Chiricahua scouts. During the final hunt for Geronimo, on Sheridan's instructions, Miles sent all the reservation Chiricahuas, including most of Crook's scouts, into imprisonment at Fort Marion, Florida, to prevent them from ever furnishing aid to the fugitives. Later Miles transported Geronimo and the last male holdouts to Fort Pickens, Florida, while their families were interned at Fort Marion, violating his promise to keep the families together. For the rest of his life, Crook campaigned to secure the Chiricahuas' release from these internment camps.

Sometime during Crook's second assignment in Arizona, Mary Crook and her sister, Fanny, joined him at Fort Whipple, where the two women took an active part in social affairs. Mary was at the post, in fact, to dismantle the household and pack their belongings when Crook telegraphed her that he had been relieved of command. The Crooks soon set out for Omaha, accompanied by Fanny, their Chinese cook, and the general's striker. En route, well-wishers showered the general with acclaim and receptions, much to his delight and satisfaction. In the following months, with Indian affairs quiet in the department, Crook handled administrative chores, attended dinner parties and the theater, and played euchre and poker with his friends. In addition, he soon resumed his annual fall hunting trips with Webb Hayes, the ex-president's son.

Yet Crook still chafed from Sheridan's failure to support his work. To set the record straight, he wrote two significant treatises: "The Apache Problem," which appeared in the *Journal of the Military Service Institution of the United States* in October 1886, and *Resumé of Operations Against Apache Indians, 1882–1886*, first printed in Omaha in December of that year. Over Sheridan's objection, the Government Printing Office reprinted the *Resumé* in 1887. In this publication, Crook strongly defended the record of his Chiricahua scouts, giving them the credit for ending hostilities. "I assert that these Chiricahua scouts ... did most excellent service, and were of more value in hunting down and compelling the surrender of the renegades, than all other troops engaged in operations against them, combined," he wrote. Crook continued to find other forums for airing his views, including gatherings in Boston, in 1887, where he spoke at the behest of the Boston Indian Citizenship Committee.

In the spring of 1888, Crook was promoted to major general and assigned to command the Division of the Missouri. Several influential friends pushed for his promotion, including former president Hayes, who wrote to the chief justice, "[Crook's] appointment will be especially gratifying to all who take an interest in just and humane treatment of the Indian." After entering upon his duties in Chicago, Crook was joined by Mary and her sister, and the three took up residence in the Grand Pacific Hotel.

At division headquarters, located in the Pullman Building, Crook instituted a regime of informality, which a *Chicago Herald* reporter applauded. No one was in uniform, he noted. "Everybody, from General Crook down is in citizen's dress." Visitors received a cordial welcome, often from the general himself. Crook, in fact, enjoyed greeting the many old friends who traveled through Chicago en route to Washington or postings in the West.

During this last phase of his life, Crook devoted his time primarily to two issues: the cession of Sioux land and the relocation of the imprisoned Chiricahuas. For several years the U.S. Congress had tried to acquire part of the Sioux Reservation for white expansion. Crook, as a member of the Sioux land commission, traveled to the Sioux agencies during the summer of 1889 and helped persuade tribal members to accept the government's most recent proposal: only "surplus" land would be ceded to the government, the rest to be allotted in severalty. Money derived from the sale of surplus land, an estimated 9 million acres, would be held in trust to benefit the Sioux. Crook had long supported the move to turn Indians into property owners; he believed also that Congress would never offer the Sioux more liberal terms. So, even though the land issue sowed dissension among the Sioux, Crook convinced them that the present offer "was better than nothing, and nothing was what [they] were likely to get if they did not agree soon."

In the fall, his work on the Sioux commission at an end, Crook went on an extended hunting trip with Webb Hayes and then traveled to the East Coast, where he consulted with Gen. O. O. Howard about the condition of the Chiricahua Apaches. The two generals now united in pushing for Indian rights. Many Chiricahuas had died during their incarceration at Fort Marion, adversely affected by the climate and poor housing facilities. Herbert Welsh of the Indian Rights Association, with the support of Crook and Crook's former aide, John G. Bourke, had pressured the government to relocate the Apaches to the supposedly better climate of Mount Vernon Barracks, near Mobile, Alabama. Conditions there were no better; the high mortality rate continued. In late December 1889, with Howard's endorsement, Crook was authorized to find a more suitable location. Accordingly, he traveled to Mount Vernon Barracks to learn firsthand the grievances of the Apaches. The Chiricahuas greeted him warmly, as described in the diary of Crook's aide, Lt. Lyman Kennon: "The Apaches crowded about the General, shaking hands, and laughing in their delight. The news spread that he was there, and those about us shouted to those in the distance, and from all points they came running in until we had a train of them moving with us."

In his report, submitted in early January, Crook decried the injustice of sending into exile his loyal Apache scouts as well as the vast majority of Chiricahuas who had stuck to farming and refused to join in the outbreak of 1885. Admitting that hostility in Arizona against the Chiricahuas made it impractical to send them there, he recommended instead that they be relocated in Indian Territory where the land more closely approximated their homeland. Responding to Crook's report, Senator Henry Dawes soon introduced a Senate joint resolution, authorizing the removal of the Chiricahuas to Fort Sill, Indian Territory. Almost immediately, Crook was caught up in a heated controversy with General Miles, who was angered by the proposed relocation since it seemed to vindicate Crook and repudiate his own actions. Until the day he died, on March 21, 1890, Crook worked relentlessly for passage of the resolution, traveling to Fort Sill in February to inspect the area and writing supportive letters. Four more years would elapse, however, before the Apaches finally were transferred to Fort Sill—still as prisoners of war.

Crook suffered from poor health after his return from Indian Territory, yet he felt well enough to speak on Indian matters at the Chicago Art Institute on March 11 and to attend the theater the night before he died. On the morning of March 21, Crook arose before 7:00 A.M. and went into his dressing room as he usually did to exercise with dumbbells. Suddenly, he had trouble breathing and called out to Mary for help. He died shortly afterward of heart failure at the age of sixty-one.

Funeral services were held at the Grand Pacific Hotel on a Sunday afternoon, with many of Crook's friends and comrades in attendance. Webb Hayes accompanied his father to Chicago, where the former president served as an honorary pallbearer. A special train draped in black took the coffin to Oakland, Maryland, for burial. Among the many on hand to pay respects and console the widow were Webb Hayes, Lt. Lyman Kennon, Capt. John G. Bourke, Fanny Reade, and Crook's brother, Walter. On November 11, 1890, Crook's remains were reinterred in Arlington National Cemetery, also the final resting place of Mary Crook, who outlived her husband by five years.

After Crook's death, two of his former aides, Capt. John G. Bourke and Maj. Azor H. Nickerson, wrote flattering accounts of the general, and their works are often cited by military and western historians. Crook, of course, had his detractors, especially among officers who envied his rapid advance in rank. Modern scholars try to give a balanced picture of the general but are hampered by significant gaps in the Crook papers. Correspondence between Crook and his wife, for example, is missing, and only two volumes of his diaries, for the years 1885–1890, have been located. His unfinished autobiography, which abruptly ends with the Battle of the Rosebud, shows him to be a man of action (like most military men) not given to introspection.

Without doubt, Crook was one of the most successful officers in the nineteenth-century army. His success stemmed, in part, from his understanding of military politics, as he had learned early in his career that a favorable press and influential backers helped advance military careers. Although he did not court politicians and reporters as assiduously as did some of his more flamboyant fellow officers, he won the support of powerful statesmen, including Rutherford B. Hayes and Ulysses S. Grant, and numerous journalists who followed his campaigns. His wife, Mary, also played a role in his climb to success. By heeding General Sherman's advice to young wives to follow their officer-husbands west, she made Crook's life more comfortable than it might have been otherwise and helped create a congenial atmosphere within the military communities where the Crooks resided. Politically astute herself, Mary did not hesitate to approach powerful people on behalf of her husband.

His fame, however, rested on his exploits as an Indian fighter. Because he learned to counter the guerilla warfare of the Apaches with unconventional tactics, Crook has been called the "most original thinker" in the frontier army. His great success came from employing Apaches to fight Apaches, recognizing the psychological impact this action had on the warring bands. "To polish a diamond there is nothing like its own dust," Crook told journalist Charles F. Lummis in 1886. "It is the same with these fellows. Nothing breaks them up like turning their own people against them."

Despite Crook's success as an Indian fighter, his greatest legacy to the nation was his work as a humanitarian, seeking justice for American Indians and urging fellow citizens to treat them as human beings. Although like other reformers of his day he embraced the doctrine of white supremacy and believed that Indian customs must give way to the dominant society, he was sincerely interested in the Indians' welfare and implemented practical programs to help them adjust to changing conditions. The two sides of Crook's career—as humanitarian and fighter—were aptly depicted in Rutherford B. Hayes's eulogy to his friend:

> [Crook was] a man of wonderful character and gifts. No seeker after popularity, he was loved by all sorts and conditions of men. With all of the essential and usual virtues of the soldier, he had modesty, sincerity, tenderness, absolute integrity, and veracity. He wears the double wreath—the soldier's and the humanitarian's.

General George Armstrong Custer

The Waging of Total War in the American West

Shirley A. Leckie

On May 23, 1865, following the Grand Review of the victorious Army of the Potomac in Washington, D.C., twenty-five-year-old Gen. George Armstrong Custer bade farewell to the soldiers of the Third Division of Cavalry. He basked in their adulation that day for he loved nothing so much as praise. Beside him was his wife, Elizabeth, two years younger than he and better known as Libbie. Her black velvet riding cap, with a red feather that echoed the color of her husband's necktie, and her dress, adorned with military buttons, showed her identification with her husband's career. The men of the Third Division also wore red neckties, thereby displaying their emotional affiliation with the Union Army's famous "Boy General." Happy and magnanimous on that occasion, Custer credited his soldiers with winning the victories they had shared together.

Many of the men present undoubtedly recalled the battles and campaigns they had fought since Custer had become their commander the previous September. Most notably, they had participated in the fall 1864 Shenandoah Valley campaign in which the young general had done what he did best. Desiring accolades, he had faithfully implemented the commands of his superior, Gen. Philip A. Sheridan, the cavalry commander of the Army of the Potomac. Following Sheridan's instructions, which emanated from Ulysses S. Grant, commanding general of the Union Army, Custer had inflicted total war on a civilian population. That meant that he and his men had cut a wide swath of destruction as they burned crops and farms in the breadbasket of the Confederacy. Most important of all, by transforming the valley into a "barren waste," they had destroyed the civilian will to continue supporting the Confederate cause. The Union victory at Cedar Creek on October 19 that ended the campaign had brought Custer his second star. In the recent spring campaign, the Third Division had played an important role in the final battles against the Army of Northern Virginia. The men of

Brevet Brig. Gen.George A. Custer, pho-
tographed here with his sabre in 1864. Although
he was known as the Boy General with the long
golden curls, he had cut his hair for his marriage
to Elizabeth Bacon in February 1864. (Courtesy
of the National Park Service, Little Bighorn
Battlefield National Monument, #575)

the Third Division knew that they had contributed more than their share to the Confederacy's defeat.

Had Custer's military career ended at this point, later historians would have chronicled him as the northern cavalier of the Civil War. Undoubtedly, some scholars would have raised questions about the high losses of life and limb under the youthful general's leadership. During the spring campaign of 1864, for example, which began with the Battle of the Wilderness, Custer's troops had sustained casualties of 45 percent, the highest of any Union cavalry in the entire war. None of Custer's immediate superiors, however, had objected. Indeed, General Sheridan had applauded his subaltern who, despite his recent marriage to Libbie, still charged with the same ferocity and disregard for safety as he had as a single man.

As for the men who had served under Custer, their memories of shared combat, although costly and bloody, had created a strong bond between them and their commander. They remembered that the Boy General with the long golden curls had always placed himself in the front of his troops, rather than commanding from a distance. Clad in his broad-brimmed hat, red necktie, and uniform, heavily trimmed with gold braid, he had escaped Confederate sharpshooters only by staying constantly in motion. Even then, eleven horses had been shot from under him and bullets had grazed his cheeks. Yet, despite the terrible losses of the Civil War, most soldiers in the Army of the Potomac probably agreed with Grant and Sheridan that a willingness to take such casualties was the only way the North could have won that conflict. Thus, the majority of soldiers were grateful to Custer for his courage and leadership. Among his fervent admirers that day was Maj. Albert Barnitz of the Second Ohio Cavalry. An aspiring writer, he would soon join the peacetime army to serve again under his beloved commander.

Libbie Custer, gazing at the crowd, felt immense pride in her choice of a husband. Her father, Daniel Bacon, a retired Monroe, Michigan, probate county judge, had hated him initially. The son of Emanuel Custer, farmer and blacksmith, and Maria Kirkpatrick Custer of New Rumley, Ohio, George Armstrong Custer came from a lower social class than the Bacons. Worse yet, the youth had a well-deserved reputation as a rake. Stories circulated, for example, that he had attended West Point because of an irate father. Alexander Holland, according to one account, had prevailed on Congressman John Bingham to support the youth's application, after intercepting his letter to his daughter Mollie asking her to meet him "at the trundle bed." At the academy, after barely escaping dismissal for numerous demerits, Armstrong had graduated last in a class of thirty-four. Finally, the first time Daniel Bacon had laid eyes on him in the winter of 1862–63, Custer, then a lieutenant on leave from the Fifth Cavalry, had been careening drunkenly down Monroe's main street. It mattered little that he later took the temperance oath and kept it religiously. The austere judge adamantly rejected him as a suitor for his daughter's hand in marriage.

But Armstrong's star was in ascendancy. His willingness to undertake dangerous intelligence-gathering activities and his ability to write clear

George Armstrong Custer's military service and various engagements in the West during the Indian wars captured the imagination of novelists, poets, and painters for decades to come. In this 1904 print, "Attack at Dawn," the artist Charles Schreyvogel depicts the opening moments of the Seventh Cavalry's attack on Black Kettle's village on the Washita River in Indian Territory in November 1868. (Courtesy of the National Park Service, Little Bighorn Battlefield National Monument, #56)

reports had earlier brought him to the attention of George McClellan, commanding general of the Army of the Potomac. Although Lincoln dismissed McClellan from his command a second time after the Battle of Antietam, Custer's fearlessness and initiative in battle won him promotion to brigadier general in June 1863. On the third day of the Battle of Gettysburg, as Gen. George Pickett was assaulting the Union center at Cemetery Ridge, Custer's Michigan Brigade played a vital role. Because of their headlong charges, Gen. James Ewell Brown (Jeb) Stuart and his Confederate cavalry came no closer to the Union lines than two and a half miles. The victory that followed gave the North a new hero: the Boy General. By September 1863, Daniel Bacon's opposition to Custer's courtship of his daughter had evaporated. On February 9, 1864, George Armstrong Custer married Elizabeth Bacon in one of Monroe, Michigan's most elegant weddings. In the fifteen months since, Libbie had waited for her husband in Washington, D.C., except for brief periods between battles or in winter months when she had joined him in the field. Now that the war was over, she looked forward to enjoying her husband's companionship without the constant anxiety of another looming campaign.

Her joy was short-lived. Soon after saying goodbye to the men of the Third Division, Armstrong, with Libbie accompanying him, was sent to Louisiana. There he assumed command of a division of volunteer units assembled for possible intervention in Mexico against Napoleon III's Austrian puppet, Prince Maximilian. The intervention never occurred, but another difficult battle ensued. The volunteers who had served in the western theater of the war almost mutinied because of the mistreatment they received from Custer.

The problems started less than twenty-four hours after the young general's arrival. Immediately he issued edicts forbidding the soldiers to forage from local farmers (which had not happened) and instituted flogging and head shaving as punishments, despite a congressional ban on flogging since 1861. When the soldiers of the Second Wisconsin Cavalry petitioned for the removal of Lt. Col. Nicholas Dale for allegedly rejoicing over the late president Abraham Lincoln's assassination, Custer charged them with mutiny. Relations deteriorated beyond repair, and many, if not most, of the men in Custer's command now hated him. Within weeks of his farewell to the men of the Third Division, Armstrong emerged as a petty tyrant to the midwestern troops he now commanded.

Peace, it turned out, proved more stressful for George Armstrong Custer than war. The one certain dynamic operating in his life was that he flourished when he had the opportunity to win plaudits from his superiors and the public at large. When that opportunity was withdrawn, he turned inward and became anxious and even depressed. Perhaps his inordinate need for accolades came from growing up in a household where he competed with children from his parents' former marriages (both had been widowed) and four siblings who arrived after his birth in December 1839.

Whatever the reason, now that the war was over and the applause had died down, Custer was a different man. He acted with less assurance and his former magnanimity vanished. Adding to his unease, the men he commanded were different. Having elected their own officers earlier, they thought they had the right to rid themselves of commanders they no longer respected. That idea, which ran counter to his West Point training, was anathema to Custer.

When these troops complained to Governor William Stone of Iowa and members of the Wisconsin legislature, state officials forwarded their grievances to the War Department. General Sheridan defended his protégé when General Grant pressed him for an explanation for the soldiers' allegations of mistreatment. To Sheridan, Custer was the subaltern he had always relied on. He was the one who, more than any other officer, had allowed him to inform Grant after the Shenandoah Valley Campaign in October 1864, "the people have nothing left but their eyes to weep over." Not surprisingly, Sheridan excused the young general, noting "the insubordination of his command" and adding, "If anything he has been too lenient." To Sheridan, George Armstrong Custer, the officer who had unflinchingly implemented total war against the Confederacy, could do little wrong.

In February 1866, after several months of Reconstruction duty in Austin, Texas, which followed his duty in Louisiana, Custer's rank in the regular army reverted to captain. With that drop in pay and prestige, the former major general headed east to seek a better position. During his absence, he wrote Libbie, who remained in Monroe to care for her ailing father and stepmother, that he was "very anxious to leave the army provided I can enter some business or employment which is certain to bring me an increased income." When no such opportunity materialized, Custer accepted an appointment as lieutenant colonel in the Seventh Cavalry. Although Sheridan requested a full colonelcy for his protégé, Grant consented only to the lesser rank.

The Seventh was one of the new regiments formed to police the trans–Mississippi West. There, in an area once known as the Great American Desert, the Plains Indians—Sioux, Cheyennes, Arapahoes, Kiowas, and the Comanches—were fighting for their existence as a people. Since the beginning of the overland trails in the 1840s, the livestock of migrating families had diminished the forage available to the buffalo. At the same time, it had also introduced new diseases and parasites that had taken an additional toll on the herds, the mainstay of the Plains Indians' way of life. A severe drought in 1863; the continuing incursions of miners, farmers, and town builders onto Indian lands; and the appropriation of pastureland and streams by ranchers had left the nomadic tribes of the Great Plains in dire straits.

Recent events had made matters worse. In November 1864, the Colorado militia under Col. John M. Chivington had massacred a band of Cheyennes camped along Sand Creek in present-day Colorado who were led by the peace chief, Black Kettle. The resulting war had unleashed new violence throughout the Great Plains. Subsequently, the Treaty of the Little Arkansas in October 1865 had brought an uneasy peace. The Cheyenne Dog Soldiers, a society of young warriors, wanted war and, angered by construction of the transcontinental railroad, threatened the crews of the Union Pacific, Eastern Division. They understood that the railroads would separate the buffalo herds and would bring non-Indian hunters onto the plains to reduce their numbers even further. Farther south, their allies, the Kiowas and Comanches, struck at the settlements that were expanding into their Texas hunting grounds since the end of the Civil War.

At Fort Riley, headquarters of the Seventh Cavalry, Col. Andrew Smith left the training of officers to his new lieutenant colonel, Custer, especially after he assumed command of the District of the Upper Arkansas early in 1867. Custer and his company commanders faced severe challenges as they struggled to instill discipline in the army's new recruits. The low pay and status assigned to soldiering in peacetime meant that the army now attracted many recent immigrants from Ireland and Germany who faced discrimination and limited economic opportunities in their adopted land. Among the native-born recruits, some were fleeing a criminal past or an unhappy marriage and were poor candidates for military discipline. Others would desert at the first opportunity to seek their fortunes in the western mines. Taken altogether, they were a far cry from the often-worshipful men Custer had commanded in the Civil War.

Feuding among the officers was more serious in the Seventh than in many regiments. In addition to the usual divisions between West Pointers and those from volunteer units in the Civil War, the officers came from varied backgrounds, educational levels, and nationalities. As Libbie Custer later recalled, they included an Irish immigrant who had served as a papal Zouave (a French soldier assigned to protect the papal states); a Canadian; an "educated Indian, part Scotch and part 'Six Nations'"; and one officer who had risen from the ranks of the enlisted men. Forging such "incongruous elements" into a cohesive regiment would have been difficult under any circumstances, but Custer himself was an additional source of conflict. Although many officers resented taking orders from so youthful a commander, others almost idolized him. Two cliques—the anti-Custer and the pro-Custer—formed immediately. Armstrong assured Libbie, however, that the regiment would become unified once it experienced combat, for "it was on the battle-field, when all faced death together, where the truest affection was formed among soldiers."

Combat appeared imminent. In December 1866, Sioux warriors under Oglala chief Crazy Horse had ambushed and killed Capt. William J. Fetterman and the eighty men accompanying him not far from Fort Phil Kearny in Montana Territory. Although chiefs of the Plains Indians usually wanted peace, the younger men often raised their voices for war. In that context, Custer trained his men in anticipation of a spring campaign under Gen. Winfield Scott Hancock, commander of the Department of the Missouri. Like Custer, Hancock had made his reputation at Gettysburg, but his ability to fight Indians remained unknown.

Hancock, seeking to "overawe" the Indians, began by concentrating 1,400 infantry, cavalry, and artillery at Fort Larned. There he planned to meet with chiefs from the Cheyennes and the Brulé and Oglala Sioux who had migrated southward following the Fetterman massacre. When a snowstorm delayed a council set for April 9 and only two chiefs and a few tribesmen appeared three days later, Hancock instructed Custer to cordon off a Cheyenne and Sioux village on Pawnee Creek. Arriving at the village, Custer found it deserted except for a blind old man and a young girl, although dog meat still simmered over the fires. Ordered to pursue the fleeing Indians, Custer discovered, after a rapid chase northwestward, that their tracks crisscrossed in all directions. Further pursuit was futile, and he now learned an important lesson: fighting Indians was far different from fighting Confederates. Once they eluded their pursuers, they were almost impossible to intercept. Still, intercept he must, for Hancock had burned the Pawnee Creek village, thereby reigniting Indian warfare on the Great Plains, from the Platte River in the North to the Red River in the South.

By May, Custer was at Fort Hays waiting for the rivers to subside and supplies and forage to arrive so that he could continue his pursuit. The whereabouts of the Cheyenne and Sioux remained a mystery, a situation that left him depressed. He was discovering that the Plains Indians fought as they hunted. Using stealth and surprise, they raided outlying farms and telegraph stations and disappeared as swiftly as they had appeared. What chance was there for glory when one confronted not massed armies but expert guerilla fighters?

Faced with this new kind of warfare and the loss of his sense of self as a heroic and admired figure, Custer reverted to the dictatorial behavior that had proved so disastrous in Louisiana. With provisions, especially vegetables and fruit, inadequate, some of the Seventh's soldiers suffered from scurvy. When they visited the post sutler to purchase canned fruit against their commander's orders, Custer punished them by parading them around the post with their heads half shaven. Not surprisingly, ninety men deserted over the next six weeks. Albert Barnitz, now a disillusioned captain in the Seventh, wrote his wife, Jennie, "No man but an incarnate fiend could take pleasure in such abuse of authority." In his view, Custer was fast losing the confidence and respect of his men as well as officers.

On June 1, when supplies finally arrived, Custer left Fort Hays with six companies of the Seventh Cavalry. He began a series of marches that make no sense in retrospect. That is, they make no sense until one realizes that all he really wanted was the opportunity to rejoin Libbie. She alone could compensate for his feelings of loss and give him a sense of security. Thus, when William T. Sherman, commander of the Division of the Missouri, instructed Custer to march toward Fort Sedgwick where he would find supplies and provide protection for the Platte River construction crews of the Union Pacific, Custer headed instead for Fort Wallace. After all, he had asked Lt. William Cooke to escort Libbie there despite the dangers of traveling on the Kansas plains. Learning en route that she was not there, however, he headed back toward Sedgwick until new instructions caught up with him telling him to march toward Wallace. Weary and disgusted with all this frantic marching to no specific place or purpose, many of his men hit the trails leading to the western mining camps. At Riverside Station, Custer ordered all deserters shot. Shortly after, three men were shot while fleeing. When the surgeon approached them, Custer ordered him away as a warning to others. Later, he told the surgeon to care for the wounded men in secret. Lacking water, the surgeon could do little, and one man died.

On July 13, Custer and six diminished companies arrived at Fort Wallace in western Kansas. In his autobiographical *My Life on the Plains*, published in 1875, Custer claimed that he reached a post that was under siege, dangerously low on supplies, and in the throes of a cholera epidemic. Facing those dire circumstances, he left on July 15, with seventy-six officers and enlisted men and the command's best horses. He was determined, he wrote, "to open a way through to Fort Harker" to resupply the post and relieve its suffering.

War Department records belie all of his statements. The post was not under siege, for additional companies had arrived. Indian attacks were less frequent, mail stages were coming through about once a week, and supplies were on hand for a month. Furthermore, cholera did not strike Fort Wallace and the Seventh Cavalry until July 22. Finally, as temporary commander of Fort Wallace, Custer had no authorization to leave his post. Nonetheless, above all else, he was determined to rejoin his wife. Thus, he and his men began a march that covered 150 miles in fifty-five hours and included stops at Fort Hays and Fort Harker before he entrained for Fort Riley. On July 19, he and Libbie experienced an ecstatic reunion at the post. As she wrote in *Tenting on the Plains*, her second volume of memoirs, published in 1887, "There was in that summer of 1867 one perfect day. It was mine, and—blessed be our memory, which preserves to us the joys as well as the sadness of life!—it is still mine, for time and eternity."

This grand gesture, which told Libbie that she was more important to her husband than his career, revitalized the romance of their marriage. That came, however, at a very high price. In October 1867, a court-martial found Custer guilty of being absent without leave and of "conduct to the prejudice of good order and military discipline." Among the specifications, he had overmarched men and government horses and mules. More serious, in an act of extreme callousness, he had failed to care for two soldiers Indians had shot near Downer's Station; they had been part of a detachment sent back to retrieve his favorite mare. Custer's sentence was dismissal from the army and suspension from rank and pay for one year. General Grant, characterizing the sentence as "lenient," thought that the court "must have taken into consideration his previous services." Sheridan, who replaced Hancock as commander of the Department of the Missouri early in 1868, showed his true feelings. He turned his comfortable quarters at Fort Leavenworth over to the Custers for the coming winter. In June they returned to Monroe to serve out the final months of Custer's sentence.

While they contended with these developments, changes occurred in Indian affairs. Late in October 1867, members of the congressionally appointed Indian Peace Commission signed treaties at Medicine Lodge Creek in Kansas with the Kiowas, Comanches, Southern Cheyennes, and Arapahoes. These Native peoples agreed to live on reservations away from the railroads and settlements. In return, they were accorded the right to hunt buffalo south of the Arkansas River and collect government annuities for thirty years. From the beginning, however, the agreement was compromised. Journalist Henry Stanley and Major Barnitz were both present and observed that the chiefs had little understanding of the terms of the treaty.

Moreover, Congress, absorbed in President Andrew Johnson's impeachment, failed to supply the promised annuities, thereby sentencing the Southern Plains tribes to more hunger and deprivation. By the summer of 1868, the Cheyenne Dog Soldiers were committing depredations in Kansas, especially among the settlements along the Saline and Solomon Rivers.

A telegram to Custer, dated September 24, 1868, brought joyous news. Sheridan, wanting him to participate in a campaign against Indians, had sought an early remission of his sentence. Custer boarded the first train that would carry him westward. At Fort Hays on October 4, Sheridan described his plans to Custer over breakfast. A strong column from Fort Lyon, Colorado, would push southeastward. Another from Fort Bascom, New Mexico, would drive eastward. Together they would propel the Plains Indians into the path of the third and strongest column, moving south from Fort Dodge under Custer's command.

In the dead of winter, when the tribes were most vulnerable and least expected attack, the Seventh would strike their villages. Jim Bridger, the mountain man, had informed Sheridan that such a campaign in the inclement climate of the Great Plains would result in disaster. But, as Custer had implemented "total war" in the Shenandoah Valley, he would now implement the same kind of warfare against the Plains Indians. "I rely upon you in everything," Sheridan told him, "and shall send you on this expedition without giving you any orders, leaving you to act entirely upon your judgment." It was the Shenandoah Valley Campaign all over again, only this time against the Plains Indians rather than the Confederates. Custer was elated; here was a chance to restore his reputation and revive his fame.

At daylight on November 23, despite the absence of the Nineteenth Kansas Cavalry, a volunteer unit formed especially for the campaign, and in the midst of heavy snow, Custer left Camp Supply. He followed "a fresh trail of a large war party" from a village about fifty miles southward. After fording the Canadian River, he force-marched his men. At 1 A.M. November 27, the command halted by the dying embers of a fire. Custer and Little Beaver, an Osage scout employed for his knowledge of the terrain and understanding of the Native peoples the army was seeking to force onto the reservation, ascended a ledge. It overlooked the Washita River Valley, and despite the darkness of the night, Little Beaver informed Custer, "Heap Injuns down there."

From a distance, a dog's bark, the sound of a bell, and an infant's cry pierced the night air. As frozen soldiers huddled together, unable to build a fire or even stomp their feet for warmth, Capt. William Thompson worried aloud. "Suppose we find more Indians there than we can handle," he said.

"Huh," Custer responded, "all I am afraid of is we won't find half enough." Viewing his regiment as superior in fighting ability to any other combatants, he added, "There are not Indians enough in the country to whip the Seventh Cavalry."

The morning star burned bright in the sky when Custer split his command into four battalions to encircle the sleeping Indians. At daylight, as the battalions closed, a warning shot from the village told the soldiers they had been spotted. Custer signaled the charge and the first few notes of "Garry Owen" sounded and died as the trumpeters' lips froze to their instruments. When the Seventh assailed the village, which was that of the peace chief Black Kettle, Indians, both males and females, bounded from their tents and fought tenaciously with any weapons at hand. Awakened from their sleep, however, they were at a disadvantage. In the battle that followed, Black Kettle and his wife were among those killed. The Seventh sustained few casualties, including four who suffered mortal wounds and about a dozen who were injured. As the warriors fought a running battle, Custer ordered the taking of women and children as hostages and the destruction of everything of value in the village. Pauperized, the Indians would have no choice but to move to the reservation.

About midday, Lt. Edward S. Godfrey, while rounding up ponies, the Indians' prized possessions, found himself atop a slight hill where he could view the river valley. Before him were tipis as far as the eye could see and "mounted warriors scurrying in our direction." He also heard heavy firing from across the river where Maj. Joel Elliott had led a detachment earlier. When Godfrey informed Custer of these sights and sounds, his commander hurried the destruction of all the tipis, robes, food supplies, and ponies. He also sent Capt. Edward Myers to look for Elliott and the eighteen men with him. Despite a two mile search down the valley, Myers found no sign of the lost detachment.

At dusk, Custer knew that growing numbers of Indians were massing and his supply train was still on the back trail. Aware that timidity invited attack, he marched his troops down the Washita Valley as if preparing to attack the other villages. His feint worked. The growing number of Indians, seeing the Seventh's hostages and knowing that an attack could place their own families in danger, hurried away. After nightfall, Custer reversed direction through the still-smoldering village and led his men to the next divide and north toward Camp Supply.

Having achieved the first significant victory over the Plains Indians since the Civil War, Custer entered Camp Supply as if he were a conquering general. At the front marched the scouts, then the captive women and children.

Following the Battle of Washita, Custer changed his persona to reflect his new status as a man of the plains or what his biographer Robert Utley calls, "a cavalier in buckskin." "How do you like the beard?" Armstrong asked Libbie in his letter of March 1, 1869, in which he enclosed this picture. (Courtesy of the National Park Service, Little Bighorn Battlefield National Monument, #633)

Finally, the Seventh Cavalry passed in review with colors flying and the band playing "Garry Owen" before General Sheridan and his staff. Henceforth, Custer had another persona: he was a frontiersman—an identity he expressed by donning an elaborately fringed buckskin jacket. He sent Libbie a photograph, noting that she might not recognize her husband and asking, "How do you like the beard?"

Nonetheless, many of the bands were still off their reservations. Thus, Custer and the Seventh—now reinforced by the Nineteenth Kansas, delayed earlier by a blizzard—continued campaigning. As the Seventh returned to the Washita battlefield, soldiers came upon the nineteen stripped and mutilated bodies of Major Elliott and his detachment on December 11. The numerous spent cartridges close by testified to a prolonged fight in which the longed-for aid had never arrived. The matter of Elliott's disappearance and Custer's failure to search for him before leaving the Washita battlefield left Sheridan disturbed. He now muted his praise for Custer's recent victory. As for the Seventh's officers and men, undoubtedly some agreed with Captain Benteen's bitter remarks. Appearing anonymously in the St. Louis *Missouri Democrat* on February 8, 1869, his comments charged Custer with deserting his men. Custer viewed combat as a means of bringing the Seventh closer together, but the Battle of the Washita deepened its divisions. Benteen's description of besieged and despairing men left some in the Seventh fearful that one day they too might suffer the same fate.

Custer wrote Libbie, warning her to be prepared for criticism from eastern humanitarians. Samuel Tappan, one of the commissioners at Medicine Lodge, noted that Congress had been derelict in funding the promised annuities. Moreover, many advocates of a more humane policy toward Indians were distressed that Custer had attacked Black Kettle's village four years after the Sand Creek Massacre. "Surely," Libbie wrote her aunt Eliza Sabin in upstate New York, "you do not believe the complaints against Autie. If you only knew the depredations and unspeakable crimes these Indians commit." Unfortunately, both husband and wife were learning that the divisions within American society regarding Indian policy guaranteed a mixed reaction to his success at the Washita.

For Custer, however, the lessons of the Washita were not derived from Elliott's fate or the criticisms of eastern humanitarians. Rather, he had won the battle by defying conventional military wisdom and forgoing the usual reconnaissance. With no prior knowledge of either the strength of his adversaries or the terrain, he had struck a village. Had he followed rules he learned at West Point or in Civil War combat, his adversaries would have detected him. Then, he was certain, they would have fled.

Throughout that winter, Custer, determined to build on his Washita victory and win new laurels as an Indian fighter, led the Seventh and the Kansas militia as together they forced bands of Kiowas and Arapahoes onto reservations at Fort Cobb and a new site, Camp Wichita. (Later it became Fort Sill.) With the less exhausted half of his command, he then doggedly pursued Cheyenne bands who were still out in the Texas panhandle. In March, after days of slogging through rain and mud, he located the village of Chief Medicine Arrows and later that of Chief Little Robe on Sweetwater Creek. Learning that Little Robe's village held two female hostages whom members of the Nineteenth Kansas—including a brother of one of the women—hoped to recover, he seized Little Robe and three of his party. Unless the women were set free, Custer informed the Cheyennes, he would hang his hostages. Three days later the women were released to the soldiers. These Cheyennes were so close to starvation that Custer left them to come onto the reservation on their own. When their ponies gained enough strength from the spring grasses to permit them to travel, they willingly complied.

Whatever the controversies surrounding the Washita victory, Custer now emerged in the public's mind as the nation's foremost Indian fighter. He gloried in his renewed prominence, especially when visitors from far and wide arrived on the Kansas plains to hunt buffalo with him and Libbie, who observed events from her own carriage. Among their hunting parties in 1869 and 1870 were members of the British Parliament and circus magnate P. T. Barnum. Such company as well as newspaper reports of their activities added to Custer's reputation as an expert frontiersman of the Great Plains.

By the 1870s Custer had emerged as a scholarly soldier by publishing essays about his adventures on the plains. He always insisted that Libbie sit beside him while he wrote, and the two are shown here in Armstrong's study at Fort Abraham Lincoln in 1875. (Courtesy of the National Park Service, Little Bighorn Battlefield National Monument)

During an extended leave in 1871, Custer visited the East and once more sought a more lucrative alternative to military service. In New York City, he peddled stock in the Stevens Silver Mine in Colorado to bankers and entrepreneurs, such as August Belmont and John Jacob Astor. Again, as in 1866, no alternative career presented itself, so he returned to active duty in Kentucky. The Seventh Cavalry had been sent there to curb the activities of the Ku Klux Klan. To Custer such service held little appeal, especially since it gave him no chance to win widespread acclaim. John Burkman, the "striker," the soldier who served as a servant to the Custers during his off-duty hours by taking care of their forty or so hunting hounds, recalled something else. Although Armstrong often engaged in practical jokes with Libbie and his brother Tom, a lieutenant with the Seventh Cavalry, "They was times when we were alone together I seen a kinda unhappy look in his eyes that worried me considerable."

Often bored, Custer turned to raising racehorses. All were "off their time," and he lost money gambling on them. To engage him in a more wholesome and less costly activity, Libbie encouraged him to write about his service on the plains. Beginning in 1867, his "Nomad" pieces, describing wildlife on the plains and buffalo hunts, had appeared in *Turf, Field and Farm*, thereby laying the foundation for his reputation as a "gentleman hunter" in the West. The new essays, covering his exploits in the Hancock and Washita Campaigns and his views on Indian policy, were published in *The Galaxy*, a New York journal. Later, Sheldon & Company compiled these writings in the volume entitled *My Life on the Plains*.

Early in 1873, Custer returned from Louisville, where his duties frequently called him, and began whooping and shouting. He had received orders transferring the Seventh to Dakota Territory and was ecstatic. Now that the Seventh was assigned to the northern Plains to protect the construction crews of the Northern Pacific Railroad from the Sioux Indians, he saw new possibilities for adding to his fame as an Indian fighter.

Since the signing of the Treaty of Fort Laramie in 1868 between the Sioux and the U.S. government, work on the Bozeman Trail and construction of three posts that led into the Montana goldfields had halted. In return, the signatory chiefs, mainly the followers of Oglala chief Red Cloud and the Brulé chief Spotted Tail, and representing about 15,000 Sioux, had agreed to live on the Great Sioux Reservation west of the Missouri River in present-day South Dakota. Article 12 of that treaty also specified that no part of "their permanent home" could be ceded by future treaty unless "at least three fourths of all the adult male Indians" gave their consent. The United States, however, could build roads, including railroads, across the reservation.

About 3,000 Sioux, led most notably by Hunkpapa Sitting Bull and Oglala Crazy Horse, refused reservation life entirely and never signed the treaty. Nonetheless, the treaty identified a territory "north of the North Platte River and east of the summits of the Big Horn Mountains" as "unceded territory." There bands could hunt and roam at will and no outside settlements could be established without Indian permission. The line between treaty and nontreaty Sioux, moreover, remained permeable. The nontreaty Indians often joined their relatives in the winter to draw rations, arms, and ammunition at the various agencies. In summer, members of the reservation bands often hunted with their nontreaty kin in unceded territory.

By 1873, both treaty and nontreaty Indians were angry. The previous summer, surveyors and construction crews for the Northern Pacific Railroad had begun work on the south bank of the Yellowstone River. The Sioux considered that area off limits for road building, according to their understanding of the Fort Laramie Treaty. They were, in addition, fully aware that the appearance of the "iron horse" in unceded territory would doom their way of life based on buffalo hunting. Predictably, skirmishes had already occurred between Indians and construction crews; they would only increase once work resumed that summer. When railroad officials requested army protection, Sherman, now commanding general of the army, and Sheridan, now commander of the Division of the Missouri, gladly complied. Railroad lines, by separating the great buffalo herds, would bring in their wake farms, cities, and commerce that would destroy the Plains Indians' economy. That, in turn, would drive the nontreaty or, as they were often called, the Sitting Bull bands, onto reservations where, in the generals' view, they belonged.

On June 20, the Seventh Cavalry and the Seventeenth and Twenty-second Infantries left Fort Rice in Dakota Territory under the command of David S. Stanley, colonel of the Twenty-second. The expedition seemed like an extended picnic and hunting expedition until August 4. Custer, eager to engage Sioux warriors, deliberately allowed his advance detachment of two companies to be drawn into combat. For hours, he and his men managed to hold off their adversaries. With the sun setting and ammunition running low, the fortuitous arrival of the rest of his command sent the Indians fleeing. That close call was repeated on August 11 when Custer and his command, in pursuit of his earlier assailants, were attempting for the second day to ford the Yellowstone River three miles from its source. As heavy gunfire erupted from across the river, Custer realized that the Sioux were also crossing above and below his encampment. Only his skilled deployment of officers and men repulsed the attack until Stanley's infantry arrived. The Sioux then retreated with the soldiers in hot pursuit for several miles.

In both battles, Custer won fresh laurels, as the national press publicized his newest feats. Undoubtedly that proved gratifying after years of lackluster duty in the South. Privately, however, he might have pondered the meaning of what he had encountered, for it challenged some of the conclusions he had reached in his combat with Native peoples in the past. Custer expected Indians to flee, but the Sioux, well armed with repeating rifles, had not done so. Instead, with their wives, children, and elders observing the battle from a nearby bluff, they had fought tenaciously in defense of their land. Reading the Associated Press accounts, Libbie wrote Armstrong from Monroe, "Oh Autie who could envy such a day as I have spent. The pride and glory I feel in you is mingled with such thrills of fear and such terrified thoughts at what risks you run to achieve your victory."

The Seventh's new headquarters when Custer returned from the Yellowstone Expedition was Fort Abraham Lincoln. There, on the west bank of the Missouri River not far from Bismarck in present-day North Dakota, the Custers moved into a newly constructed commanding officer's home, magnificent by frontier army standards. After the first dwelling burned to the ground in February 1874, its replacement, boasting a large bay window in the parlor that Libbie filled with plants, was even more impressive. With a piano rented from St. Paul, Minnesota, the couple enjoyed the ongoing companionship of Tom Custer and another sibling, Maggie (Margaret) Custer, now married to Lt. James Calhoun. They also frequently entertained the other post officers and their wives and visiting dignitaries. Although no couple ever enjoyed the idyllic life Libbie later described in her books, she was truthful when she wrote, "Of all our happy days, the happiest had now come to us at Fort Lincoln."

In July 1874, ten companies of the Seventh and two from the Seventeenth and Twentieth Infantries set out on another expedition, this time through the Black Hills. Officially they were seeking a suitable location for another fort on the Great Sioux Reservation, since the Sioux still threatened railroad crews and had committed recent depredations. Less publicized but more important, the expedition would determine if the rumors of gold in the Black Hills were true.

For decades stories of gold in the hills had circulated. Now Dakota boosters increasingly pressured the federal government to conduct a survey that would answer that question once and for all. True, the Black Hills belonged to the Sioux according to the Treaty of Fort Laramie, but 1874 marked the nation's second year of depression. The Grant administration, under increasing pressure for its Reconstruction policies in the South and revelations about corruption among members of the president's cabinet, was loath to turn citizens away from western goldfields. Thus, in addition to those experts who would select the best site for the new fort, the expedition included two "practical miners"—William McKay and Horatio Nelson Ross—as well as journalists from New York and Chicago newspapers and one from the *Bismarck Tribune*. On July 30, Ross discovered the first evidence of gold while panning in French Creek. Two days later, Ross and McKay issued statements that prospecting for gold might prove worthwhile after all. That same day, Custer sent Charley Reynolds, a noted army scout, to Fort Laramie to file reports from journalists. These included one from William E. Curtis, correspondent for the Chicago *Inter-Ocean*, which proclaimed, "From the grass roots down it was 'pay dirt.'" The *Bismarck Tribune* now characterized the Black Hills as a veritable "El Dorado." Before long, miners were invading the region despite the Grant administration's orders that no intruders be allowed on this Indian land.

When a follow-up expedition in 1875 under Walter Jenney confirmed these reports, Secretary of the Interior Alonzo Delano sent a commission under Senator William Allison to persuade the Sioux to sell the Black Hills. The commission, meeting with these Indians in September 1875, found them deeply divided over the question. Red Cloud suggested selling the Black Hills for $70 million. That figure, which was much higher than the $6 million the commission offered, would, in his view, give the Sioux a firm economic foundation for seven generations. Those from the nontreaty bands adamantly opposed the sale and threatened harm to others who even considered the idea at any price. Obviously three quarters of adult males would never agree to give up the sacred hunting grounds they called Paha Sapa. Faced with this reality, commission members returned to Washington and advised Congress to set a price and force the Sioux to accept it.

On November 3, 1875, President Grant; the new secretary of the Interior, Zachariah Chandler; Commissioner of Indian Affairs Edward Smith, and Generals Sheridan and Crook—the latter, since April, the commander of the Department of the Platte—met in Washington, D.C. Although the ban against entering the Black Hills remained in place, the army, they decided, would no longer evict miners from that region. Moreover, because members of the Sitting Bull bands were the most vehemently opposed to selling the Black Hills, they would be forced out of unceded territory and into reservations. That, along with the increasing numbers of miners moving onto the hills, would render non-Indian occupation a fait accompli. In December an order went out to dispatch runners into unceded territory. They were to inform the Sitting Bull bands that they had until January 31, 1876, to report to the agencies. Failing to comply, the bands would be viewed as Indians off their reservation. More specifically, that meant they would be categorized as "hostiles" and thus subject to military action.

Custer, on leave during the winter of 1875–76, visited New York City with Libbie. Still avidly pursuing wealth, he entered into a reckless speculation with Emil Justh, a Wall Street broker. In transactions amounting to $389,983 and involving borrowed money, he engaged in what a court later called "pretended purchasing" and "pretended sale" of railroad shares. Had his gamble paid off, he would have pocketed the profit. Instead he was left owing $8,578. On February 10, 1876, he signed a six-month promissory note at 7 percent to Justh and Company. To repay the heavy debt, Custer planned to lecture for the Redpath Speakers' Bureau for $200 a lecture, four to five nights a week, after his campaign against the Sioux.

The campaign was now a foregone conclusion. On February 1, Interior Secretary Chandler, aware that the nontreaty Sioux had failed to come in to the agencies, turned them over to the War Department. By now, many agency Indians, increasingly angered by the poor rations they received and the growing number of miners pouring into the Black Hills, planned to join their nontreaty cousins in unceded territory for hunting as soon as weather permitted.

On March 15, shortly after the Custers returned to Fort Lincoln, Heister Clyman, who chaired a congressional committee investigating corruption in the War Department, summoned Armstrong to Washington, D.C. William Belknap, secretary of war, had been involved in the sale of a post tradership at Fort Sill. The House of Representatives, controlled by the Democrats, sought additional information to increase the embarrassment of the Republican Grant administration. Custer gave hearsay testimony that spring that implicated President Grant's brother Orvil and his brother-in-law John Dent in ongoing corruption. As he prepared to return to Fort Lincoln, however, he was summoned to appear at Belknap's impeachment hearing. When Sherman, as commanding general of the army, asked Alphonso Taft, the new secretary of war, to allow Custer to rejoin his command to begin the Sioux Campaign, President Grant intervened. Someone else, he told Taft, would lead the campaign against the Sioux.

Custer, anxious to return to Dakota Territory, sought unsuccessfully to gain an audience with Grant. When he visited Sherman's office, the general was away in New York City. However, an adjutant and an inspector general in the War Department assured him that he could return to his post and he started westward. As he boarded a train at Chicago for St. Paul on the way to Fort Lincoln, Custer received a message from Sherman, dictated by Grant. Custer had left Washington improperly it said, since he had not seen Sherman and the president first. Thus, he was to be halted to "await further orders; meantime," the message continued, "let the expedition proceed without him." Astounded, Custer repeatedly telegraphed Sherman until at last he received permission to proceed to departmental headquarters at St. Paul.

There he met with Gen. Alfred E. Terry, commander of the Department of Dakota. As Terry later recalled, Custer pleaded, "with tears in his eyes," for his support. The general, who had never fought Indians, wanted Custer along for the coming campaign and drafted a telegraph for the lieutenant colonel's signature. It beseeched Grant "as a soldier to spare me the humiliation of seeing my regiment march to meet the enemy and I not to share its dangers." Terry added his own notation: "Lieutenant Colonel Custer's services would be very valuable with his regiment." That request, seconded by General Sheridan who endorsed Custer's qualifications (while reprimanding his anti-administration statements) and by press criticism of Grant's actions against Custer, led the president to relent. Custer could lead the Seventh under Terry's overall command.

On May 17, the Seventh, under Custer and with Terry as field commander, departed from Fort Lincoln with two companies of the Seventeenth Infantry, one of the Sixth, and forty Arikara (Sahnish) scouts from the Fort Berthold Reservation. The Arikaras, at war with the Sioux for decades, had allied themselves with the United States against their enemy. Libbie, who felt more anxious about this campaign than any other, accompanied her husband that first night. The following morning he assured her that his famed "Custer's luck" would hold this summer, and they said goodbye. As he rode off with his regiment, Libbie recalled that he "turned around, stood up in his stirrups and waved his hat. Then they all started forward again and in a few seconds they had disappeared, horses, flags, men, and ammunition."

The Sioux Campaign bore similarities to the earlier winter campaign that had struck Black Kettle's village in 1868. The overall strategy relied on converging columns that would find the Indians from the Sitting Bull bands and force them onto the reservation. One column, consisting of the Seventh Infantry and companies of the Second Cavalry under Col. John Gibbon's command, had already left Fort Ellis on April 2. It patrolled the north bank of the Yellowstone River to prevent the Sitting Bull bands from fleeing into Canada. The second column, under Terry and Custer, was also in motion and moving toward Montana. Later that month, General Crook, as field commander of a force that included ten companies of the Third Cavalry, five companies of the Second Cavalry, three companies of the Ninth Infantry, and two of the Fourth Infantry, would move northward from Fort Fetterman. These columns planned to converge, not simultaneously but as elements that would be in place to prevent the Sitting Bull bands from fleeing northward into Canada or southward into the Bighorn Mountains. Everyone participating in this campaign believed that any one of the three columns could easily defeat any number of Indians it encountered.

Terry, convinced that the Sitting Bull bands were on the Little Missouri River or somewhere between it and the Yellowstone, marched the column along the survey line of the Northern Pacific Railroad. By May 30, Custer wrote Libbie that they had encountered no Indians on the Little Missouri. At Fort Lincoln, however, Libbie was unnerved; rumors had reached her that reservation Indians were joining the Sitting Bull bands.

On June 9, Terry and Custer met with Colonel Gibbon aboard the Yellowstone steamer and supply ship, the *Far West*. When Terry learned that scouts had sighted parties from the Sitting Bull bands in the Rosebud River Valley, he ordered Gibbon back to the mouth of that river. Simultaneously, to determine that the "hostiles" had not moved east, Terry instructed Seventh Cavalry major Marcus Reno to explore the Powder and Tongue River Valleys. After resting, Terry and Custer moved to the Tongue River where they were encamped by June 17.

That same day, Crook's column, having left Fort Fetterman on May 29, stopped for a morning break along the banks of the Rosebud. Suddenly, Sioux warriors, led by the Oglala chief Crazy Horse, appeared. Although

Crook drove them off, fearing an ambush farther north, he retreated with his wounded to his camp on Goose Creek. By June 21, Libbie had heard of the Battle of the Rosebud and wrote her husband from Fort Lincoln that the Indians Crook had met had been "very bad and don't seem one bit afraid." She also pleaded with him to take care of himself. "With your bright future and the knowledge that you are [of] positive use to your day and generation, do you not see that your life is precious on that account, and not only because an idolizing wife could not live without you." Custer never received her letter.

That day, encamped midway between the Tongue and Bighorn Rivers, he and Terry evaluated Major Reno's report after he had returned from exploring not only the Powder and Tongue river valleys, but the Rosebud River Valley as well. In the Tongue valley, Reno had seen the remains of a month-old village, and along the Rosebud, a more recent site. Custer now knew that the Sitting Bull bands no longer camped on the Rosebud. Most likely, to avoid encountering another of their traditional enemies—the Crow Indians—they had moved toward the Little Bighorn River.

Plans now changed. The mobile Seventh would locate the "hostiles" and drive them against Gibbon's infantry. Thus, Terry instructed Custer "to move directly up the valley of the Rosebud," while he, with Colonel Gibbon's command, would simultaneously proceed by steamer up the Bighorn River "as far as the boat can go." To increase Custer's chances of finding the "hostiles," he gave him six of Gibbon's Crow Indian scouts and the army scout Mitch Boyer, a mixed-blood Sioux who was married to a Crow woman. Custer retained his Arikara scouts as well.

The next day, Armstrong wrote Libbie, noting that he would soon set out on his assigned march. He included an extract from Terry's orders to him that read, "It is of course impossible to give you any definite instructions in regard to this movement, and, were it not impossible to do so, the Department Commander places too much confidence in your zeal, energy and ability to impose on you precise orders, which might hamper your action when nearly in contact with the enemy." The portion Libbie did not see continued, "He [Terry] will, however, indicate to you his views of what your action should be, and he desires that you should conform to them unless you shall see sufficient reason for departing from them."

Custer's move up the Rosebud would continue until he knew in which direction the Indian trail was moving. If it was heading toward the Little Bighorn, which Terry thought "almost certain," Custer "should still proceed southward, perhaps as far as the headwaters of the Tongue, and then turn towards the Little [Big] Horn, feeling constantly, however, to your left, so as to preclude the possibility of the escape of the Indians to the south or south-east by passing around your left flank." Terry noted that his and Gibbon's column would move toward the mouth of the Bighorn River and from there would "cross the Yellowstone and move up at least as far as the forks of the Big and Little [Big] Horns. Of course," he added, "its future movements must be controlled by circumstances as they arise, but it is hoped that the Indians, if upon the Little [Big] Horn, may be so nearly inclosed by the two columns that their escape will be impossible."

Thus written, these orders became the source of unending controversy. Clearly they gave Custer broad flexibility in unforeseen circumstances. The fifteen days of rations he carried with him, moreover, meant that if the "hostiles" fled, he was expected to pursue them. Still, Terry had spelled out a plan, subject to changing circumstances. Custer was to follow the Indian trail southward up the Rosebud. If it turned west toward the Little Bighorn, his instructions were to continue on the Rosebud, to prevent the Indians from escaping to the south or east. At or not far from the Tongue's headwaters, he would move west toward the Little Bighorn.

Terry knew that Gibbon's forces needed time to march westward and then southward along the Bighorn River before they could arrive on the Little Bighorn. He estimated that he and Gibbon would arrive on that river on June 26. None of the officers present knew that Crook, the third element in this campaign, was no longer moving northward.

As Custer said goodbye to Terry, he declined the latter's offer of a battalion of the Second Cavalry and two Gatling guns. Reno had reported seeing 380 lodges during his recent reconnaissance, which meant that the Seventh could expect to encounter about 2,700 to 3,000 Indians. And although Indian women were known to fight (as Cheyenne women had done at the Washita), Custer and most officers thought only of battling against men. He calculated that, with about 600 men in his regiment, he would encounter about 800 Indian men in battle. Even if he met twice that number, he believed he would easily triumph. Well-trained soldiers, he was sure, were superior to Indians as combatants. As for the Gatling guns, this heavy equipment would impede his progress over difficult terrain.

Moving up the Rosebud, Custer struck Reno's earlier trail on June 23. Following it, he came upon a large abandoned village where troopers found a white scalp and the scouts saw evidence of a recent Sun Dance. As the Seventh pushed on, soldiers saw that the trail widened and crisscrossed in confusing ways. Many of the pony droppings were fresher. The soldiers found the signs unfathomable, but the Arikara scouts probably understood. Immense numbers of Indians had come together and, more important, were staying together. Furthermore, the distance between themselves and this large and growing assemblage was narrowing.

When the Crow scouts returned from their reconnaissance on the night of June 24, Custer learned that the Indian trail turned west toward the Little Bighorn River. Terry had instructed him to march southward up the Rosebud, based on the supposition that the Sitting Bull bands were located on the upper Little Bighorn. Custer now knew that they were camped directly ahead on the lower Little Bighorn. With this new information, he changed his plans. Rather than continuing south and approaching the Indian encampment from that direction, which might allow them to escape, he would follow the trail westward that night. When he arrived at the divide between the Rosebud and the Little Bighorn, he would rest his command in that protected spot and attack the village on the morning of June 26 when Terry and Gibbon were within striking distance from the north.

After an all-night march, the weary soldiers flung themselves down for a much-needed rest. The Crow scouts, meanwhile, ascended a promontory known as the Crow's Nest. With their sharp eyesight, they identified a huge village by the "worms in the grass" or the immense pony herd on the Little Bighorn River to the west. They also saw small parties of warriors, which led them to conclude that the command had been sighted. Custer heard other distressing news. His brother Tom, now a captain, informed him that hardtack had fallen from the mule pack the night before. In retracing their steps, soldiers had come upon several Sioux prying open a box and gunfire had been exchanged. The Sioux had fled and were actually headed for the reservation, but Armstrong concluded that his command had been detected and the village would soon be alerted. He now decided to attack that day. Forgoing advance reconnaissance of the enemy and the terrain, he marched his regiment as a reconnaissance in force toward the Little Bighorn.

Reaching the headwaters of the creek now known as Reno Creek, Custer assigned one company of about 86 men, including officers, to the pack mules and then divided the remainder of the regiment into three battalions. He instructed the first battalion, about 125 men under Captain Benteen, to explore to the left where high bluffs obscured his view. They were to make certain that no satellite Indian camps were on the upper Little Bighorn. Custer assigned three other companies, consisting of 145 men, to Major Reno. The rest, numbering about 225, remained with him. (Some, such as the Crow scouts, would later depart, and soldiers, later carrying messages to Benteen or the pack train, would remain with those units.) As Benteen moved out to reconnoiter the Little Bighorn valley, Custer and Reno marched down Reno Creek on opposite sides of the stream.

Historian Larry Sklenar argues that Custer had a plan at this point. He had ascended the Crow's Nest earlier that day, not once but twice, a fact that earlier historians have overlooked. The second time, he had peered through high-powered spyglasses that permitted him to see tipis in the distance. Sklenar maintains that Custer, concluding that the tipis were the nucleus of a small satellite village on Reno Creek, planned to seize it. By holding the women and children of the village hostage, he could use them to persuade the larger village beyond the bluffs to surrender to government demands. Certainly having hostages at the Washita had proved valuable when Southern Plains tribesmen had been gathering in the villages along the river. Hostages could serve a similar function with the larger village before him.

If that was Custer's plan, it failed entirely. When he reached the camp, all that remained was one lone tipi. Inside was the body of an Indian killed in battle and still-smoldering cooking fires. As Custer and Reno conferred, the Arikara interpreter, Fred Gerard, caught sight of about forty Sioux. Waving his hat toward the last fleeing inhabitants of the now-deserted Sans Arc camp, he called out, "Here are your Indians, General, running like devils!"

Custer ordered Reno to pursue these Indians, who now headed toward the larger village just beyond the bluffs while he followed behind. When Custer caught sight of the fleeing Indians again on the slopes of the bluffs, to his right, he sent instructions to Reno to attack the southern end of the village. Reno later stated that he understood he would "be supported by the whole outfit." Custer, however, had decided to split his forces, as he had done at the Battle of the Washita, to attack the village from a different direction.

Shortly before 3 P.M., Reno reached the west bank of the Little Bighorn River and began his charge. Nearing the village, he saw increasing numbers of Indians and no sign of Custer. Rather than continue the charge, Reno ordered his men to dismount and form a skirmish line. When the Indians threatened to turn his left flank, Reno, fearful of being overpowered, formed a defensive position in thick underbrush and trees along the river. As the Indians ignited the shrubs and fired heavily from all sides, the major became rattled. After the Arikara scout Bloody Knife was shot in the head, and bone, flesh, and brains splattered across Reno's face, he lost all composure. He ordered his men out of the timber to the high bluffs across the river. In the din of battle, many never heard the order, which Reno countermanded and then repeated. A disorganized retreat now turned into a panic-stricken rout. When Reno reached a high bluff on the Little Bighorn's east bank, his battalion had sustained heavy casualties, including thirty killed, thirteen wounded, and others who were missing.

Custer, meanwhile, had turned his battalion to the right along the bluffs until he reached a point where he could view the river valley. To his front stretched an enormous village harboring Hunkpapas, Miniconjous, Oglalas, Blackfeet, Sans Arcs, Santees, and Brulés, along with Cheyennes and some Northern Arapaho allies. The entire village, a huge one by Plains Indians' standards, included about 1,000 tipis and numbered about 7,000 people. On that basis Custer could expect to meet 1,500 to 1,800 warriors. Numerous reservation Indians, including women needed for their skills as butchers and tanners of the buffalo, and children, who were learning the ways of their people, had joined the Sitting Bull bands for summer hunting.

At this point Custer realized that his battalion desperately needed the pack train and additional men as quickly as possible. After sending a courier to hasten the pack train, Lt. William Cooke, as Custer's adjutant, dispatched Trumpeter John Martin, a recent immigrant from Italy, to carry a message to Benteen. Cooke, not trusting Martin's ability to make himself understood, hastily scribbled, "Benteen. Come on. Big Village. Be Quick. Bring packs. W. W. Cooke, P. bring pacs [sic]." As Martin departed, he glanced back one last time and saw the soldiers of Custer's battalion descending Medicine Tail Coulee.

Benteen, having completed his reconnaissance to the left, had found no Indians. Rather than rejoining the regiment as quickly as possible, however, he was proceeding at a leisurely pace. Responding to Cooke's message, he speeded up, but halted when he came upon the survivors of Reno's fight on the hill bordering the bluffs. There the captain encountered a demoralized major. Assuming virtual command, Benteen set up a defense perimeter and remained with these men rather than joining Custer as ordered. So too did Capt. Thomas McDougall, as commander of the pack train. When calm was restored, Capt. Thomas Weir, at first with only Company D, but later joined by the others, moved toward the firing downriver in an attempt to reunite with Custer. The appearance of a large number of Indians forced all of them back to Reno Hill.

All day on June 26, the Reno-Benteen forces fought off Indian assaults, which subsided only when darkness fell. As they awaited rescue, some wondered if Custer had abandoned them, as Benteen thought Custer had abandoned Elliott years earlier at the Washita. Finally, the Indians took down their tipis and wickiups and moved south toward the Bighorn Mountains. When Terry and Gibbon arrived on the June 27, the survivors on Reno Hill had lost a total of fifty-three men in three days of engagement. Only now did they learn the whereabouts of Custer's battalion.

The bodies of 210 officers and enlisted men were scattered along a ridge down the Little Bighorn River some four miles from Reno Hill. Armstrong; his brothers Tom and Boston (the latter employed that summer as a civilian worker for the army); a nephew, Autie Reed, along as "herder"; and four other officers lay on Custer Hill. With Reno in retreat, the Indians in the huge village, including boys, old men, and women who "fought with stone clubs and hatchet knives," according to Hunkpapa combatant Chief Gall, had turned their attention to Custer's forces. The lieutenant colonel, having divided his command, had found his battalion isolated as he faced able, determined, and tenacious defenders of their village that day. The entire Battle of the Little Bighorn had taken no more than two hours from start to finish. Chief Gall remembered it as lasting for about half an hour.

Lt. Edward S. Godfrey was among those examining the bodies on June 28. He later reported that Custer, though shot in the left temple and in the chest, was not mutilated like the rest of the men. Rather he was lying on his back and looked as if he were taking an afternoon nap, a statement that may have been crafted to comfort Libbie. Whatever the condition of his corpse, the soldiers buried him and the others on that battlefield as hastily as possible. Their most pressing concern was to evacuate the wounded to the steamboat, the *Far West*, so that they could reach Fort Lincoln as swiftly as possible for medical care.

On July 6, at about 2 A.M., Capt. William S. McCaskey, Twentieth Infantry, opened a message at Fort Lincoln from General Terry. Custer and five companies had been killed on June 25 at the Little Bighorn River in a battle with Sioux Indians and their Northern Cheyenne allies. A few hours later, McCaskey; J. V. D. Middleton, post surgeon; and Lt. C. L. Gurley, Sixth Infantry, met with Libbie Custer, Maggie Calhoun, and Emma Reed, Autie Reed's sister, in the Custer parlor. As McCaskey read his dispatch, the women wept, but Libbie arose and accompanied the men as they made the rounds to give the other widows the sad news.

When the American public learned of the battle in newspaper reports published on July 7, many responded with outpourings of grief and condolences. On July 10, Walt Whitman's "A Death Song for Custer" appeared in the *New York Herald* and praised him as Americans remembered him from earlier days. No longer a boy general and with his thinning hair cut short, Custer had not been "thou of the tawny flowing hair" as he breathed his last. Painters, novelists, and other poets nonetheless would portray him that way for decades to come. Ten days later, local leaders in Will County, Illinois, named a town they were establishing after the fallen soldier. On July 28 a resolution from the Texas legislature thanked the late Custer for his services during the Indian wars and extended sympathy to his family who had lost three sons, a nephew, and a son-in-law in the recent battle. By now, the *New York Herald* was already accepting donations to build a monument to him. Individuals as young as twelve were sending their contributions to the newspaper.

Others, however, blamed Custer for the battle's outcome. In a confidential report to Generals Sheridan and Sherman dated July 2, General Terry stated that he had instructed Custer to march up the Rosebud until he came upon the trail Reno had struck earlier. If it led to the Little Bighorn valley, Custer's orders were to march south approximately twenty miles before sweeping north and west to coordinate his column's arrival with Gibbon's. Had Custer done so, Terry added, both columns would have arrived in the vicinity of the battlefield on June 26 and the campaign would "have been successful." (How "successful" is debatable as Terry and Gibbon's forces did not arrive at the battlefield until June 27.) Terry's report, which the press intercepted and published in the *Philadelphia Inquirer* on July 7, established the charge that Custer had disobeyed orders. In doing so, it reported, he had led his men into unnecessary disaster.

Custer's reputation suffered more when Samuel Sturgis, the colonel commanding the Seventh Cavalry, lashed out in grief over the loss of his son, Lt. James Sturgis, a casualty at the Little Bighorn. He denounced Custer as "a very selfish man" who was "insanely ambitious of glory." Even worse, on September 2, President Grant characterized the recent battle in the *New York Herald* as "a sacrifice of troops brought on by Custer himself, that was wholly unnecessary—wholly unnecessary." Thus, early on, the lines of argument that persist to the present day were laid out. One side saw Custer as a martyr who had gone down fighting to the last and against great odds for his country against "savage foes." The other saw him as a foolhardy leader. Vainglorious, he had doomed his men by disobeying orders and hastening to meet the enemy a day early to avoid sharing a victory with any other commander.

By the late summer of 1876, Elizabeth was already intervening in the debate, but in Victorian-era, ladylike fashion, behind the scenes. She gave her husband's personal papers to the dime novelist Frederick Whittaker. By Thanksgiving, his work, *The Complete Life of Gen. George A. Custer*, was in bookstores. In it Whittaker presented Reno as a coward for failing to sustain his separate charge and accused Benteen of ensuring a disastrous outcome by failing to come quickly to Custer's aid. Even President Grant, in Whittaker's view, bore responsibility for the debacle. By relieving him as field commander, he had undercut Custer's authority with his subalterns, Reno and Benteen, and left him reporting to Terry, who knew little about fighting Indians.

Elizabeth Custer, through her three books and appearances on the lecture tour in the 1890s, transformed her husband into a hero for boys and a martyr whose sacrifice at the Little Bighorn paved the way for the spread of "civilization" across the West. She was sixty-eight when she posed in June 1910 for this picture, taken in Monroe, Michigan. (Courtesy of the National Park Service, Little Bighorn Battlefield National Monument, #1171)

From 1885 to 1890, Elizabeth published three books: *"Boots and Saddles"* (1885), *Tenting on the Plains* (1887), and *Following the Guidon* (1890). In these works, which were her own monument to Armstrong, she transformed him into an ideal husband and an exemplary commander. In 1901, Charles Scribner's and Sons published Mary Burt's condensation of Libbie Custer's three books as *The Boy General*. It sold as a textbook that would teach middle school children civic virtues and boys "lessons in manliness."

Army men who were critical of Custer planned to speak out about him and the Battle of the Little Bighorn after Elizabeth died. She lived, however, until April 4, 1933, four days short of her ninety-first birthday. By then, only Charles Varnum, among all the officers who had participated in the Battle of the Little Bighorn, was still alive. A year later, Frederic Van de Water published *Glory-Hunter*, the first iconoclastic biography of Custer.

Since then, assessments of the general have often reflected the social currents of the time, the military's standing in the nation's eyes, and public sensitivity to the question of justice for racial minorities. In all the disputes, however, certain facts remain true. Custer and the Seventh Cavalry were in Montana Territory on June 25, 1876, because of decisions made in the highest councils of government. Moreover, although the battle was a tragedy for the soldiers and their families, it was even more tragic for American Indians. Not only were they left to mourn their dead, but by August a presidential commission under George W. Manypenny gave the reservation Sioux assembled at the Red Cloud Agency an ultimatum: to sell their sacred

Black Hills or face the loss of their annuities and, hence, endure starvation. At the same time, the army followed its defeat with retaliatory strikes that forced the nontreaty Sioux and their Northern Plains allies onto reservations. The one band that escaped to Canada under Sitting Bull encountered such privation that it returned to the United States in 1881 to accept the confinement and poverty of life on the shrinking Sioux Reservation.

The role of Custer in all of this was the same as it had been when he had waged total war for Sheridan in the Shenandoah Valley. Later, he had performed the same function for Sheridan against the Southern Plains Indians at the Washita. When Custer died at the Little Bighorn, he was attempting to wage the same kind of total war against the Sitting Bull bands. In the end, however much he had welcomed the opportunity to engage the Indians in order to add to his laurels, he was not the one who decided to war against the Sioux and their allies. Earlier, he had not been the one who conceived of the plan to burn the crops, fields, and farms of the Confederates in the Shenandoah Valley. The significance of his life and career is that he was the commander whom the architects of total war could rely on to implement the harsh and often brutal measures that would attain their objectives. He did so because he was at home in the world only when he drew praise from his superiors and acclaim from the public at large.

His opportunities to gain such praise came because, in its relations with its indigenous people, the United States often resorted to total war as a way of solving conflicts that stemmed from cultural differences. Ethnocentric in their thinking, most U.S. citizens—George Armstrong Custer included—thought the solution to the "Indian problem" was that Indians should cease being Indians, give up their homelands, and become assimilated into the larger society. If they resisted—as the Plains Indians resisted—they were turned over to the military. The army then destroyed their homes, food supply, and ponies so that they were so impoverished they had no choice but to move to reservations. Once there, agents and other staff sought to destroy their culture and traditions.

Total war as a policy drove the Sitting Bull bands onto reservations. It also succeeded in taking from all the Sioux—reservation and nontreaty alike—their land, including not only their Black Hills but over time, most of the Great Sioux Reservation. The effectiveness of total war ended there, however. By the early twentieth century, the Sioux were initiating court cases to contest the taking of their sacred land. In 1980, after decades of disappointment and reversals, the Supreme Court of the United States heard their case. Based on historical evidence, including information on the November 3, 1875, meeting of President Grant, Generals Sherman and

Crook, Secretary of the Interior Chandler, and Commissioner of Indian Affairs Smith, it rendered a ruling. In an eight-to-one decision, *U.S. vs. Sioux Nation* held that the U.S. government had violated the Fifth Amendment rights of the Sioux by taking the Black Hills from them without adequate compensation. The Sioux were entitled to $106 million.

To the day of this writing, the Sioux, who remain among the nation's poorest people, have not accepted that award. Perhaps if the figure were substantial enough to give seven generations of Sioux a firm economic foundation, as Red Cloud had sought when he had asked for $70 million for the hills in 1875, they would accept it. But it is not, and the Sioux leave their just compensation award in the U.S. Treasury where it continues to gather interest. Total war may have taken from the Sioux their land and their freedom to roam and hunt buffalo. But, as was true in 1875, for these people the sacred Black Hills are still not for sale.

RANALD MACKENZIE

War on the Plains Indians

DURWOOD BALL

No one expected the boy to stay the rigorous course at the U.S. Military
Academy when he left home in the summer of 1858. Relatives and acquain
tances anticipated failure; an uncle admonished him about "the great
disadvantage" of being "found deficient." Even the family's clergyman, who
labeled him "bright," predicted doom. Professional soldiering seemed a poor
fit, for the boy was "very shy and reserved," spoke slowly and indistinctly,
and deferred to a brilliant younger brother. Family and friends believed that
the law, not the army, was the proper profession for the reticent eighteen-
year old. Four years later, he silenced the naysayers. In the U.S. Army he
found an environment receptive to the manly code he had internalized as a
child and that would guide him through a career as the most brilliant combat officer in the post–Civil War army.

During his career, Mackenzie successfully distinguished himself among
the highly competitive officers of the U.S. Army. Outside the Civil War, the
nineteenth-century army was a small, often static institution in which
opportunities for distinction, particularly combat, were few and far between.
In the postwar service, the top-heavy ranks of the officer corps made promotion glacially slow, especially for subalterns. Professional preferment—
promotion to higher grades, assignment to high-profile commands, or posting to easy and desirable duty—often depended on the advocacy of powerful
superior officers. Personal courage, devotion to duty, and professional honor
were plentiful among Mackenzie's peers, but like other exceptional soldiers,
he possessed the talent, will, charisma, and luck to transform himself from a
raw West Point cadet into one of the most preeminent combat officers in the
post–Civil War frontier army. The irony of Mackenzie's life was that he
beat the professional odds to advance rapidly through the ranks of the U.S.
Army only to be struck down at a relatively young age by what was likely a
youthful indiscretion.

Ranald Slidell Mackenzie was brought into a world of federal service. He was born on June 27, 1840, to Alexander Slidell and Catherine Robinson Mackenzie in New York City. Alexander was a U.S. naval officer and popular writer; Catherine was the daughter of a wealthy New York banker. Shortly after Ranald's birth, the couple relocated thirty miles north to Mount Pleasant. Ranald, the oldest child, had two brothers and two sisters. Alexander taught the boys hunting and sailing and spun tales of Mackenzie military glory. Although he was born Alexander Slidell, he idolized his Scottish ancestry and would add Mackenzie, his mother's maiden name, to his own as a young man. Other martial influences in Ranald's family included his uncle Matthew Perry, a U.S. Navy commodore and the son of Oliver Hazzard Perry, a naval hero in the War of 1812. Alexander probably envisioned a military future for his eldest son. At the age of six, Ranald entered Mount Pleasant Academy, a preparatory school that enforced a martial regimen, an experience that he cherished throughout his life.

When Ranald was eight, Alexander died of a sudden heart attack, leaving his young family with burdensome debts. After burying her husband, Catherine resettled the children near her family in Morristown, New Jersey. Her uncle William A. Duer, a lawyer and former president of Columbia University, pushed Ranald to prepare for the legal profession, but a white-collar future left him flat. After two unspectacular years at Williams College, he accepted a berth at the U.S. Military Academy in 1858, partly to relieve the financial strain on his mother and to fulfill a dream—his father's and his own—of becoming a professional man of arms. From his father and from his uncle Commodore Matthew Perry, Ranald had learned to associate manliness with courage, duty, honor, and sacrifice. Those values would motivate him for the remainder of his military career.

The U.S. Army ignited Ranald Mackenzie's manly ambition. He graduated at the top of the class of 1862, earning first-place finishes in engineering, and ordnance and gunnery, the two most esteemed fields in the peacetime army. After graduation, Second Lieutenant Mackenzie went straight to the Corps of Engineers in the Civil War's eastern theater, while his brother, Alexander Jr., served in the Union Navy. Ranald's service would be a panorama of major battles, excepting Antietam, from Second Manassas to Appomattox. During Second Manassas, the young Mackenzie was shot off his horse and left to die. Recovered the next morning, he was transported to Washington, D.C. Catherine rushed to the hospital, gathered her son, and took him to Morristown, where she nursed him back to health, as she would on several subsequent occasions.

At Gettysburg, with chief engineer Gouverneur K. Warren, Mackenzie helped identify Little Round Top as critical Union ground. He then guided the infantry brigade that first occupied the position to protect the Union left flank against surging Confederate forces.

His gallantry at Gettysburg earned him a brevet to major in the regular army, but Mackenzie was still a staff officer. The army identified staff corps such as the engineers with the rear, ground far less dangerous than the line. Only peripherally engaged in combat at best, First Lieutenant Mackenzie yearned to measure his courage while taking fire and life on the line. His cool, obedience, zealousness, and intelligence led to a promotion to colonel of the Second Connecticut Heavy Artillery, a combat regiment, on June 10, 1864. Under the twenty-four-year-old Colonel Mackenzie, the Second Connecticut, in fact an infantry unit, operated in northern Virginia and the Shenandoah Valley. Promoted to brigadier general in March 1865, he next led a cavalry division in the final campaign that climaxed with Robert E. Lee's surrender at Appomattox. Afterward, Mackenzie helped disarm rebel troops and occupy northern Virginia. The cavalry would remain his preferred combat arm.

By war's end, Mackenzie's courage was apparent to everyone but possibly himself. He was wounded six times, twice in staff missions, and earned brevets, honorary promotions for valor, to brigadier general in the regular army and major general in the volunteer service. At Second Manassas, while performing courier service, he was hit in the "right shoulder," the ball scarring his back. Evacuated to Washington, D.C., he reassured his mother, "I am wounded in the back, but I was not running away." During Cedar Creek in fall 1864, he took three wounds in several hours. Maj. Gen. Phil "Little Phil" Sheridan ordered him off the field, but the young officer "implored permission [to remain] till success was certain." Mackenzie's bravery and honor so impressed Little Phil that, from that day forward, he stewarded the young man's professional fortunes. At the close of the Civil War, Lt. Gen. Ulysses S. Grant considered Mackenzie the "most promising young officer" in the U.S. Army.

Indeed, during nine months in the line, the reticent Mackenzie seemed to smile only when laughing down death "in a fight." Like many combat officers, he recklessly exposed himself to enemy fire, but unlike many, he skillfully maneuvered troops to minimize his casualties. Regulars such as Mackenzie believed that fierce discipline created unit cohesion critical to supple maneuvers on the battlefield; he delivered harsh punishments for even small infractions in his infantry and cavalry units. An officer from a neighboring regiment recalled "cutting down" a Second Connecticut offender who was hanging by his thumbs. The exhausted man collapsed.

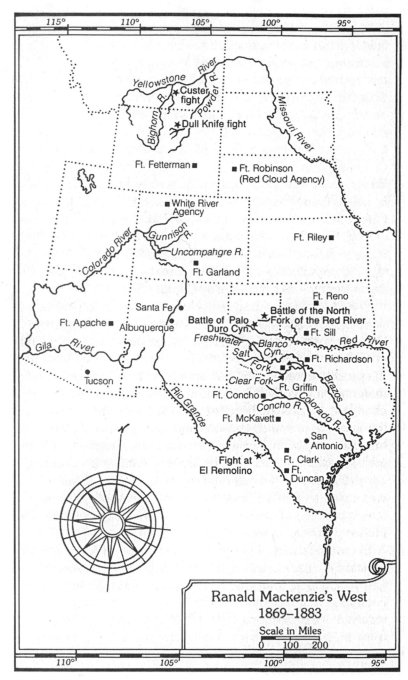

From Michael D. Pierce, The Most Promising Young Officer: A Life of Ranald Slidell *Mackenzie (Norman: University of Oklahoma Press, 1993), 59. (Map reproduced by permission from the University of Oklahoma Press. All rights reserved)*

The men of the Second Connecticut cavalierly talked about shooting Mackenzie in the back, but his skill and their courage in the hottest battlefield at the Third Winchester erased those malevolent fantasies. Officers and enlisted men alike later regretted Mackenzie's transfer to the cavalry.

With the war won, the U.S. Congress began demobilizing the volunteers and reorganizing the regulars. By the end of 1866, there were forty-five regiments of infantry, ten of cavalry, and five of artillery to contend with southern Reconstruction and western expansion. This new establishment returned Brevet Major General Mackenzie, twenty-six years old, to the Corps of Engineers at his regular rank of captain, until the army appointed him colonel of the Forty-first U.S. Infantry, a black regiment, in March 1867. He wanted a cavalry berth, but General in Chief Ulysses S. Grant assured Mackenzie that commanding the Forty-first would soon reward him with a mounted regiment. Dispersed along the lower Rio Grande in Texas, the Forty-first became a "crack regiment" under endless drill and strict discipline. In March 1869, further army reductions sent Mackenzie to the Twenty-fourth U.S. Infantry, another black regiment.

Despite his zealous attention to garrison administration, Mackenzie longed for frontier combat. The close of the Civil War had renewed national interest in the West, where U.S. priorities were building railroads and transforming American Indian homelands into farms, ranches, mines, and towns. In that vision, Native Americans would cede land, relocate to reservations, and ultimately assimilate. In 1869 President Grant launched the Peace Policy to convert Indians to civilization through charity and example. Fort Sill, Indian Territory, agency headquarters for Comanches, Kiowas, and some Apaches, became a policy showcase, but Indian resistance to the reservations made conflict inevitable. The Departments of War and of the Interior fought in Congress for control of Indian affairs, with the latter retaining the upper hand. In the meantime, frontiers from Canada to Mexico, including Texas, erupted in violence between Indians and whites. The federal government deployed the regulars to chastise "hostile" Indians, restore peace, and maintain order.

On June 7, 1869, from Fort McKavett, Mackenzie led a mounted scout that crushed Lipan and Mescalero Apaches, whetting his appetite for a horse command. A lengthy leave eventually landed him in Washington, D.C., in fall 1870, an opportune time. The Fourth Cavalry's colonel retired on December 15, and President Grant gave Mackenzie the regiment, which was then chasing Texas Indians with little success. President Grant and General in Chief William T. Sherman hoped that the thirty-year-old Mackenzie would transform the Fourth into a ferocious strike force.

Colonel Mackenzie now had the vehicle to seek war, test his courage, and ride to glory.

In early April 1871, he passed burnt-out homesteads on the road between San Antonio and Fort Richardson, where he established his headquarters. One month later a Kiowa war party destroyed a wagon train at Salt Creek near Fort Richardson. Just hours before, General Sherman and his escort had passed through Salt Creek under Kiowa observation. The outraged Sherman immediately ordered four companies of the Fourth to hunt, punish, and capture the Kiowas and "bring them" to Fort Sill, the next stop on his inspection of the military frontier.

The following day, drenched by a downpour, Mackenzie's sickened regulars interred the butchered, bloated corpses at Salt Creek. The Kiowa trail dissipated in heavy rain, thick mud, and buffalo tracks just south of the Red River. On June 4, Mackenzie led his men over the river and on to Fort Sill, which was administered by the Bureau of Indian Affairs (BIA). Solid evidence—including boasts by Kiowa leader Satanta—implicated the Fort Sill tribes in "many of the murders and depredations," Salt Creek included, in Texas. Their atrocities, citizen outrage, and army disgust were conspiring to destroy Grant's humanitarian experiment.

Before the Fourth's arrival, Sherman and Col. Benjamin Grierson had dramatically confronted and arrested Kiowa leaders Satanta, Satank, and Big Tree at the agency headquarters. Mackenzie was ordered to transport the three Kiowas to Texas for a criminal trial. A mile south of Fort Sill, Satank worked free of his bracelets but was shot by Cpl. John B. Charlton. Resuming travel, Mackenzie escorted Satanta and Big Tree to Jacksboro, Texas, where a "cowboy jury" convicted the warriors of murder and sentenced them to death, but the governor commuted the sentence to imprisonment at Huntsville.

The Salt Creek carnage and Satank's defiance persuaded Mackenzie to hound the Comanches and Kiowas in their panhandle homeland until they capitulated. Granted the authority, men, and transportation, he gathered the Fourth's ten troops in August 1871 and campaigned with Grierson's Tenth Cavalry against Kiowas in southwestern Indian Territory. No Indians were found, but the Fourth learned valuable lessons about campaigning with pack trains in choking dust, brutal heat, and rugged desert terrain. In particular, they learned the necessity of campaigning on the plains desert on its spartan terms. Mackenzie and his officers were astonished to see the Tenth hauling luxuries, including ceramic china, into the field for its officers. Such comforts, Mackenzie believed, only diminished unit speed and efficiency.

Even before pulling into Fort Richardson on September 13, 1871, he had secured permission to operate on the Llano Estacado, "staked plains." The Kiowas and Comanches, still defiant, had intensified their raids in Texas. From the headwaters of the Brazos River on October 2, the Fourth picked its way to the Freshwater Fork and settled in a narrow valley for the night. At one in the morning, Kwahadi Comanches, "yelling like wild demons," stampeded sixty-six mules and horses, including the colonel's "fine gray pacer." Early the next morning, Lt. Peter M. Boehm's Tonkawa scouts, rescuing a patrol, drove 200 Kwahadis onto a nearby butte. When Mackenzie and the Fourth galloped up, the Kwahadis, led by Quanah Parker, fled into the Llano.

Still fuming over the stampede, Mackenzie ordered a pursuit up Cañon Blanco and onto the Llano Estacado, the broad plateau of high plains grassland stretching from the headwaters of the Red and Brazos Rivers to the Pecos River in New Mexico Territory. The Llano was habitat for the southern buffalo herd, the critical source of meat for Comanches and Kiowas. The Fourth followed, "west and northwest," a "very broad and distinct Lodgepole and stock trail" made by the entire Kwahadi "outfit" or village. Angry warriors nipped at the regulars, but the disciplined Mackenzie bore down on the women, children, and elders, who were now in clear sight and whose capture would strengthen his bargaining position with the Kwahadi leaders.

On the cusp of the battle, however, a norther—driving wind, rain, and sleet—blanketed the regulars and Indians in "inky blackness." To the dismay of the officers, men, and scouts, Mackenzie prudently halted the attack and deployed his men in a circle around the horses and pack train. A few minutes later, a Kwahadi party, whooping and yelling, galloped "at breakneck speed" through the position and into the darkness. The regulars sheltered themselves under "robes," "blankets," and "tarpaulins" and hung on to the

Ranald S. Mackenzie, a Boy General, during the Civil War. (Courtesy of the Massachusetts Commandery Military Order of the Loyal Legion and the U.S. Army Military History Institute, Carlisle Barracks, Pennsylvania)

reins of cold, nervous horses and mules. Mackenzie, his Civil War wounds throbbing, hugged himself in a soaked campaign blouse until someone "wrapped his shivering form in a buffalo robe."

Dawn filled the Llano with warm sunshine. Mackenzie resumed the chase, but the Kwahadis' headstart and the Fourth's jaded horses forced an about-face. At Cañon Blanco, he dispatched a fire team after two Comanches surrounded in a ravine by his Indian scouts, but his manly code compelled him to risk his life by directing the fire in person. A few minutes later, he limped back with an arrow lodged in his thigh. The squad killed both Comanches; one other regular was wounded. Still determined to punish the Indians, Mackenzie organized a small scout toward the Pease River, but his new wound drove him back to Duck Creek. The scout returned empty-handed on November 8, and Mackenzie broke up the expedition.

During this fighting season, the Kiowas and Comanches witnessed a possessed soldier who boldly led his men into the Native heartland. He stood five feet, nine inches tall and weighed only 140 pounds, but his intense gaze, boiling like a warrior's, shot far into the Llano. The unostentatious officer wore a plain blue undress uniform, smiled or laughed little, and spoke impatiently to everyone. The Indians also noticed a peculiar disfigurement. His right hand, with which he vigorously gestured, was missing two digits—both lost to a Confederate missile at Petersburg. When angry or anxious, he vigorously snapped the stumps. Thereafter, they called him Mangomhente, or Bad Hand. He became the white soldier most feared by Indians and most admired by whites on the Great Plains.

At Fort Richardson the young colonel found War Department endorsements of his mission. First, the department replaced Mackenzie nemesis Col. J. J. Reynolds with Brig. Gen. Charles C. Augur as commander of the Department of Texas. Before launching his last campaign, Mackenzie had complained to his superiors about contract irregularities endorsed by Reynolds. Adamantly denying the charges, Reynolds accused Mackenzie of ignoring accession protocols for rations and ammunition and failing to report his movements. Second, the same orders added the Department of Texas to the Division of the Missouri, and Indian Territory between Texas and Kansas to the Department of Texas. Those changes placed Texas under Lt. Gen. Phil Sheridan's divisional command, opened Indian Territory to Fourth Cavalry invasion, and declared the confidence of Grant, Sherman, and Sheridan in Mackenzie.

After a winter respite, Comanches, Kiowas, and Apaches vigorously renewed their depredations in spring 1872. One Kiowa attack alone killed seventeen employees of a wagon train at Howard's Wells, Texas. To curb raids, Mackenzie deployed Fourth Cavalry patrols, one of which captured an eighteen-year-old *comanchero*, Polonio Ortíz, from La Cuesta, New Mexico, in March. At Fort Concho, Ortíz admitted to coming east with other *nuevomexicanos* to steal horses and cattle and trade with Indians. Indeed, since the late eighteenth century, New Mexicans had seasonally crossed the Llano to barter with Indians—especially Comanches—and hunt buffalo. Ortíz explained, "There is plenty of water on the Staked Plains, it is permanent, the road is a good one." Ortíz guided Capt. Napoleon B. McLaughlin—an old regular who began as a dragoon private in 1850—and 92 troopers to Muchaque, a conical mountain one hundred miles northwest of Fort Concho, where they found an abandoned village of "150 or 200 lodges … with at least 1000 animals." The reconnaissance recorded valuable data on water, grass, and geography north of Fort Concho.

Mackenzie's summer campaign became ever more imperative when, on June 9, 1872, Kiowas killed four settlers and abducted three children at a homestead near Fort Griffin. Headquartered in Chicago, Sheridan bellowed for "some authority to manage and punish the Kiowas." Throwing up his hands, the Fort Sill agent sanctioned the Kiowas, Kwahadis, and Mow-way (Comanche) band for "attack and capture" by the army. Sheridan promised to "settle their hash" if civilian authorities stayed out of Mackenzie's way. The Fourth's colonel aimed to chastise the Comanches and Kiowas and disperse the *comanchero* trade. Chomping at the bit, he believed that "vigorous measures" alone would chasten the Fort Sill tribes and bring "quiet" to north Texas.

By early July, six companies of cavalry and five of infantry had rendezvoused at the supply camp on the Freshwater Fork of the Brazos. Scouts in force found Indians neither at the Freshwater and Brazos headwaters, at Muchaque, nor on the Red River, but they regularly found wood and water along the way. Upon returning from the Red River on July 19, Mackenzie concluded that, far from a barren waste, the "edge of the Staked Plains" easily supported the Indians in winter and that the upper North Fork of the Red River and the Washita would "answer at any time." His next objective was "the head tributaries of the main Red River," where Ortíz said Indians could "always" be found.

However, Mackenzie approached the Red's far reaches from the west. On June 28, with Ortíz as guide, five companies of the Fourth, one company of infantry, and a small quartermaster train climbed onto the Llano to explore a wide *comanchero* trail west to New Mexico. Mackenzie's men found plenty of holes, lakes, and buffalo wallows recently recharged by heavy rains. By August 7 his regulars reached Las Cañaditas in New

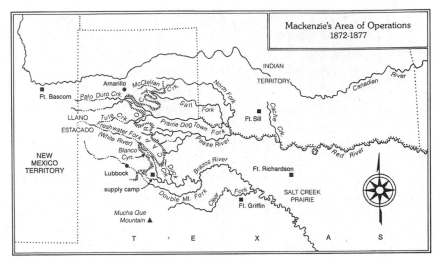

From Michael D. Pierce, The Most Promising Young Officer: A Life of Ronald Slidell Mackenzie *(Norman: University of Oklahoma Press, 1993), 110. (Map reproduced by permission from the University of Oklahoma Press. All rights reserved)*

Mexico. While Capt. Henry Lawton, the Fourth's tireless quartermaster, took the wagons to Fort Sumner, Mackenzie led the Fourth to Puerta de Luna, where he intended to arrest merchants who supplied the *comancheros*. However, they had already fled ahead of angry Texas cowboys searching for stolen stock. With the quarry flushed, Mackenzie marched his men north to Fort Bascom.

He now turned eastward. Many troopers were suffering hangovers when the Fourth set off on August 17. Their colonel berated no one for overimbibing but likely swelled with pleasure when heavy rains sobered them that afternoon. Three days previously, an Eighth Cavalry scout had embarked toward the Red River, so Mackenzie's unit scoured its "southern tributaries" along the northern *comanchero* road. At Quitaque Creek the column turned southwest to the Freshwater Fork and reached the supply camp on September 2. Mackenzie reported, "This route has permanent and excellent water across the Plains and no distance of more than thirty miles between water." The Palo Duro River (Prairie Dog Town Fork), the colonel concluded, was "undoubtedly the Upper red river [sic]." With Ortíz's critical services, he had opened the Llano to the regular army.

Exploration did not satisfy the warrior in Mackenzie, and he immediately led a column north to find and punish the Indians. Abandoning the wagons at the Red's North Fork on September 24, 223 troopers and 9 Tonkawas rode twenty miles to McClellan Creek, "a small tributary of the North Fork." Here, a fresh trail took the Fourth to an Indian camp in a "beautiful valley along the creek." While one troop and the scouts cut out the horse herd, the balance of the Fourth drove into the village of approximately 275 lodges. Concealed behind a creek embankment, warriors fired small arms and arrows until the regulars maneuvered to deliver an "infilading fire." Thirty minutes later, surviving warriors escaped through the lower village. The Fourth recovered 23 corpses and captured approximately 125 women, children, and elders. Mackenzie ordered "everything" burned. The village was Kotsoteka Comanche; their leader, Mow-way or Shaking Hand, was absent negotiating with the "peace people."

The Fourth encamped several miles away, while 1st Lt. Peter M. Boehm and the scouts guarded the captured horses in a nearby sink. That night, a Comanche counterattack stampeded the herd. Capt. Robert G. Carter recalled, "They got every horse ... and some of ours [the Fourth's]." The next morning, the men chortled at the scouts, who hiked into camp with their saddles stacked on burros, but the sizzling Mackenzie plucked at his stumps. Eight Comanche captives, wounded during the fight at McClellan Creek, died en route to the supply camp. On October 11, Mackenzie broke up the expedition and returned to Fort Richardson. Comanche and Kiowa raiding subsided dramatically, and Kotsoteka warriors came to Fort Sill to seek peace and secure the release of their families.

Mackenzie was fair to and hard on his men in equal measure. Nine enlisted men, recommended for "favorable consideration" by Mackenzie, received the Medal of Honor for gallantry in the McClellan Creek fight, but none was Sergeant Charlton. His squad had charged into the thickest Comanche fire. Two men died, two were seriously wounded, and all four received the medal. Charlton simply survived. Nearly fifty years later, he bitterly complained that his many hardships and services had received only "a few caustic remarks" from Mackenzie. The colonel was quick to upbraid men and officers whose devotion to the service fell victim to intemperance, unruliness, or inattention. In his mind the honor was to serve with the Fourth and share its combat victories. A high standard of unit discipline, he knew from experience, often translated into efficiency in the field. Battlefield successes brought martial glory, institutional accolades, and public recognition to the regiment, the men, and the officers, including Mackenzie.

The Old Man, as the Fourth soon began calling Mackenzie in private, was indeed a harsh disciplinarian, but officers throughout the army inflicted cruel sentences on errant enlisted men. The Fourth's punishments, standard in the regular army, included hauling the log, hanging by the thumbs, spreading eagle on a wheel, and dunking in a water tank. Stringing men up by their thumbs was a common measure that Mackenzie had learned during the Civil War. His combat victories during and after the rebellion probably magnified his fierce reputation among his peers and superiors, who pondered the secret of his skill and the Fourth's prowess. In the 1920s, Charlton still bristled at Mackenzie's punishments and remonstrances, hoping that at some point, "some one [had] dared ... to *talk back to the 'Old Man.'*"

Nineteenth-century officers such as Mackenzie practiced severe discipline in part to condition their recruits to daily deprivation. Frontier soldiering demanded strong, hardened men. Some combination of poor diet, substandard housing, killer diseases, backbreaking labor, mind-numbing boredom, and brutal campaigning dogged every private soldier in the frontier army and eroded unit efficiency at any frontier post. Despite his martial vinegar, Mackenzie vigorously worked the army bureaucracy—generally with success—to feed, house, clothe, arm, and mount his regiment at a high standard. Few troopers in the Fourth Cavalry died in battle, a testament to Mackenzie's skill and the Fourth's high level of fitness. A soldier in any combat regiment was more likely to succumb to disease—dysentery, scurvy, diarrhea, cholera, yellow fever, malaria—than to an arrow or ball fired by an Indian.

Mackenzie's extraordinary attention to his regiment still could not overcome the despair that generally infected the enlisted ranks. Traditionally suspicious of the professional standing army, the American people scorned enlisted men as drunks, loafers, and parasites. In 1871, Congress struck the private's monthly stipend from sixteen to thirteen dollars per month, the basic sum awarded monthly in 1861. Escape into alcohol—even among officers—was a common response to the physical, emotional, and financial stress. Among private soldiers, desertion was an often successful recourse. From 1867 to 1891, 15 percent of the enlisted ranks deserted annually. The celebrated Fourth Cavalry lost 171 men in 1871, a year in which almost one-third of enlisted men, angered partly by a pay cut, fled the army. A year later, General Sherman eagerly endorsed the Medals of Honor for Mackenzie's men to show the soldiers that their sacrifices were "appreciated."

In addition to army culture, the source of Mackenzie's edginess was likely physical discomfort. Although he loved the cavalry, he was not a superlative horseman, and the jolting and bouncing took a daily toll on his body. By the mid-1870s he was often in visible pain at the end of a day in the saddle. On one occasion, he invited Sergeant Charlton to join him for a swim in a nearby "little stream." When Mackenzie disrobed, Charlton quietly gasped: "His scars were plainly visible and by looking, when he wasn't looking, I learned much of what he had suffered and would suffer until his dying day." The irritation of old wounds may have partly explained why

Mackenzie slept and ate little, especially when on campaign. A shy, retiring man, he struggled courageously to hide physical pain behind placidity in society but unleashed that same anguish in angry outbursts at officers and men on duty. Some male fits of temper that would otherwise be proscribed in polite society, civilian or military, however, were acceptable from commissioned and noncommissioned officers in garrison, on campaign, and in battle.

Turbulence along the Texas-Mexico border soon consumed the army and, ultimately, Mackenzie's Fourth. Kickapoos, Pottawatomies, Mescalero Apaches, and Lipan Apaches in Mexico routinely stole cattle, horses, and sheep in southwestern Texas. U.S. authorities futilely demanded Kickapoo removal to Indian Territory. By 1873, while dispatching diplomats to northern Mexico, the Grant administration quietly embraced the military solution and ordered the Fourth to the Rio Grande. Sherman noted, "The President is doubtless influenced by the fact that Col. Mackenzie is young and enterprising. ..." After the Fourth occupied stations along the Rio Grande in early spring, Mackenzie hosted Secretary of War William W. Belknap and General Sheridan at Fort Clark, the Fourth's new headquarters.

Over two days the three men huddled in private to sketch countermeasures. At some point Sheridan verbally ordered Mackenzie to inflict "annihilation, obliteration and complete destruction" on the depredators by whatever means possible. By whose orders or authority? Mackenzie asked. Pounding the table, Sheridan barked, "Damn the orders! Damn the authority! ... You must assume the risk. We [Grant and Sheridan] will assume the final responsibility should any result." When Sheridan and Belknap departed on April 12, Mackenzie's scouts were already identifying Indian camps and reconnoitering "roads" in northern Mexico. Meanwhile, the Fourth's officers prepared men and horses for an unknown destination. On May 20, Sheridan endorsed Mackenzie's report on a recent Kickapoo raid: "There is in my opinion only one way left to settle the Mexican Frontier ... to cross the Rio Grande and recover our property, and punish the thieves."

Mackenzie had already struck. In the late evening of May 16, 1873, his scouts reported the "location" of Kickapoo and Lipan camps over the border. The following day, he outlined the mission to officers at the confluence of the Rios Las Moras and Grande. At dusk he led 400 troopers and 34 Seminoles over the Rio Grande to Mexico. In a column of fours, the regulars crossed the bleak alkali desert lit by a hazy moon. When the pack train fell behind, the stressed Mackenzie exploded, ordering the "packs cut away." In less than ten minutes, troopers filled their pockets with hard bread and cartridges, re-formed in fours, and trotted onward. Toward dawn, the Fourth inhaled refreshing breezes from the Santa Rosa Mountains and descended into a "lovely valley." Three Indian villages, Kickapoo and Lipan Apache, lay before them.

Mackenzie put the Fourth into battle formation and ordered the charge. The cheering troopers attacked by platoons and fired in volleys. Bolting from sleep, the Kickapoos scattered across the valley. Units in the vanguard knifed through the first village, while others in the rear dismounted, covered the flank, and ransacked lodges. Captain Carter recalled, "It was short work." In less than thirty minutes, the Fourth rounded up several hundred horses and forty Kickapoo prisoners—women, children, and elders. Mackenzie counted nineteen dead Indians, many of whom were probably women and children. Surprise partly explained the quick victory, but most Kickapoo warriors, he knew, had departed several days before on a raid to Texas. The Fourth's attack failed to reach neighboring camps before their inhabitants had escaped into the nearby mountains. Mackenzie grimly ordered torches lit and the three camps burned. As flames, ash, and smoke rose into the sky, troopers, scouts, and prisoners retreated through nearby Remolina, whose residents cursed the "gringos," and trotted into the blazing desert.

The ride through darkness seemed "interminable." Anxious officers darted up and down the column to shake and rap exhausted regulars, forty-eight hours "without sleep," into consciousness. Drowsy captives were lashed to their mounts. His nerves frayed but still taut, Mackenzie showed no sign of fatigue. At dawn the Fourth opened a "farm gate" to ford the river, a great sigh washing over officers and men, now some thirty-two hours and 159 miles in the saddle. A short time later, Captain Lawton's quartermaster train rolled into camp, bearing fresh rations and forage. Mackenzie threw out a defensive perimeter above the river with sharpshooters covering the ford. A few hours later, "large bodies" of horsemen, berating and gesturing at the Americans, appeared on the opposite bank but moved off. Irritating some of his officers, Mackenzie ordered "several buckets" of mescal, intended for the men's consumption, spilled onto the ground. Still on duty, he declared, the "exhausted" troopers were unfit to consume the powerful "stimulant."

That night, Capt. Eugene B. Beaumont queried Mackenzie about his orders. The colonel had none. The officers, the indignant Beaumont and McLaughlin declared, would have had the right to refuse to invade Mexico. Mackenzie flared, "Any officer or man who had refused to follow me across the river I would have shot!" (Mackenzie's father had hanged at sea the son of a secretary of war for mutiny in 1842.) Capt. Wirt Davis, the Fourth's best shot, snorted, "*That would depend, Sir,* upon who *shot first!*" Mackenzie dropped the issue on the banks of the Rio Grande. The officers and enlisted men tacitly acknowledged that "success" had cut their colonel's orders and would rally his superiors. Mackenzie led his column into Fort Clark at noon on May 21.

The Grant administration publicly endorsed Mackenzie's raid and Sheridan congratulated him. Although kept in the dark, a furious Sherman still defended and praised the operation. The U.S. public and newspapers generally applauded Mackenzie's bold strike. Likewise, the Texas state legislature voted a resolution of "grateful thanks" to Mackenzie and the Fourth. Besieged by political unrest, Mexican president Sebastian Lerdo de Tejada filed only a lukewarm protest. Mackenzie's operation persuaded approximately 350 Kickapoos to return to the United States, while some 280 relocated farther south in Mexico. In the raid's wake, depredations launched from Mexico declined sharply.

The Fourth's officers clearly had a love-hate relationship with Mackenzie. They were proud to serve under him and in the Fourth Cavalry, respectively the army's best frontier combat officer and combat force. On campaign or in garrison he worked himself to exhaustion for the welfare of officers, men, and horses. Lt. James Parker wrote, "Mackenzie had an unusually magnetic influence on his officers. ..." Until his death in the Philippines, Lawton still asked himself, "What would Mackenzie do?" when he found himself "in a tight place." The Fourth's officers marveled at Mackenzie's boundless energy. Captain Carter remembered how little the colonel slept "during an Indian campaign," when everyone else, drained by the day's ride, napped any chance they had. Young officers especially appreciated Mackenzie's attention to retiring "disabled" officers, a practice that speeded up promotions in the Fourth. He also assigned mentors to officers with drinking problems and loaned others money, interest free, to pay off debts. The unmarried Mackenzie wanted his officers to devote their undivided attention, as he did, to equipping, training, and leading the Fourth Cavalry.

His fussiness, however, just as often vexed his officers. He was, Carter explained, "rather hard to serve with." That "ceaseless energy" also made him edgy, "irritable," "impatient," "impulsive," "nervous," "explosive," and "oftentimes irascible"—qualities compounded by his habit of ignoring rest and meals, particularly when he was in the field. Although he gave his officers and men wide latitude to execute orders, Mackenzie quickly poured his boiling temper on anyone he suspected of or witnessed shirking his duty. On one occasion, the colonel berated Carter for ignoring the herd guard placed under his care: "I see only two men out there, where is the other man?"

Having left the herders "in charge of a good Corporal," Carter assumed the third man was "absent" for a "good" reason and replied, "I don't care to be accused of neglect.'" The agitated Mackenzie returned the indignity: "Sometimes you get a little insubordinate and you must not talk to me in that way." Standing his ground, the captain declared, "I shall not, Sir, unless you choose to reflect upon my performance of duty." Sure enough, the captain recalled, a private dispatched by the sergeant quickly appeared to replace the "herder who had taken sick." Mackenzie stalked "away" without uttering a word.

Despite his reputation as a tough nut, he also displayed humility, warmth, and humor. According to Carter, the colonel was no West Point martinet. The army was legendary as a battleground of frustrated, touchy officers who waged mutual vendettas over the smallest slight, sometimes real but more often imagined. Although dogged in his performance of duty, Mackenzie never hounded any man into his grave. Nor did he seek "to inflict an injury" on any officer or enlisted man. He retreated equally rapidly from officer or private—often apologetically—if his tongue-lashing turned out to be unwarranted. In society, although he never became "unduly familiar or intimate with his officers," Mackenzie was congenial and solicitous to them and their wives and children. At gatherings he was still generally quiet and aloof, but, when cajoled enough, he would "indulge in reminiscences to which all eagerly listened." Capable of gregariousness, he could be mischievous. At Fort Richardson, Texas, Captain Carter and his wife raised a large "hospital tent" as their private quarters. One morning, when walking by, Mackenzie stuck his head in the "upper half of the door," called "Mrs. Carter to him," and solemnly stated, "Look here, I told Carter he could put up some tents on the line, but I did not intend that he should use up all the canvas in the Army." Fearing he was serious, she sighed when he let out a big smile.

Hard campaigning triggered "inflammatory rheumatism" in Mackenzie. In September he took four months' leave in the East and returned to a tranquil border early the next year, but Indian-white violence had returned to Texas's northern frontier. At the Fort Sill and Reno Reservations, Comanches, Kiowas, and Cheyennes became infuriated by white livestock thieves, slaughter of the southern buffalo herd, and spoiled rations. A Kwahadi medicine man, who foresaw a Native American revival that would expel the whites from the plains, inspired warriors to wage war in Texas and Indian Territory during the spring of 1874. The state of Texas demanded Mackenzie's services on the northern frontier.

On July 20, 1873, Interior and War Department officials agreed to unleash the army. Sheridan quipped, "I propose now, if let alone to settle this Indian matter in the Southwest forever." He planned total war against people, property, and resources. "Friendly" Indians had until August 3 to submit. Afterward, five columns—from Forts Sill, Dodge, Griffin, Concho, and Union—converged on the upper Red River country to harass "unfriendlies" into starvation and submission. From August to December, regulars fought Indians or destroyed villages at the Anadarko Agency, near Mulberry Creek, in Palo Duro Canyon, near Gageby Creek, near Washita River, at McClellan Creek, at Elk Creek, and at Muster Creek. These operations under Lt. Col. John W. "Black Jack" Davidson, Col. Nelson A. Miles, Maj. William R. Price, Lt. Col. George P. Buell, and Col. Ranald S. Mackenzie endured blistering heat in the summer and knifing cold in the fall and winter. All operations were hampered by logistical shortages on the vast southern plains, but the Red River war also finished the Southern Plains tribes.

No operation was probably more prosaic and destructive than Mackenzie's campaign to the sources of the Red River. Brigadier General Augur, still commanding the Department of Texas, instructed Mackenzie "to follow the Indians wherever they go." If his pursuit entered the Fort Sill Reservation, he could take "entire Control of the Indians there." After arranging for critical supplies at Fort Griffin, Mackenzie joined his southern column—eight companies of Fourth Cavalry, three of Tenth Infantry, and one of scouts (whites, Seminoles, Tonkawas, Lipans, and a *nuevomexicano*)—at Duck Creek on September 19.

The following morning, Mackenzie led his men and Lawton's supply train along the edge of the Staked Plains northward to the Pease River in search of Comanches, especially Kwahadis. Rain slowed all movement, chilling both men and beasts. Mackenzie's men climbed onto the Llano five days later and then marched northwest twenty-five miles to the rim of Tule Canyon the next day. Fresh Indian trails ran in all directions. During the night of September 26, the Fourth easily repulsed an attack by approximately one hundred Comanches and Kiowas. Twenty-eight hours later, Mackenzie's men went into camp near Palo Duro Canyon.

Near camp, the scouts spied "a very large trail" leading to the "yawning chasm." The canyon was half a mile across and 1,500 feet deep. Strung along the Prairie Dog Town Fork for two or three miles were four or five encampments: Comanche, Kiowa, and Cheyenne with "hundreds of horses." The scouts found a narrow switchback descending to the canyon floor. Mackenzie ordered Lt. William A. Thompson and his scouts down the trail to open the fight. Troops E and A pressed closely behind. Everyone led their mounts. Near the bottom, an Indian popped up to wave a red blanket, fire a gun, and cry danger. He was killed. Still, the Indians were slow to wake to the danger, until Thompson's scouts charged down the canyon. Taking cover behind the riverbank and in timber and rockslides, warriors furiously skirmished to screen the flight of women and children. The scouts and Troops E and A captured 1,400 Indian ponies.

Mackenzie joined the battle with Troops H and L. He rode through camp after camp littered with "Buffalo robes, blankets, and every imaginable thing." Warriors laid down a hot crossfire from the canyonsides. Mackenzie countermanded Capt. Sebastian Gunther's order to clear Indians from a rock formation. Everyone, the colonel roared, would die. About noon, he secured the switchback and threw a skirmish line across the canyon. The balance of the Fourth heaped and burned Indian belongings, food stocks, and lodges. In the early afternoon, Mackenzie withdrew his troops and captured horses up the switchback to the Llano. His only casualties were a wounded trumpeter and three dead horses. The Indians lost three warriors and nearly all of their horses, property, and stores.

The colonel had crushed the Native spirit. Across the Llano his regulars drove the pony herd to Lawton's supply camp at Tule Canyon. At sunup the scouts cut out several hundred animals. Afterward, army volleys slaughtered more than a thousand of the remaining horses. Captain Carter explained, "It was the surest method of crippling the Indians and compelling them to go into and stay upon their reservations." The mound of bones, surviving into the twentieth century, was a grim monument to the brilliant but brutal campaign.

Mackenzie gave "the Indians as little rest as possible." From nearby Tule Creek, his southern column crossed the head of Palo Duro Canyon, scouted the opposite rim, and marched southeast to Mulberry Creek and the Pease River drainages, reaching the supply camp at the Freshwater Fork on October 23. His men saw only a few Indians at a distance and encountered a few *comancheros*. His third operation south to Laguna Rica smashed into a small Comanche camp on the northeastern loop, killing two warriors and capturing 19 women and children and 144 horses. On November 8, his battalion, battered by cold, snow, and rain, lumbered into the supply camp. However, Mackenzie wrote, "There have not been, so far as I have heard, enough of them killed." On December 3 a fourth operation, stalled in snow at the head of Freshwater Fork for ten days, started southward through Yellowhouse Canyon to Cedar Lake. Near Muchaque, a small detail killed two Indians and captured another. Battling wet, muddy conditions, Mackenzie and the Fourth reached Duck Creek sixteen days later.

With the assistance of Mackenzie and the Fourth, Sheridan's campaign crushed the Comanches, Kiowas, and Southern Cheyennes. Death, destruction, hunger, and fear fueled their capitulation from September 1874 to June 1875. Satanta brought 145 Kiowas to Fort Reno on October 4. Another 500 Kiowas and Comanches surrendered at Fort Sill about the same time. Most Southern Cheyennes submitted at Fort Reno in late February and early March—820 alone on March 6. Comanche leader Mow-way, whose people the Fourth had assaulted on McClellan Creek in 1872, brought in 200 Kotsotekas and Kwahadis to Fort Sill. Four hundred more Kwahadis—Quanah Parker among them—arrived on June 2, 1875. An additional blow to the Native spirit was Sheridan's eventual imprisonment of 72 warriors at Fort Marion, Florida, an arbitrary policy to extract the war faction from the defeated tribes. The Southern Plains Indian wars were finished.

Unhappy with the security at Fort Sill, Sheridan replaced Davidson with Mackenzie. The divisional commander wrote, "I'm sure if McKenzie [sic] can have the entire control, we will have no more trouble with these Indians." Mackenzie took over in March 1875 but soon complained that both Forts Sill and Reno ought to be under his command. Annoyed at his subordinate, Sheridan nonetheless ordered the change. At Fort Sill, Mackenzie threw himself into stabilizing the Indians under his care. Like nearly all army officers, he believed that they had to surrender their traditional way of life and assimilate into white society, but also that the federal government had to honor its promises to ease their transition with adequate food, clothing, and housing. He cooperated with Indian agents to develop sheep and cattle raising among the Comanches, Kiowas, and Cheyennes, but BIA mismanagement, Indian hunger, and white cattle rustlers scuttled the efforts. Chastising the BIA, Mackenzie wrote, "The position of a jailer to a vast band of half-starving criminals can never be very pleasant."

The depth of Mackenzie's anger became apparent in spring 1876 when a *New York Times* article singled out Fort Sill for abusing reservation Indians. The unsigned article labeled the post "a young Sodom" and its officers and enlisted men "tosspots." The regulars were a poor example—licentious and unbridled—of Christian civilization to the Indians. The piece coincided with a congressional investigation into corruption in the army contract system by the Clymer Committee, which also reopened the Reynolds-Mackenzie dispute. In Mackenzie's mind, the charges were a personal attack orchestrated by the friends of Colonel Reynolds in Texas and Washington. Through official channels the Fourth's colonel filed a series of letters defending himself and demanding an investigation to unmask the article's author. His choleric and belabored explanations aggravated Sheridan and Sherman, who contended with insulted officers and professional feuds on a weekly basis. Mackenzie was too good an officer, they groused, to be bothered by such inflammatory drivel. To his good fortune, the Clymer Committee, now amassing evidence for Belknap's impeachment, dropped the issue, while Reynolds faced a court-martial over a separate matter.

The last great Indian war on the northern plains soon occupied Mackenzie. Since the Civil War's end, the Sioux and Northern Cheyennes had held at bay Anglo expansion into the northern plains, but white miners, ranchers, and settlers demanded the region be opened to development. Yielding to pressure, Sherman and Sheridan concluded to break the Indian resistance. The army's converging columns, however, were checked on the Powder River, at the Rosebud, and on the Little Bighorn in spring and summer 1876. Horrifying the American people, who were celebrating the 1876 Centennial, Sioux, Cheyennes, and Arapahos led by Crazy Horse and Sitting Bull annihilated Lt. Col. George Armstrong Custer's Seventh Cavalry in late June. One month later, the Interior Department surrendered "all Indian agencies within the theater of war." Wanting vengeance, Sheridan also deployed trusted officers to destroy the recalcitrants. To that end, he transferred Mackenzie and Col. Nelson A. Miles to the northern plains. Mackenzie brought six companies of the Fourth and took over Fort Robinson, Nebraska, on August 17.

His first mission was to round up and disarm the bands of Red Cloud and Fall Leaf. On October 22 he led eight cavalry troops through a bitterly cold night to Chadron Creek. Dividing his force, Mackenzie captured both villages at dawn. He dismounted and disarmed the surprised Sioux and marched them back to Fort Robinson. Sheridan was infuriated, however, when Maj. Gen. George Crook let the friendly agency Sioux and Cheyennes retain their ponies and arms, and enrolled them as scouts for his next campaign against their relatives—a successful tactic that he had used against the Apaches in the Southwest.

During the winter, Sheridan wanted to destroy the Sioux and Cheyennes hiding in the Bighorn, Yellowstone, and Powder River drainages. One wing under Miles harassed Indians in the Bighorn and Tongue river valleys. A second wing under Crook was instructed to scour the Powder River country. Mackenzie commanded Crook's cavalry, eleven companies including six of the Fourth. The Powder River expedition—52 officers, 1,500 enlisted men, and 6 surgeons—was outfitted with "a full kit of the latest cold-weather gear." Also attached were 168 supply wagons, 7 ambulances, and a mule remuda. Sioux, Cheyenne, Arapaho, and Pawnee scouts hunted for villages. The weather was windy and snowy. On November 14 Crook's men launched northward from Fort Laramie, reaching Cantonment Reno one hundred miles away in a ferocious blizzard four days later. Here, one hundred Shoshones, traditional Sioux enemies, joined the scouts.

On November 20 scouts brought in a Cheyenne boy who stated that Crazy Horse's camp lay on the Rosebud, but a Red Cloud agent informed Crook that a large Cheyenne village was hidden in the Bighorn range. Crook unleashed Mackenzie, who led ten companies of cavalry (23 officers, 790 enlisted men, 4 interpreters, and 363 scouts) down Crazy Woman's fork to Beaver Creek. Mackenzie's scouts reported the Cheyenne village as located on the Red Fork. Through the night of November 24, he drove men and horses over snowy, icy mountains and struck the Red Fork eight miles below the village. The regulars could hear the dull thud of Cheyenne drums beaten to celebrate a recent military victory.

Envisioning a "bloodless capture," Mackenzie hoped to envelop the village and force Native capitulation before shooting started. At dawn, when the drumming ended and the Cheyennes went to sleep, Mackenzie attacked down both banks, but an ever-narrowing trail slowed the charge. Granted precious time, the Cheyennes retreated into nearby ravines and rock formations, from which they poured a galling fire. Mackenzie wisely avoided frontal assaults on the Cheyennes' "improvised rifle pits," instead maneuvering men to enfilade and flank places of concealment. The combatants fought often muzzle to muzzle and sometimes hand to hand. During the battle, Mackenzie raced his "iron-gray mount" across the snowy plateau between Double Buttes and Red Butte as Cheyenne warriors blasted away at his hunched figure. By midafternoon, however, the regulars controlled the village, and Indian scouts drove in 700 horses.

Mackenzie won the "prize" of the entire Sioux campaign: 200 lodges belonging to Dull Knife's Cheyennes. Plundering troopers and scouts recovered artifacts stripped from the dead of Custer's Seventh Cavalry. Indeed, Dull Knife's Cheyenne had participated in that terrible battle. Fires, now a routine weapon, consumed "buffalo robes and hides"; "tons of dried buffalo meat"; "hundreds of bladders and paunches of fat and marrow"; "cooking utensils, warlike trappings and horse equipments"; and other property. Leaving behind twenty-five dead, the Cheyennes trekked for three weeks to Crazy Horse's hard-pressed camp on the Tongue River, where they met a chilly reception. Mackenzie's column lost five enlisted men to death and twenty-three to wounds. One officer, Lt. John A. McKinney, a Mackenzie favorite, was killed.

The following morning, with heavy snow falling, Mackenzie's column moved out with the wounded men carried on mule-drawn travois and frozen dead packed on mules, and pulled into Crook's camp on Crazy

Woman's fork several days later. On December 2, the entire expedition tramped twenty-eight miles through snow to Cantonment Reno, where Crook sent part of the command back to Fort Fetterman to ease forage and supply shortages. With Mackenzie's remaining cavalry in tow, Crook made an additional scout, but forage deficiencies forced his command to spend most of December at Belle Fourche. On December 29, he ordered the Powder River Expedition back to Fort Fetterman. He marched his own men on to Fort Laramie, where the Fourth would find forage for its horses. When Mackenzie placed Lieutenant McKinney's body on the train for shipment to his family in Memphis, the colonel "testified to his admiration and affection for him by weeping like a child."

With Crook and other officers, Mackenzie rode to Cheyenne, Wyoming, where the army was trying Colonel Reynolds for incompetence during his attack on Indians at the Little Powder River in March 1876. Lingering only briefly, Mackenzie was summoned to Washington, D.C., by the Grant administration to command troops should the disputed presidential election of 1876 explode in national crisis. The Compromise of 1877, however, gave the election to Republican Rutherford B. Hayes in return for withdrawing federal troops from the South and ending Reconstruction. Mackenzie returned to Fort Robinson in March 1877. The following month, Dull Knife's people, 500 destitute Cheyennes, surrendered to him at the Red Cloud Agency. Moved by their desperate plight, the colonel immediately provisioned and clothed them. Over the spring and summer, other Sioux and Cheyennes surrendered to Mackenzie and Miles. On May 6, Crazy Horse led the Oglalas to the Red Cloud Agency. With Sitting Bull and his people in Canada, Crazy Horse's submission concluded the Great Sioux War.

In late May 1877, Mackenzie returned with the six companies of Fourth Cavalry to policing the agencies in Indian Territory. Several months later, he received 900 sullen Northern Cheyennes at Fort Reno. They would flee, he predicted, unless the federal government adequately housed, clothed, and fed them. A heavy guard alone, he argued, checked Indian violence. Mackenzie believed that "*force*" was the cornerstone of "moral restraint, respect for the laws, [and] enforcement of discipline." In summer 1877, through an interpreter, he threatened to ride out to Comanche camps and "kill them all" if the chiefs did not deliver unregistered Kwahadis who had infiltrated the Fort Sill Reservation. Riding hard to their villages, the awestruck chiefs gathered and handed over the Kwahadis.

Mackenzie remained at Fort Sill until December 1877 when border violence in southwestern Texas brought him back to Fort Clark. Indians, specifically the Lipan and Mescalero Apaches, had resumed violent raids from camps in the Santa Rosas in 1876. Penetrating as far as San Antonio, they claimed forty-eight lives between October 1877 and October 1878. With some success, Col. William R. "Pecos Bill" Shafter led forays into northern Mexico in 1876 and 1877, but the new government of Porfirio Díaz demanded their cessation and the withdrawal of a War Department order sanctioning the "hot pursuit" of depredators into Mexico. The Texas congressional delegation simultaneously demanded the return of Mackenzie, a soldier of "unflinching courage and firmness," to the border as a condition for voting against further army reductions. Mounting civilian casualties, Texas pressure, and the prospect of war with Mexico finally forced the Hayes administration to transfer Mackenzie and six companies of the Fourth to the Texas-Mexico border on December 3, 1877. The troopers toiled through heavy sleet, snow, and mud to reach their stations in February and March 1878.

After conferring with Maj. Gen. Edward O. C. Ord in San Antonio, Mackenzie returned to Fort Clark. As he prepared to cross the border, he tried to cultivate the cooperation of Gen. A. R. Falcon but, lacking authority, the latter flatly refused to help. Flying pickets of the Fourth Cavalry, operating from a screen of stations, helped dampen Apache depredations. Mackenzie's tactical plan was to establish a supply base near the Santa Rosas and scout the mountains for Lipans and Mescaleros. He rode with the strike force commanded by Capt. Samuel Young and composed of four companies of Eighth Cavalry, two of Fourth Cavalry, and a unit of Seminole scouts. On June 11, 1878, Young's men crossed the Rio Grande near Devil's River "without mishap" and reached the Burro Mountains three days later. Here, water was scarce and Mackenzie's guide became ill. Another day of frustration compelled Mackenzie to fall back, uniting with the second column—Shafter's infantry and supply column—along the Rio San Diego on June 17.

Instead of proceeding to the Santa Rosas, Mackenzie led his troops to Remolina on the Rio San Rodrigues. A Mexican garrison made a show of resistance but stood aside. Mackenzie's force, politely trailed by the Mexicans, descended the river. On June 21, at Monclava, the Mexican skirmishers occupied a "high hill" overlooking the Rio Grande ford Mackenzie intended to use. Col. Jesus Nuncio demanded "some apology or reparation for the presence" of U.S. troops on Mexican soil. Mackenzie punctuated his refusal by deploying skirmishers to dislodge the Mexicans, and the U.S. regulars crossed the river in peace.

The belligerent Ord instructed Mackenzie to recross the river and humiliate the Mexicans. Although he was urging war to resolve outstanding issues with Mexico, his own honor would not permit him to cross the river simply to settle an empty score with Nuncio. On July 4 Mackenzie led a unit over the Rio Grande, but the War Department called him back, explaining that President Díaz had agreed to punish Indian and Mexican raiders. During the summer, scouts of regulars and Seminoles still pursued livestock thieves over the border, even occupying New Town in mid-August. The following month, however, Mackenzie negotiated a cooperative agreement with Lt. Col. Felipe Vega: American troops would pursue thieves to the river; Mexican troops would pick up their trail on the other side. Joint pursuit made dramatic inroads into Indian marauding that fall. Mackenzie loosed no other campaigns to northern Mexico.

Called to Washington, D.C., to sit on a board in December, he returned to Fort Clark in late April 1879. The Fourth waged no summer campaign, and Mackenzie traveled to Lawrence, Kansas, for a civil proceeding in mid-September. That month, a Ute uprising in northwestern Colorado claimed the lives of ten regulars and ten BIA employees. The Indians also took two women and three children into captivity. The violence captivated the public nationwide. Federal authorities feared the spread of unrest to other Ute bands, Navajos, and Apaches farther south. In response Sheridan concentrated overwhelming force at White River, Fort Lewis, and Fort Garland, but Secretary of the Interior Carl Schurz rushed Commissioner Charles Adams to negotiate peace with Ute leader Ouray. In the meantime, the army, wanting vengeance, fumed.

As Texans howled in protest, Mackenzie and six troops of the Fourth were transferred to Fort Garland, Colorado, in October 1879. In the winter he assembled troops and supplies for the spring campaign. Marching westward on May 16 and 17, 1880, Mackenzie's command, sixteen companies of cavalry and infantry with a supply train, crossed Cochetopa Pass, descended into the Uncompahgre River valley, and arrived at the Los Pinos Agency two weeks later. In Mackenzie's opinion the government's conciliation simply coddled White River Ute murderers, but he lent assistance to the negotiations. With little to do the colonel drilled his command, reconnoitered central western Colorado, and entertained his champion, Sheridan. He accompanied Little Phil to Gunnison City and traveled on to Fort Garland and to Fort Riley, Kansas. The peace commissioners had settled with the White River and Uncompahgre Utes, who agreed to relocate to Utah the following spring. Leaving the infantry at Los Pinos, the Fourth Cavalry followed Mackenzie to Fort Riley.

In the fall, Mackenzie traveled east on army business and took leave. In August the office of chief signal officer had become vacant and Miles,

Mackenzie, and Wesley Merritt were recommended for the post, but it ultimately went to William B. Hazen, a senior colonel. An even more bitter pill was the promotion of Miles, an unceremonious grandstander, a non–West Pointer, and Mackenzie's chief rival, to brigadier general, the retired Ord's old slot, on December 15, 1880. As a rule, Mackenzie let others campaign publicly for his preferment. Crook, Pope, Sheridan, Sherman, and others advocated for him, but his self-serving proofs and pleas, routinely submitted through official channels, irritated Sheridan and Sherman for years, and when a higher grade opened, the young officer always materialized in the East. The army consoled Mackenzie by creating and assigning him to command the Department of Arkansas. When the jurisdiction was abolished in May 1881, he followed the Fourth Cavalry to Los Pinos in western Colorado.

There the Utes, facing removal, were in an ugly mood. With only eight companies available, Mackenzie felt especially vulnerable. The stress exacerbated his irascibility, which now began to take the form of a persecution complex. In early June, he wrote Pope, "For a considerable period of years ... I have found it so very difficult to procure what is essential without the risk of being regarded as captious and troublesome." Tensions escalated when the Utes learned that their new home would be the southeastern corner of the Uintah Reservation in northeastern Utah. Federal agents scheduled removal for late August. Both White River and Uncompahgre Utes balked, a few entrenching on a nearby mountain.

On August 24, Mackenzie received orders to relocate the Utes with force. After outfitting the cavalry with ammunition and rations, he met with some two dozen armed Utes the next day. The colonel dutifully read Secretary Schurz's order to leave in two days. When Ute denunciations became violent, Mackenzie abruptly rose to deliver an ultimatum: "All I want to know is whether you will go or not. If you will not go of your own accord, I will make you go." With hat in hand, he stalked out. Stunned silence gave way to animated deliberations. Three hours later the Utes offered a compromise, but Mackenzie declared, "No, if you have not moved by nine o'clock tomorrow morning, I will be at your camp and *make* you move." The following morning, the Indians began their migration to the Uintah Reservation. Mackenzie's cavalry followed to push them along. Whites claimed their land.

On September 2, 1881, a rider handed Mackenzie an order to take his regiment to Arizona without delay. Traveling mostly by rail, the Fourth marched the last 138 miles over a rain-soaked road to reach Fort Apache two weeks later. Mackenzie had received little information. Troops of the Sixth Cavalry, Col. Eugene A. Carr's regiment, had arrested an Apache medicine man and clashed with Apaches at Cibecue Creek. A day later, regulars beat off an Apache assault on Fort Apache. Maj. Gen. Orlando B. Willcox, the Arizona commander, feared an uprising of 4,000 Apaches at the San Carlos Reservation. The fed-up Sherman wanted Mackenzie to crush the Apaches, inadvertently pitting the colonel against Willcox.

Each subsequent professional clash raised the pitch of Mackenzie's sense of persecution. The command structure in Arizona vexed Mackenzie, who outranked Willcox and Carr by brevet rank. In a few days he and Willcox were sparring over jurisdiction and authority. Mackenzie concluded that Willcox's spineless panic, not a genuine military crisis, had brought the Fourth to Arizona. The rankled Sherman intervened to give Willcox the department and Mackenzie the field, but the new arrangement only heated their mutual recriminations. His fears of persecution roiling, Mackenzie offended the adjutant general with a stream of invective about his "false position" in Arizona. By this point in early October, most off-reservation Apaches had fled to northern Mexico. Seeing few, if any, hostile Apaches in the territory, Mackenzie requested the Fourth's transfer to New Mexico. Partly to end his letter writing, Sherman and Sheridan ordered the move. In late October he and the regiment marched toward Fort Wingate.

Mackenzie was granted the District of New Mexico, his first real administrative command. His mother and sister Harriet joined him in Santa Fe and became active members in the community. Throwing himself into district affairs, Mackenzie monitored the restless Navajos, negotiated cooperative agreements with Mexican officers, and supported operations against Apaches in southern New Mexico and northern Chihuahua. A jurisdictional dispute with Pope, his departmental commander, was his major fight in New Mexico. Without consulting Mackenzie, Pope had granted one of his officers leave. Throwing a fit, Mackenzie complained that Pope's intentional act had "injured" his command. Sheridan labeled his accusations "extraordinarily" excessive, and Sherman perceived it as "supersensitiveness." Such outbursts began to raise questions about the colonel's emotional stability.

Still, Mackenzie's impetuosity did not impede his rise. Brig. Gen. Irvin McDowell's retirement on October 15, 1882 opened a brigadier's slot. The congressional delegations of Colorado and Texas, the New Mexico Republican Party, and influential men such as Sheridan campaigned for Mackenzie. Ex-President Grant's praise, however, most moved President Chester A. Arthur. Grant stated that Mackenzie's promotion was a "personal favor" to him and a "matter of simple justice." On October 26, 1882 Arthur awarded him the brigadier's star. Immediately going on leave, he reported that his health had been worse "in the last two years than anyone"

knew. Physical deterioration, particularly rheumatism, may have partly
explained his reluctance to campaign
against Apaches in Arizona. Upon
his return to Santa Fe in February
1883, New Mexico affairs did not
overtax him for the remainder of the
year, but he did suffer a bout of
"cerebral trouble" possibly related to
the death of his mother, who had
provided emotional ballast in his life.

Now a brigadier, Mackenzie
hoped for an eastern assignment,
but the army posted him to the
Department of Texas, duty that ultimately satisfied him. He now owned
a home in San Antonio and a ranch
in Kendall County. However, after
taking command on November 1,
1883, Mackenzie's "erratic" behavior
began to puzzle his officers. A former officer noted that his carriage

Ranald S. Mackenzie at the end of his military career. (From the L. P. Bradley Collection, courtesy of the U.S. Military History Institute, Carlisle Barracks, Pennsylvania)

was slumped and that he was losing weight. By early December, the
abstemious general was drinking heavily and raging frequently. To some he
was plainly mad. On the night of December 18, his raving provoked several
civilians in town to beat him and lash him to a cart wheel. Town constables
found the delirious Mackenzie the next morning.

The departmental medical director examined him over the next three
days. The general was alternately lucid and delusional. On December 22
departmental adjutant Thomas M. Vincent concluded that Mackenzie could
no longer command and had to enter an asylum. Three other doctors con-
curred. Exploiting the general's delusions of grandeur, Vincent, General in
Chief Sheridan, and Adj. Gen. R. C. Drum lured him to Washington, D.C.,
ostensibly to confer on army reorganization. Only he, Mackenzie boasted,
could assist Sheridan with the task. On December 26 a Pullman car rolled
away with Mackenzie, Harriet, Vincent, Dr. Passmore Middleton, two
aides-de-camp, and two orderlies. Tragically, the brigadier left behind his
fiancée, Florida Tunstall Sharpe, whom he had been scheduled to marry on
December 19.

A bachelor throughout his army career, Mackenzie had courted no one until Sharpe. Their romance startled everyone. There was some speculation that he had pursued Florida when they first met at San Antonio in 1868, but no romance flourished and she soon married an army surgeon, Redford Sharpe. In fact, the Fourth Cavalry boasted a reputation as the "Bachelor Regiment." Frontier soldiering—done well—often demanded the uncompromised devotion of a Mackenzie. He believed that frontier combat stations, spartan, rugged, and unrefined, offered a poor environment for family life, although many officers still brought their spouses and children. He counseled young officers to put off marriage until they had retired their debts and their careers had seasoned. His devotion to administering and leading the Fourth left little room for a woman. During his career, he appeared to be professionally consumed and financially stable, if a little lonesome.

At the same time, women did figure into Mackenzie's life. Wives, daughters, sisters, and laundresses were present at nearly all frontier stations, and, ever the gentleman, he was polite and solicitous to all, but never indulged in flirtations with any women, even unattached ones. The most important woman in Mackenzie's life was his mother, Catherine, who lived in New Jersey for many years. He always visited her when he went on leave in the East. Also important to him was his sister Harriet, a spinster, with whom he kept in close contact. His mother's death was a profoundly grievous blow to Mackenzie, and Harriet became his principal caregiver at the end of his life. During his many years in the West, Catherine and Harriet had helped the professionally driven officer retain some tangible connection to family, home, and domesticity.

As the army wrestled with Mackenzie's case in the late fall, Harriet asked Sheridan to place her brother in the government asylum in Washington, but other family diverted him to Bloomingdale Asylum in New York, where he arrived on December 30. Nearly two months of observation gave Dr. Charles A. Nichols little hope for the general's recovery. On March 5, 1884, Maj. Gen. Winfield Scott Hancock convened the Retiring Board to consider the case. Mackenzie denied his insanity and pleaded to remain in the army. Dr. Nichols diagnosed him with "General paresis" or "General Paralysis of the Insane." The cause was "wounds received and exposure in the line of duty." The board agreed, but Mackenzie felt dishonored: "The Army is all I have got. ... I think it very harsh if I am left out of the Army ... for a few months sickness." The army retired him on March 24, 1884.

Mackenzie remained at Bloomingdale until June 14, when Harriet relocated him to the family home in Morristown, New Jersey. A year and a half later, he was moved to Morris Duer's home at New Brighton. His condition steadily declining, he became childlike and walked only with help. On January 19, 1889, the forty-eight-year-old Mackenzie passed away peacefully. The official cause was "general paresis" but, in the light of modern medicine, his cerebral paralysis was likely caused by syphilis, a sexually transmitted disease, for which he demonstrated classic symptoms: "irritability, restlessness, poor emotional control, and dipsomania" in the early stages, and slurred speech, incoherence, physical deterioration, physical aggression, and delusional fantasies in later stages. He also fell into the age group, thirty to fifty, at which general paresis usually strikes. No historical evidence indicates where he might have contracted the infection, but bachelors commonly visited prostitutes for sexual release in the nineteenth century, and Mackenzie might have called on brothels during his leaves of absence on the East Coast. With modest public acknowledgment, Ranald Slidell Mackenzie was laid to rest at West Point alongside Civil War cavalrymen John Buford and Judson Kilpatrick.

Throughout his military career, Mackenzie sought fields for the demonstration of personal courage, which was his guiding principle and the fountain of duty and honor. Profoundly influenced by military men in his family, he devoted his life to exploring bravery in the army and war, and he drove his officers and men, individually and collectively, to exercise their manly strength in battle, the most stressful of human environments. Under his leadership, his regiments, particularly the Fourth Cavalry, performed superbly in campaigns and battles. At the same time, Mackenzie demonstrated command prudence, another characteristic of soldierly courage, when he suspended the Fourth's assault against the Comanches during a storm on the Llano Estacado, even in the face of grumbling officers and men. Over the next five years, the intact Fourth compiled a distinguished record of combat victories over Comanches, Kiowas, Apaches, Kickapoos, and Cheyennes. Still another demonstration of the soldier's courage was that in spite of however many men and horses he lost on campaign, Mackenzie refused to abuse and humiliate defeated enemies. Even when doubting their honor and intentions, he sought to succor and protect the Indians under his care. In his mind, the courageous officer, the manly soldier, was no cold-blooded killer but a humane leader of men and a conscientious protector of the vanquished.

As a combat officer, Colonel Mackenzie stood shoulder to shoulder with other frontier-army luminaries such as George A. Custer, Nelson A. Miles, and George Crook. All four officers distinguished themselves in the line during the Civil War, and their battlefield commands earned the respect and admiration of Grant, Sherman, and Sheridan, the three greatest martial legends in the victorious Union Army. On the western frontier, Mackenzie, Custer, Miles, and Crook skillfully maneuvered their men and supplies through rugged terrain and harsh climates to strike elusive Indian warriors and societies, earning well-deserved reputations as superb frontier campaigners. Their dependability in warfare against Indians explained why Grant, Sherman, Sheridan, and Pope invested them with critical combat operations in the West after the Civil War.

What differentiated Mackenzie from the other three was that he had less history and fewer obstacles to overcome in his professional career. Mackenzie's first place in the West Point class of 1862 gave him near mystical status in the regular army, while Miles's lack of formal military training often attracted the scorn of his West Point peers. With only three years in the service by the Confederate surrender at Appomattox, Mackenzie had far less time to entrench himself in army politics and engage its institutional rancor than did Crook, who had entered the army from West Point in 1852. Mackenzie enjoyed the almost unanimous support of his immediate superior officers, especially that of Major General Sheridan, whose divisional jurisdiction embraced Mackenzie's field. However much the young colonel's entreaties exasperated his divisional commander, he had enjoyed Sheridan's profound respect and trust as a frontier campaigner and combat officer.

As a commander of cavalry, Mackenzie was tactically uncontroversial. Despite his many combat successes, Crook skirmished with edgy civilians and skeptical peers over his deployment of entire units of Apache scouts to fight their relatives in the Southwest. Although Mackenzie always employed some Indian scouts in his frontier campaigns, his Fourth Cavalry regulars performed the lion's share of the actual fighting. Unlike Lieutenant Colonel Custer who lost more than 200 men in the Battle of the Little Bighorn in 1876, Mackenzie suffered no major disasters in the West, although his second armed incursion into northern Mexico was more frustrating than successful. In general his skill and luck persisted through the 1870s, his most active years as a frontier combat officer and his methodical reduction of the Comanches and Kiowas on the southern plains earned him a lasting place in the history of frontier campaigning and of the post–Civil War U.S. Army.

NELSON A. MILES

The Soldier as Westerner

ROBERT WOOSTER

Joe B. Frantz, president of the Western Historical Association, once proclaimed the American West to have been a "child of federal subsidy." "From start to finish," he said, the westerner "was subsidized from his brogans to his sombrero." As the government's most visible agent in the nineteenth-century West, the U.S. Army was often the source of these subsidies. Military scientists explored and mapped it; blue-coated regulars conquered its earlier inhabitants and paved the way for its non-Indian settlement; army purchases of food, grain, hay, and countless other items to supply far-flung garrisons underwrote its economy.

Of course, the relationship went two ways. Just as most non-Indian westerners of the nineteenth century hoped to profit from their association with the military, so did many officers see their western assignments as something from which they too might benefit. Success in western battle could lead to professional advancement; life in western garrisons could spell relief from the drudgeries of the East; speculation in western lands could yield financial gain; exploitation of western resources—both tangible and intangible—could mean untold opportunity.

The career of Nelson Appleton Miles exemplifies this symbiotic relationship. Born in 1839, Miles overcame a lack of formal military training to emerge as one of the North's most effective combat leaders of the Civil War. But he would be best known for his western activities. Courageous in battle and tenacious on the trail, driven by his desire for fame and fortune, Miles contributed mightily to the defeat of the Cheyennes, Comanches, Kiowas, and Sioux. He also bested Chief Joseph and the Nez Perce, oversaw the final campaigns against Geronimo and the Chiricahua Apaches, and helped to prevent the Ghost Dance outbreak from exploding into a bloodbath even more horrific than the slaughter at Wounded Knee. During the Spanish-American War, as commanding general of the army, Miles conducted a nearly flawless conquest of Puerto Rico. But as a shameless self-promoter, he sought to parlay his battlefield successes into personal glory; an inveterate booster of things western, he hoped to ally his own interests with those of the region's rich and powerful. After all, he enjoyed access to potentially lucrative sources of military patronage. In so doing, Miles assiduously, if somewhat clumsily, associated himself with the opportunities emerging from the conquest of the American West.

Little in his early years hinted at these relationships with the military and the West. Born to an upper-middle-class family in Massachusetts, as a teenager he left his parents' rural Westminster home for the excitement of big-city Boston. With some assistance from relatives there, he sold fruit and crockery in a variety of retail stores and attended night school. "My prosperity ... has not amounted to much," he admitted in a letter written shortly after the move. "I have some hard time[s] to go through. But as it was my choice to come into this city I mean to put it through if I can." Miles kept at it, and by 1860 he had moved to a boardinghouse near fashionable Temple Place and had placed his name in the city's business directory. Perhaps with an eye to the nation's looming sectional conflict, he and several fellow enthusiasts began military drills under the tutelage of a retired French army officer.

Following the North's defeat at the First Battle of Bull Run (July 21, 1861), the twenty-two-year-old Miles joined the army. With a thousand dollars given to him by his father and another 2,000 loaned by an uncle, he organized and outfitted Company E, Twenty-second Massachusetts Infantry. The men elected their patron as captain, but Governor John A. Andrew refused to commission this unknown youth to such a high rank. Smarting from this snub, the first in a long saga of clashes with political superiors ("I was cheated out of it," he concluded bitterly), Miles had to settle for a first lieutenancy. He saw his first combat at the Battle of Fair Oaks, Virginia (May 31, 1862), where, ignoring a foot wound, he helped stem the retreat of a regiment of Pennsylvania volunteers. His exploits throughout the Seven Days' battles (June 25–July 1) and at the Battle of Antietam (September 17) led to promotions to lieutenant colonel and colonel, respectively. Miles then suffered a severe neck wound while assaulting strong Confederate positions in the Battle of Fredericksburg (December 13).

Colonel Miles's six-foot frame, intense blue eyes, and steely gaze already reflected his increasingly martial appearance. He spent the spring of 1863 convalescing from his wound and politicking for higher command. Although he had no formal military training, his aggressive nature, instinctive tactical aptitude, and bravery under fire suited him ideally for the Civil

War battlefield, where soldiers expected their officers to visibly demonstrate their leadership. "That officer will get promoted or get killed," one superior had observed. His physical wounds healed, but his failure to gain promotion irritated the scars from his earlier clash with Governor Andrews. "It all goes by political favor," Miles explained bitterly to his brother. Fortunately, his battlefield excellence matched his desire for promotion. During the Battle of Chancellorsville (May 2–4, 1863), he skillfully conducted his division's skirmishers until nearly killed by a Rebel bullet that ripped through his stomach and bowels. Thirty-nine years later, the War Department awarded him the Medal of Honor for his gallantry there.

Upon his return to active duty, Miles once again distinguished himself in the Battles of Spotsylvania (May 11, 1864), Cold Harbor (June 2), and Reams' Station (August 25), securing an appointment as brevet major general in the process. Further acclaim poured in the next year. "Miles has made a big thing of it," wrote Ulysses S. Grant about the former's role in the victory at Sutherland's Station (April 2, 1865), "and deserves the highest praise for the pertinacity with which he stuck to the enemy until he wrung from them the victory." Another success at Sayler's Creek (April 6) netted Miles's division two enemy cannon, four battle flags, and 250 supply wagons.

Still a youthful twenty-six, Miles emerged from the Civil War a major general of volunteers. Based on his outstanding combat record, he was assigned to oversee security arrangements at Fort Monroe, Virginia, for the government's most famous prisoner, former Confederate president Jefferson Davis. Better suited to the finality of combat than to the subtleties of public relations, he placed the enfeebled ex-president in irons. The shackles were soon removed, but the resulting furor hinted of Miles's limitations off the battlefield.

Following the wholesale reductions in the postwar regular army, Miles was appointed colonel of the Fortieth Infantry, one of six regiments reserved for black enlisted men and white officers. Although a personal disappointment because he had not obtained a higher rank, the assignment was consistent with the sharp cutbacks of the day, when Civil War veterans saw their ranks slashed by several grades. In spring 1867, he took up Reconstruction duties in North Carolina. Sympathetic to the plight of former slaves, he championed political change in the South, used his troops to monitor labor contracts, and protested the spread of pseudomilitary organizations like the Ku Klux Klan.

Colonel Miles also continued his relentless self-promotions, finding every excuse to curry favor with potential patrons in Washington. On one such sojourn he met an attractive and very eligible young woman: Mary

By his mid-thirties Col. Nelson Miles looked every bit the soldier. Here he sports some of his winter garb. (Courtesy of the Montana Historical Society, #943-884)

Hoyt Sherman, niece of Senator John Sherman and Gen. William T. Sherman. Following a year's courtship, the couple were married in 1868. "A perfect lady" and congenial hostess, Mary would prove a valuable asset to her husband's very public career. For his part, Miles tried to use the familial relationship with the powerful Sherman family to further his own professional life. To General Sherman, who wanted to divorce the army from politics, such boorish behavior was unbecoming an officer and a gentleman; to Miles such entreaties seemed normal for a man on the make.

Changing national priorities promised new opportunities and challenges. Frustrated by the difficulties of Reconstruction and eager to slash military spending, in March 1869, Congress reorganized the army once again. In the resulting shuffle, Miles was transferred to the Fifth Infantry Regiment, then stationed in Kansas. The move thus spared him many of the controversies of Reconstruction, allowing him instead to take advantage of the opportunities associated with western development. As the colonel's wife, Mary set the tone for polite society in the regiment, entertaining guests and select post residents and occasionally accompanying her husband on organized hunts. She also bore their first child, Cecilia, in September 1869.

Miles saw his first combat against Indians during the Red River war of 1874–1875. Commanding more than 700 officers and men, he marched south from Fort Dodge on August 14 against the Southern Cheyennes, Comanches, and Kiowas. After sixteen scorching days, his scouts located several hundred Indians along the Red River south of Camp Supply, Indian Territory. A sharp skirmish up Tule Canyon and onto the Staked Plains followed, but concerns about his supply lines and a sudden rainfall that transformed dry creekbeds into raging rivers prevented effective pursuit. Characteristically, Miles blamed others for his failure. Many junior officers, he charged, had failed to keep up a sufficient march pace; in the rear, malingering bureaucrats had left him without supplies.

As Miles limped back to camp, Col. Ranald Mackenzie dealt the Indians a sharp defeat at Palo Duro Canyon, Texas (September 28). A lean thirty-four-year-old with a superb Civil War record of his own, Mackenzie had destroyed almost the entire pony herd of a large Cheyenne, Comanche, and Kiowa encampment. Stung by the challenge posed by a rival like Mackenzie, Miles resolved to involve himself more closely in the details of future operations. He took the field later that year determined to reclaim his status as among the army's top young colonels. Even as frigid weather forced others to retire to winter quarters, he led three companies of hardy infantrymen on a final, defiant foray, returning to a temporary cantonment on the Washita in early February. Although no clear battlefield victory ended the Red River wars, the army's constant campaigning had drained the resources of the Kiowas, Southern Cheyennes, and Comanches, who eventually turned themselves in to reservations. And Miles, too, had made his point: troops under his command would invariably outmarch those led by rival officers. Gen. Phil Sheridan, in whose division most of the operations had taken place, proclaimed that Miles had "exceeded expectations."

Developments on the northern plains posed new challenges. Following the annihilation of George Custer's column at the Little Bighorn, Montana (June 25, 1876), Miles and his regiment were transferred north to the Yellowstone River valley, where they erected a temporary cantonment and scoured the region for signs of the enemy. His Fifth Infantry soon drove the Indians back in a running fight along Cedar Creek (October 20–21). As was often the case in Indian-army combat, the skirmishing produced few immediate casualties—the bodies of five Indians were found, and three infantrymen were reported wounded. But the regulars had captured much of the Indians' winter stores and had clearly bested foes once thought invincible. "I believe we can wear them down," Miles concluded, even as he peppered his superiors with a barrage of complaints about the lack of logistical support.

Miles and his rugged infantrymen, who had frantically secured every scrap of clothing in the Tongue River region, kept up the pressure all winter. Undaunted by the subzero temperatures, they repulsed an attack by Crazy Horse's Oglala and Cheyenne followers at Wolf Mountain (January 8, 1877). Their colonel's victory reports counted fifteen Indians dead and thirty wounded and concluded with the customary allegations of mismanagement behind the lines. The staff's "criminal neglect" had forced his troops "to march through blinding snow storms, in piercing winds, with insufficient underclothing, and feet bound up in grain sacks, and in the skins of wild animals."

Heavy Montana snows did not deter Miles and his Fifth Infantry from pursuing Sitting Bull and Crazy Horse. Miles is in the middle, surrounded by several junior officers, on the event of their 1876 campaign from the Tongue River Cantonment. (Courtesy of the U.S. National Archives, public domain)

As had been the case following the Red River war, active campaigning petered out as thousands of exhausted Indians turned themselves in to the various government agencies that now dotted the northern plains. But Lame Deer's Miniconjous vowed to continue the struggle. Now leading a mixed force of Indian scouts, cavalry, and infantry, on May 7, Miles struck Lame Deer's encampment along Muddy Creek. The resulting melee left fourteen Sioux (including Lame Deer) and four soldiers dead. Most significantly, in their frantic escape the Miniconjous had left behind most of their lodges and ponies. "The best thing that has been done since hostilities commenced," reported Miles's immediate superior, Gen. Alfred Terry. Sitting Bull and about 4,000 followers had fled to Canada, but Sioux and Northern Cheyenne resistance south of the Forty-ninth Parallel had been broken.

That summer, as Miles bombarded superiors with demands for promotion or greater responsibility (on one occasion, Miles asked General Sherman to name him secretary of war), disputes between the government and Chief Joseph's Nez Perces, escalated into open warfare. The Nez Perce had fled their homelands in Oregon's Wallowa Valley, winding their way through Idaho, Montana, and Wyoming. Oliver O. Howard, on whose staff Miles had served in the early days of the Civil War, had been unable to block their escape and called upon his old comrade at Tongue River for assistance. At the head of four companies of mounted infantry and six troops of cavalry, on September 30, Miles intercepted the Nez Perce in the northern ranges of the Bear's Paw Mountains, forty miles from the Canadian border.

Fearful that the Nez Perce would yet elude his grasp, he promptly attacked. A hail of well-directed fire from Indian marksmen hidden in the rocks and ravines forced his men back. Wheeling up a Hotchkiss mountain gun and a twelve-pound Napoleon cannon, Miles settled in for a siege. Howard arrived five days later, with early snows presaging the onset of another brutal winter. Determined to maintain their way of life to the end, about 200 Nez Perce broke through the soldiers' defenses and escaped to Canada. But the 1,700-mile trek had exhausted the others. Joseph, along with 87 men, 184 women, and 147 children, surrendered on October 5, trusting that Miles could make good his assurance that they could return to the Northwest the following year.

"We have had our usual success," gloated Miles. Yet this triumph did not extend to the government's acceptance of his surrender terms, and the Nez Perce were dispatched south to the Indian Territory. Impressed by Joseph and the Nez Perce, Miles protested the decision with characteristic vigor. "Fraud and injustice" had caused the war, he insisted to General Terry. "I believe that Joseph is by far the ablest Indian on the continent and if they can be fairly treated will rank as loyal friends of the govt. as they have been dangerous enemies," added Miles in a letter to Sherman. These efforts proved futile; Joseph died in 1904, still longing to return to his beloved Wallowa River valley homeland.

In helping to defeat the most powerful tribes of the plains, Colonel Miles had established a splendid military record. At the same time, his jealousy and immense ego had made many enemies; he seemed constitutionally unable to cooperate with anyone. "I ... have fought and defeated larger and better armed bodies of hostile Indians and at the same time have gained a more extended knowledge of our frontier country than any living man," went a typical report. His criticisms of War Department staff officers were legion. Miles had also broken with Howard, his old superior, in a squabble about who most deserved credit for Joseph's defeat. Likewise, he had clashed with Ranald Mackenzie, victor at Palo Duro Canyon, and George Crook, whose record fighting Indians in Oregon and Arizona was, to date, as good as anyone's. The army's small size meant that the promotion of one necessarily came at another's expense, driving Miles to challenge any real or imagined slight. His rivals invariably responded in kind, leading an exasperated General Sherman to urge his ambitious nephew-in-law to "keep quiet."

The disputatious Miles was also leaving his mark on the western landscape. As the Joseph campaign closed, the army relocated the temporary cantonment on the Tongue River to a more permanent site two miles away, Fort Keogh. Miles City, the settlement that developed around the garrison, was named in the commander's honor and became the region's economic hub. There, Mary Miles once again entertained with a style and grace suitable to the needs of her ambitious husband. In time-honored western tradition, he cultivated alliances with territorial officials like Governor Benjamin F. Potts (who owed his appointment to Miles's uncle-in-law, Senator John Sherman) and delegate to Congress Martin Maginnis. Expanded responsibilities for Miles would not only satisfy his own ambitions, but also pump much-needed federal dollars into the Montana economy. Indeed, these lobbying efforts exemplified the complementary roles played by the federal government, army officers, and local politicians in boosting the non-Indian development of the American West.

Emerging was a western consciousness that Miles, never hesitant to voice his opinion, expressed loudly and frequently. A much-sought-after commentator on Indian and western affairs, he testified before Congress, spoke to reform groups, and published essays in influential journals like the *North American Review* and the *Journal of the Military Service Institution of the United States*. Like many, he believed that the West must be opened to non-Indian development at almost any cost. The southern plains "should be swept of these miserable savages and opened to settlements," he had proclaimed during the Red River Campaign. "There is scarcely any part of it not adapted to pastoral or agricultural purposes." Further, he joined almost all of his comrades in supporting the return of Indian affairs from the Interior to the War Department, a move that would allow army officers to replace the political appointees of the Indian Bureau.

Even so, most Indian reformers welcomed Miles as one of their own. Capt. Richard Henry Pratt, whose Carlisle Indian School epitomized their faith in the "civilization" process, complimented Miles for having attempted to bring "justice to the Indians." Taking his cue from contemporary anthropologists such as Lewis Henry Morgan, Miles believed that most American Indians had advanced from a state of "savagery" to one of "barbarism." A selected number of "localized" tribes, most notably the Choctaws and the Creeks, had even achieved "civilization"; the vast majority, however, still needed to be disarmed and encouraged to adopt herding as a necessary step toward civilization. For its part, the government needed to emulate the Canadian model, where a "permanent, decided, and just" system had helped to limit violence. Miles also supported the cause of land-in-severalty, whereby tribal reservations were broken up in favor of grants to individual Indians. Such a move, championed by many reformers of the period, was designed to speed the assimilation of Native Americans into white society.

In December 1880, Miles finally received his first general's star and with it command of the Department of the Columbia, encompassing Oregon, the Washington Territory, most of the Idaho Territory, and the district of Alaska. From his headquarters at Vancouver Barracks, Washington, the new brigadier general once again curried favor with politicians and businessmen and proclaimed the region's virtues. The 1,600 soldiers garrisoning the department hardly matched its strategic and economic importance, argued Miles. Larger military posts, more railroads, and improved telegraphic networks would stimulate development. And the nation need not stop at the Forty-ninth Parallel. British Columbia residents would "vote for annexation tomorrow," he predicted in 1881. Army explorations could, moreover, quicken the conquest of Alaska, whose "industrial and commercial resources ... are attracting the interest and attention of the Pacific Coast." While at Vancouver, Mary bore the couple's second child, Sherman, in 1882.

Transfer to the sprawling Department of the Missouri, which contained the states of Colorado, Missouri, Kansas, and Illinois, as well as the New Mexico Territory, came in 1885. The new department and its fine headquarters at Fort Leavenworth suited not only his family's comfort but his enormous ego. Characteristically, Miles attributed his new position to his personal interview with President Grover Cleveland. The promotion led him to redouble his efforts on his own behalf. Smug in his new promotion, it thus came as quite a shock to learn that his rival, Crook, had secured the transfer of New Mexico to his own Department of Arizona. Strategically, the move made sense, as it would enable Crook to better coordinate his southwestern campaigns against Geronimo, who neither respected nor understood the military's boundaries. Miles, however, took the shift of New Mexico out of his jurisdiction as a personal affront and undoubtedly rejoiced at Crook's inability to crush the Apaches.

In 1886, Crook's transfer to the Department of the Platte gave Miles his chance. Promising to rely more heavily on regular troops than had Crook, who had employed swarms of Indian auxiliaries, Miles was dispatched to Arizona and soon commenced field operations. Teams of regulars, supported by civilian packers, mules, and Yuma scouts, combed suspected Apache hideouts. Meanwhile, Miles hoped to moderate the government's insistence on unconditional surrender. Negotiations, he suggested, would be a more practical means of restoring order against an unconventional enemy like the Apaches, whose mobility, knowledge of the terrain, and disdain for traditional supply lines made for an elusive foe indeed. His effort to change policy sparked a bewildering series of instructions, observations, proposals, and counterproposals among the War Department, the commanding general's office, departmental headquarters, officers in the field, and prominent Apache leaders.

Events came to a head late that summer even as interested parties were still trying to sort out who had promised what. On Sheridan's orders, the family and friends of Geronimo's followers were removed from their homes at the San Carlos Agency and sent by rail to Fort Marion, Florida. Meanwhile, using methods more suggestive of Crook's tactics than his own, Miles dispatched Lt. Charles B. Gatewood, a respected figure among the Apaches, to meet with Geronimo. As delicate talks between Gatewood and Geronimo continued, Miles arrived on September 3, anxious to conclude a settlement before the Chiricahua leader fled again. "So long as you are our prisoners," he later remembered having assured Geronimo, "we shall not kill you but shall treat you justly."

Exhausted by their travails and dispirited by the news that their loved ones had been removed from Arizona, Geronimo and his followers agreed with Miles's terms. On September 6, the general sent back word that the prisoners expected "banishment from this country." Fearing that the Apaches would escape, Miles wired Sheridan of his intention to relocate them to Florida. But officials back east thought otherwise. More interested in restoring order than in ensuring justice, President Cleveland wanted to hold the Indians in Arizona to await civil prosecution.

Claiming not to have received Cleveland's final instructions, Miles, still worried about an escape, hustled Geronimo and the others onto eastbound railroad cars. Administration officials, joined by Howard, Crook, and Adj. Gen. Richard Drum, denounced Miles's actions. After several weeks' delay in San Antonio as the government figured out what to do, the Indians finally completed their trip to Florida. The general's subsequent attempts to regain political favor with the Cleveland administration failed miserably, and any credit that might have been forthcoming for his having helped to secure Geronimo's capture was forgotten amidst the resulting furor. Rather than a conquering hero, Miles, who had not carried out a direct executive order, seemed an uncooperative schemer more concerned about fulfilling his personal ambition than the president's policies.

Fortunately for him, his continuing military success rendered any official public censure impossible. So as the behind-the-scenes sparring with Washington continued, he took refuge at departmental headquarters in Los Angeles, where the family took up residence at Pasadena's fashionable Raymond Hotel. There Miles counted among a growing circle of connections his old scout–turned–professional westerner "Buffalo Bill" Cody, artist and illustrator Frederic Remington, and future secretary of state John Hay. During this time, daughter Cecilia completed her education back east while the precocious young Sherman kept the general's staff busy. The shuffling among top army brass following commanding general Sheridan's death in 1888 allowed Miles to assume command of the Division of the Pacific. Encompassing the departments of Arizona, California, and the Columbia, this posting held with it the added bonus of quarters in San Francisco.

The move inspired the inevitable torrent of local boosterism from the new division commander. Congratulations to President-elect Benjamin Harrison included an extended thesis on the importance of the West, as well as an invitation for a guided tour by the army's most successful Indian campaigner. "You will find the true American pioneer spirit in this western country," wrote Miles. Social engagements included visits with Chief Justice Stephen Field, Senator Eugene Hale, and Lewis Wolfley, territorial governor of Arizona. Speeches at various Pacific Coast ports promoted naval modernization, which would mean an infusion of federal dollars into the local economies. Inadequate seaboard defenses also required an additional half million dollars for military construction on the Pacific, asserted Miles. And a new essay for the *North American Review*, "Our Unwatered Empire," proposed that federal irrigation projects make the western deserts bloom.

However, Miles' romance with the Pacific Coast soon proved to be another temporary fling. In 1890, the death of his old rival, George Crook, made room for him to secure his second general's star as well as command of the huge Division of the Missouri. The transfer allowed him to move to Chicago, then in the midst of a tremendous building boom. This "wonderful city," he proclaimed jubilantly, might "in time become the largest in this country if not in the world."

Events at the Standing Rock, Cheyenne River, Pine Ridge, and Rosebud Reservations soon turned his attention from the refinements of big-city Chicago to the wilds of the Dakotas. Fanned by crop failures, poverty, and the government's failure to supply promised annuities, the Ghost Dance movement, which blended traditional Indian spiritualism with millennial Christianity, had spread like wildfire through many Northern Plains tribes. The skittish agent at Pine Ridge, Daniel Royer, a political hack dubbed by his charges Young-Man-Afraid-of-Indians, demanded military intervention, as did panicky whites throughout the region.

Miles hoped to calm the excitement with a decisive display of military power. But the moves must be carefully choreographed. As he prepared to occupy the Pine Ridge and Rosebud Reservations, he instructed Brig. Gen.

John R. Brooke, commander of troops in the region, not to allow his soldiers to mingle with the Indians. "One thing should be impressed upon all officers," he told Brooke on November 18, "never to allow their commands to be mixed up with the Indians." As the army swept in as planned two days later, many stunned Brulés and Oglalas fled to the agencies in favor of the isolation of the northwestern quarter of the Pine Ridge Reservation. "Do not allow your command to become mixed up with the Indians friendly or otherwise," Miles reminded Brooke on November 23, following this with a similar admonition two weeks later.

At the Cheyenne River and Standing Rock Agencies, Miles believed it best to treat with individual Indian leaders, many of whom he knew from previous campaigns. Such an approach worked well in the case of Hump, a prominent Cheyenne River figure, who denounced the Ghost Dance and pledged to support the government. But Big Foot's Miniconjou followers remained a potential threat; at Standing Rock, a bungled attempt to arrest Sitting Bull left the influential leader and thirteen others dead or mortally wounded. Hundreds of Sitting Bull's frightened people bolted following the melee.

On December 28, Col. James W. Forsyth's command of 438 cavalrymen, augmented by a platoon of Oglala scouts and four cannon, met with Big Foot and his followers at Wounded Knee Creek. The following day, Forsyth tried to disarm the Indians, who numbered about 120 men and twice that many women and children. In direct violation of Miles's repeated orders to his superior, General Brooke, Forsyth dispatched two companies to an isolated position near the encampment to conduct the weapons inspection. Shots soon rang out from the lodges, followed by more substantial volleys. Amidst a hail of often ill-aimed supporting fire from army positions overlooking the encampment, the troops who had been assigned to find the weapons fell back in disorder. Meanwhile, the Indians scrambled for safety in the tangled ravines surrounding the village as the rest of Forsyth's men joined the fray. Eighty-four Indian men and boys, forty-four women, and eighteen children were later found dead on the snow-covered battlefield. Fifty-one Indians were also wounded. The soldiers lost twenty-five killed and thirty-nine wounded.

News of the slaughter at Wounded Knee spread quickly, upwards of 4,000 Indians now having fled the reservation agencies. Furious over Forsyth's "incompetence" in having intermingled his troops amongst the Indians, Miles still preferred the combination of an overwhelming military presence and patient diplomacy to pitched battle. Although several skirmishes did occur over the coming weeks, the tactic worked. The Indians gradually returned to their reservations, and another slaughter was avoided.

As calm returned to the region, Miles organized a formal investigation of Forsyth. "I have no hesitation in saying," he thundered, "that I would not jeopardize the lives of officers and men in the hands of such an officer." Wounded Knee, he alleged, had been little more than a massacre. Despite the general's attempts to stack the military court with his allies, its report spared Forsyth any official sanctions. Rebuffed by Secretary of War Redfield Proctor and commanding general John Schofield, both of whom were eager to put the entire affair behind them, Miles had to satisfy himself with a series of letters and reports to officials in Washington and another *North American Review* essay. His complaints, however, again went unheeded. "I do not endorse the criticism made by General Miles upon the management of these Indians by the officials of the Department of the Interior," wrote Secretary Proctor.

In November 1894, General Howard's retirement allowed Miles to take over the Department of the East. Thrilled with the chance to relocate to New York, he and Mary reveled in the public acclaim wrought by Miles's western successes. He also found time to complete his first autobiography, *Personal Recollections and Observations of General Nelson A. Miles, Embracing a Brief View of the Civil War; or, From New England to the Golden Gate, and the Story of His Indian Campaigns, with Comments on the Exploration, Development and Progress of Our Great Western Empire.* Blending personal reminiscences and extracts from official reports with ruminations on anthropology, ethnology, history, and travel, the book also featured fifteen Frederic Remington illustrations. Hoping to cash in on the public's fascination with things western, *Personal Recollections* emphasized Miles's western exploits and ignored his association with Reconstruction or the imprisonment of Jefferson Davis. Indians "stood ... in the position of unruly children to indulgent parents for whom they have very little respect, at times wrongly indulged and again unmercifully punished," wrote Miles, whose views seemed a manifestation of the racist thought of the era. The Pacific Northwest possessed "natural resources capable of producing all that is required by mankind." Not to be left out, the Southwest "has been noted ever since civilized man has been there for its active, enterprising spirit." Similarly, new migrants to the northern plains "will also develop in the near future a strong, hardy, heroic race." To its author's great disappointment, however, the weighty tome failed to generate much interest.

On October 2, 1895, commanding general John Schofield turned sixty-four, the mandatory army retirement age. As the senior major general, Nelson Miles acceded to the command, which brought him to Washington.

Western affairs remained of much interest to the nation's highest-ranking army officer, who continued to lobby for increased military control over Indian affairs. Recent discoveries of gold along the Yukon River meant great riches, concluded Miles, but also the potential for warfare with the region's Native peoples. "Such has been the history of nearly all the tribes in other Territories," he warned. At his behest, army explorers traversed Alaska's far northern reaches in 1898 and again in 1899, and the War Department created a separate military Department of Alaska the following year.

Miles made relatively few changes to the army. As had his predecessors, he pressed unsuccessfully for a larger army and tried to sponsor minor structural reforms. Always fascinated by technology, he recommended that an entire regiment be equipped with bicycles and motorized wagons. Of course, a few "slight changes" in his uniform were also needed. The *Army and Navy Register* captured the full glory of the Milesian finery:

> General Miles ... added gold embroidery to the sleeves
> and collar of the full-dress coat. The design is a delicate
> tracery of oak leaves in gold. The familiar epaulets have
> been abandoned in favor of the flat Russian shoulder knot,
> without fringe, bearing the coat of arms of the United
> States and the two starts indicative of the rank of major
> general. To this is added a belt of Russian leather piped
> with gold bullion and embroidered in oak leaves to match
> the design on the collar and cuffs of the coat. The new fea-
> tures of the uniform are completed by a sash of alternate
> strips of yellow and gold, which extends from the right
> shoulder to the left side.

In 1897, the commanding general embarked upon a long European junket. Another book, *Military Europe: A Narrative of Personal Observation and Personal Experience*, followed his return from abroad, as did an essay, "The Political Situation in Europe and the East," published in the *Forum* magazine. Still, Henry Allen, a former Miles aide–turned–military attaché to Germany, noticed that his old boss seemed to have learned little over the years. "I am always astonished at the lack of knowledge of Genl. M[iles]," wrote Allen on August 10, 1897. "He reads a minimum and his opinions are not at all well founded, although he has a natural intelligence of a high order. This absence of general knowledge, his great vanity, and the unfortunate selection of an aide [Marion P. Maus] are sufficient to cause friction wherever he goes."

The outbreak of the Spanish-American War exposed Miles's weaknesses. Shocked by the War Department's outmoded bureaucracy and disappointed that Miles seemed more concerned with defending the continental United States than with organizing offensive operations, President William McKinley turned elsewhere for military advice. "God willing ... we shall end the war before the General would have us begin operations," thundered McKinley in response to a particularly frustrating memorandum from Miles. First summoning the retired Schofield back to Washington as a personal military advisor, the president eventually came to rely on Adj. Gen. Henry Corbin. Miles, quipped one Washington observer, was "accused of being strongest on millinery." "When in doubt," she continued, "Miles has his photograph taken."

A series of public relations disasters accompanied the army's efforts to mobilize for an assault on Spanish held Cuba, but William Shafter's expeditionary force finally splashed ashore on June 22, 1898. Following sharp fighting at San Juan Hill and El Caney and the destruction of Spain's Atlantic fleet at Santiago, the Spanish surrendered Cuba the next month. Miles then moved against Puerto Rico; in a lightning campaign, he occupied most of the island against ineffectual Spanish opposition. In the resulting Treaty of Paris, Spain gave Cuba its independence and ceded Puerto Rico, Guam, and the Philippines to the United States in exchange for $20 million.

The occupation of Puerto Rico went well, but it came too late to salvage Miles's reputation among administration officials. His propensity to air his grievances before the press and subsequent claims that the War Department had supplied the army with "embalmed beef" reaffirmed the president's distaste for Miles. McKinley's selection of Elihu Root to replace the ineffectual Russell Alger as secretary of war further marginalized Miles's position. Root soon tired of the general's delays, complaints, and impolitic public pronouncements. He could not check Miles's promotion to lieutenant general in 1900, but determined to bring about significant reforms to his department and the army.

Theodore Roosevelt's accession to the White House following McKinley's assassination compounded Miles's problems. The new president had once admired Miles, but the general's public questioning of Roosevelt's involvement in the famous charge up San Juan Hill had permanently soured their relationship. "What a scoundrelly hypocrite the man is!" thundered Roosevelt. Over the commanding general's strong objections, the president supported the Root reforms, which called for the abolition of the position of commanding general in favor of a general staff. The general's final public relations stunt while still on active duty—a ninety-mile horseback ride from

Fort Sill to Fort Reno in nine hours and ten minutes—recalled his past western glories, but failed to turn the tide. In August 1903, upon reaching the mandatory retirement age of sixty-four, Miles was officially retired with little public fanfare. As Root had insisted, the post of commanding general disappeared as well.

Still in vigorous health and wealthy from his investments in western land, minerals, and timber, Miles remained in the public eye. Daughter Cecilia married a former aide, Capt. Samuel Reber, and Sherman followed his father and became a professional soldier. Slowed only momentarily by Mary's death in 1904, the senior Miles unsuccessfully floated his name for that year's Democratic presidential nomination, traveled widely, and in 1911 published a second set of memoirs, *Serving the Republic: Memoirs of the Civil and Military Life of Nelson A. Miles, Lieutenant-General, United States Army*. During World War I, he advised Congress not to adopt conscription, instead advocating investments in "the new American engines of war": submarines and airplanes. In 1917, at the age of seventy-eight, Miles proposed that he be given command of an American expeditionary force to save Russia from the Bolsheviks.

Western affairs remained of great interest. As author Forrestine Hooker proclaimed, "Miles will never die. The West is his monument!" He surrounded himself with a colorful array of western paraphernalia and mementos and in 1909 floated the idea of building a giant statue of an Indian at the mouth of the Hudson River. Four years later, his old friend Buffalo Bill Cody enlisted him as historical advisor for a new moving picture project about the American West. The cantankerous old general proved to be a meticulous stickler for detail and an enormous headache for the overworked Cody. Because events at Wounded Knee had occurred in the winter, for example, he argued that filming must be done then as well. The few hundred soldiers loaned by the army as extras, insisted Miles, must be filmed repeatedly in order to replicate the thousands of soldiers involved in the campaign. To Cody's relief, Miles eventually demanded that his name be removed from the project. Although the film was completed, it never received much public attention.

Miles remained a showman to the end. On May 15, 1925, he escorted a friend and several of his grandchildren to a Washington performance of the Barnum and Bailey Circus. "You know I never miss the circus," he explained in a special meeting with the show's owner, John Ringling. "I have been coming for years." Miles and his party made their way to their third-row seats, then rose as the band struck up the "Star Spangled Banner." When the music stopped and he began settling back into his seat, a heart

Among Miles's many western friends was William F. ("Buffalo Bill") Cody. Here Cody (far left) joins a clean-shaven Miles near Pine Ridge, South Dakota, just after the Wounded Knee campaign. (Courtesy of the U.S. National Archives, public domain)

attack killed him instantly. An elaborate funeral ceremony and burial in the imposing family mausoleum he had built at Arlington National Cemetery seemed a fitting end to a life of eighty-six years.

Nelson A. Miles had played a major role in the non-Indian development of the American West. Troops under his command had been instrumental in breaking the military power of tribes of the southern and northern plains, as well as in securing the surrenders of Chief Joseph and Geronimo. For better or worse, forcing the tribes onto reservations had opened up huge expanses of land to prospective settlers, and the army's expanded presence had been a lucrative boon to frontier economics. Further, Miles had been a tireless and vocal advocate of things western, a boosterism that seemed well in line with contemporary American business culture.

Militarily, his successes had extended over three decades against a variety of foes. A natural tactician who easily adapted his methods to fit the terrain and the circumstance, Miles, driven by his craving for recognition, pushed himself and those around him hard. The personal leadership that had served him so well during the Civil War seemed even more suited for the smaller engagements in the West, where his coolness under fire was visible to all. Too, he recognized the value of good reconnaissance and thus took pains to cultivate strong ties with Native auxiliaries and civilian frontiersmen alike. This "perfect spy system," as he once described it, enabled him to act aggressively, without taking undue risks.

Nelson A. Miles, the last commanding general of the United States Army, in full military regalia. (Courtesy of the Arizona Historical Society, Tucson, #1156)

There were, of course, unattractive sides to Miles's personality. His views of Indians seem cruelly paternalistic, and his overweening ambition—anyone who had the audacity to write two autobiographies and an account of his experiences in Europe had an extraordinarily high opinion of his own importance—alienated virtually everyone around him. Critics might also point out that his promotion activities seemed a rather calculated ploy by one so open about his desire to translate his western ties into personal advancement. Such flaws were hardly unique to Miles however; indeed, his willingness to exploit the opportunities found in the West seemed part and parcel of the nineteenth-century American dream.

Sources and Further Reading

CHAPTER 1: LAKOTA CHIEF RED CLOUD

The primary and secondary sources for Red Cloud's life are more abundant and varied than those for most Native American leaders during the nineteenth century. In a culture and time when most historical evidence is in the form of oral testimony rather than written documentation, these printed sources are a real boon. Red Cloud's prominence, of course, accounts for much of this availability. He was a key figure in Lakota history, from his bold defiance at the first Fort Laramie gathering in 1866 to his disappointing effort to avoid bloodshed during the Ghost Dance crisis of 1890.

Red Cloud unwittingly made a major contribution to his own historical legacy when he responded to questions from his old friend, French Canadian trader Sam Deon, at the Pine Ridge post office in 1893. The interaction between these two companions, which lasted six months, had been arranged by the Pine Ridge postmaster, Samuel W. Allen, who envisioned as his own project a groundbreaking biography using these interviews. Allen's literary efforts eventually aided Addison E. Sheldon, former superintendent of the State Historical Society of Nebraska in Lincoln, who incorporated Allen's account, originally written in the third rather than first person, into a 135-page manuscript titled "Red Cloud, Chief of the Sioux." For decades this unpublished manuscript languished in the Lincoln archives, unacknowledged as Red Cloud's own story, even though one of Sheldon's research assistants, the famous writer Mari Sandoz, who typed the manuscript for Sheldon in 1932, referred to it in a 1962 letter as the "Red Cloud Autobiography." The manuscript was finally authenticated as Red Cloud's autobiography by R. Eli Paul, the society's former senior research historian in Lincoln, in "Recovering Red Cloud's Autobiography: The Odyssey of a Chief's Personal Narrative," *Montana: The Magazine of Western History* 44

(Summer 1994): 2–17. The autobiography, which covers Red Cloud's early life, was edited and published by Paul in a volume titled *Autobiography of Red Cloud: War Leader of the Oglalas* (Helena: Montana Historical Society Press, 1997). Robert W. Larson used much of Red Cloud's autobiographical information in his recent biography, *Red Cloud: Warrior-Statesman of the Lakota Sioux* (Norman: University of Oklahoma Press, 1997).

The best primary source for Red Cloud's years after 1864, also found in the Nebraska archives, is the collection of eighty-nine interviews conducted by Judge Eli S. Ricker during the first decade of the twentieth century. These include the testimony of Lakota and white participants, such as American Horse, George Little Wound, Clarence Three-Stars, William Garnett, and Dr. James R. Walker. There are also pertinent primary materials at the South Dakota State Historical Society in Pierre, such as the papers of Dr. Vincent T. McGillycuddy, Doane Robinson, Charles P. Jordan, and John R. Brennan, not to mention Red Cloud's own estate papers.

Because of Red Cloud's frequent interaction with government and army personnel, relevant congressional documents and annual government reports are also worth careful examination. Especially valuable for Red Cloud's well-publicized feud with Agent J. J. Saville is the *Report of the Special Commissioner Appointed to Investigate the Affairs of the Red Cloud Indian Agency, July, 1875* (Washington, D.C.: Government Printing Office, 1875). Useful newspaper sources include the *New York Times* and the *New York Herald*, particularly good for their coverage of Red Cloud's 1870 visit to Washington and New York City, and western news journals, such as the *Omaha Weekly Herald*.

Secondary sources are reasonably plentiful and varied. The most influential pioneering work on Red Cloud is George E. Hyde's *Red Cloud's Folk: A History of the Oglala Sioux Indians* (Norman: University of Oklahoma Press, 1937). More thorough and better documented is James C. Olson's *Red Cloud and the Sioux Problem* (Lincoln: University of Nebraska Press, 1965), which focuses on the Oglala chief's many dealings with the federal government. Richard White provides a good study of the early history of Red Cloud's people in "The Winning of the West: The Expansion of the Western Sioux in the Eighteenth and Nineteenth Century," *Journal of American History* 65 (September 1978): 314–43. Excellent for the reservation years of the Lakota Sioux is Robert M. Utley's *The Last Days of the Sioux Nation* (New Haven: Yale University Press, 1963). Raymond J. DeMaille, who has published numerous studies on the Sioux religion, offers excellent insights into the divisive Ghost Dance in "The Lakota Ghost Dance: An Ethnohistorical Account," *Pacific Historical Review* 51 (November 1982):

385–406. Studies on the political and social culture of the Lakota Sioux include Royal B. Hassrick, *The Sioux: Life and Culture of a Warrior Society* (Norman: University of Oklahoma Press, 1964), and Catherine Price, *The Oglala People, 1841–1879: A Political History* (Lincoln: University of Nebraska Press, 1996). Works by such scholars as Father Francis Paul Prucha and William D. Hagan are helpful in understanding the Plains Indian culture during the last decades of the nineteenth century.

Secondary accounts on the military aspects of Red Cloud's life and times include Grace Raymond Hebard and E. A. Brininstool, *The Bozeman Trail* (Cleveland: Arthur H. Clark Co., 1922), Frances C. Carrington, *Army Life on the Plains* (Philadelphia: J. B. Lippincott Co., 1910), and Jerry Keenan, *The Wagon Box Fight,* 2nd ed. (Sheridan: Fort Phil Kearny/Bozeman Trail Association, 1990), which focus on his leadership during the famous war that bears his name.

For information relevant to the continual conflict that followed Red Cloud's acceptance of the Treaty of Fort Laramie, including the Great Sioux War of 1876–1877, such works should be consulted as John S. Gray, *Centennial Campaign: The Sioux War of 1876* (Ft. Collins, Colo.: Old Army Press, 1976); Paul T. Hedren, *Fort Laramie in 1876: Chronicle of a Frontier Post at War* (Lincoln: University of Nebraska Press, 1988); Stephen E. Ambrose, *Crazy Horse and Custer: The Parallel Lives of Two American Warriors* (Garden City, N.Y.: Doubleday and Co., 1975); Paul Andrew Hutton, *Phil Sheridan and His Army* (Lincoln: University of Nebraska Press, 1985); Robert Wooster, *Nelson Miles and the Twilight of the Frontier Army* (Lincoln: University of Nebraska Press, 1993); Jerome A. Green, ed., *Lakota and Cheyenne: Indian Views of the Great Sioux War, 1876–1877* (Norman: University of Oklahoma Press, 1994); and Gregory F. Michno, *Lakota Noon: The Indian Narrative of Custer's Defeat* (Missoula, Mont.: Mountain Press Publishing Company, 1997).

CHAPTER 2: APACHE CHIEF VICTORIO

For anyone interested in Victorio and Lozen, there are two must-reads, both of which try to partially remedy the greatest lack in Apache historiography—that of Apache accounts. Eve Ball's *In the Days of Victorio: Recollections of a Warm Springs Apache* (Tucson: University of Arizona Press, 1970) presents the recollections and opinions of James Kaywaykla, the four-year-old Mimbreño present at Tres Castillo in 1880. Although professional historians have mercilessly pointed out the flaws in Ball's techniques, this oral history is useful and, perhaps most importantly, preserves Apache memories of a major event in their history. Also useful is Eve Ball, with Nora Henn and Lynda A. Sánchez, *Indeh: An Apache Odyssey* (Norman: University of Oklahoma Press, 1980), a collection of more Apache recollections, but they are mostly post-Victorio. The second important book is Sherry Robinson, *Apache Voices: Their Stories of Survival as Told to Eve Ball* (Albuquerque: University of New Mexico Press, 2000), containing what the researcher and freelance writer found in Eve Ball's unpublished papers, housed at the Brigham Young University's Harold B. Lee Library in Provo, Utah.

For military history, the grand scope of the Mimbres Apaches' campaigns is covered in great detail in Dan L. Thrapp, *Victorio and the Mimbres Apaches* (Norman: University of Oklahoma Press, 1974), whereas Joseph A. Stout Jr., *Apache Lightning: The Last Great Battles of the Ojo Calientes* (New York: Oxford University Press, 1974), concentrates on the campaigns of 1879–1880. Donald E. Worcester, *The Apaches: Eagles of the Southwest* (Norman: University of Oklahoma Press, 1979), is especially good on Apache-Spanish contact and Victorio. Although these authors used—mostly by necessity—largely Anglo records such as military reports and memoirs of white military officers, they were among the earliest writers to show sympathy with, and understanding of, Apache perspectives. More recently, Karl W. Laumbach, *Hembrillo: An Apache Battlefield of the Victorio War* (Las Cruces, N.Mex.: Human Systems Research, 2000), reconstructs—almost minute by minute—the Battle of Hembrillo Canyon through the use of archeological techniques, ranging from the interpretation of Indian petroglyphs to forensic analysis. Rich in photographs, graphs, and maps, Laumbach's report also attempts to understand Victorio's point of view.

Several overviews are also worth pursuing. Outstanding military histories regarding the U.S. Army are Robert M. Utley, *Frontiersmen in Blue: The United States Army and the Indian, 1848–1865* (1967; Lincoln: University of Nebraska Press, 1981), Robert Wooster, *The Military and United States Indian Policy, 1865–1903* (Lincoln: University of Nebraska Press, 1988), and *Nelson S. Miles and the Twilight of the Frontier Army* (1993; Lincoln: University of Nebraska Press, 1995). Equally fine surveys of Indians are Robert M. Utley and Wilcomb E. Washburn, *The American Heritage History of the Indian Wars* (New York: American Heritage Publishing, 1977), and Robert M. Utley, *The Indian Frontier of the American West, 1846–1890* (Albuquerque: University of New Mexico Press, 1984).

The complexities of the U.S.–Mexico boundary dispute are revealed in Clarence C. Clendenen, *Blood on the Border: The United States Army and the Mexican Irregulars* (New York: Macmillan, 1969); Bruce J. Dinges, "The

Victorio Campaign of 1880: Cooperation and Conflict on the United States–Mexico Border," *New Mexico Historical Review* 62 (January 1987): 81–91; William B. Griffen, *Utmost Good Faith: Patterns of Apache-Mexican Hostilities in Northern Chihuahua Border Warfare, 1821–1848* (Albuquerque: University of New Mexico Press, 1988); and, most recently, Shelley Bowen Hatfield, *Chasing Shadows: Apaches and Yaquis Along the United States-Mexico Border, 1876–1911* (Albuquerque: University of New Mexico Press, 1998). A specialist in the history of modern Mexico and the Southwest, Hatfield did extensive research in newspaper accounts, personal papers, and government documents in Mexico and in the southwestern United States.

The importance of the horse to Apache culture and warfare is pointed out in D. E. Worcester, "The Spread of Spanish Horses in the Southwest," *New Mexico Historical Review* 19 (July 1966): 225–32, and LaVerne Harrell Clark, *They Sang for Horses: The Impact of the Horse on Navajo and Apache Folklore* (Boulder: University Press of Colorado, 2001).

The roles of Apache women are discussed in Regina Flannery, "The Position of Woman Among the Mescalero Apache," *Primitive Man* 5 (April–July 1932): 26–32; Patricia Albers and Beatrice Medicine, eds., *The Hidden Half: Studies of Plains Indian Women* (Washington, D.C.: University Press of America, 1983); H. Henrietta Stockel, *Women of the Apache Nation: Voices of Truth* (Reno: University of Nevada Press, 1991); *Chiricahua Apache Women and Children: Safekeepers of the Heritage* (College Station: Texas A&M University Press, 2000); Ruth McDonald Boyer and Narcissus Duffy Gayton, *Apache Mothers and Daughters* (Norman: University of Oklahoma Press, 1992); and Virginia Bergman Peters, *Women of the Earth Lodges: Tribal Life on the Plains* (Norman: University of Oklahoma Press, 1995). Insights into the recording of Indian women's history are found in Gretchen M. Bataille and Kathleen Mullen Sands, *American Indian Women: Telling Their Lives* (Lincoln: University of Nebraska Press, 1984).

For Lozen, see Eve Ball's and Sherry Robinson's books cited above, and Eve Ball and Lynda Sánchez, "Legendary Apache Women," *Frontier Times* (October–November 1980): 8–12. Although Kimberly Moore Buchanan, *Apache Women Warriors* (El Paso: University of Texas, Southwestern Studies Series No. 79, 1986), establishes women as fighters, the study is marred by significant factual errors. A recent entry is writer Peter Aleshire's *Warrior Woman: The Story of Lozen, Apache Warrior and Shaman* (New York: St. Martin's, 2001), which uses anthropological studies, Eve Ball's writings, and military records to create Lozen's life as it may have been. Inexplicably, Aleshire largely ignores scholarship regarding Apache women.

The contributions of African American buffalo soldiers are recounted in William H. Leckie, *The Buffalo Soldiers: A Narrative of the Negro Cavalry in the West* (Norman: University of Oklahoma Press, 1967); Charles L. Kenner, *Buffalo Soldiers and Officers of the Ninth Cavalry, 1867–1898* (Norman: University of Oklahoma Press, 1969); Arlen L. Fowler, *The Black Infantry in the West, 1869–1891* (1971; Norman: University of Oklahoma Press, 1996); Major E. L. N. Glass, comp. and ed., *The History of the Tenth Cavalry, 1866–1921* (Ft. Collins, Colo.: Old Army Press, 1972); Col. C. M. Hurtt, "The Role of Black Infantry in the Expansion of the West," *West Virginia History* 40 (1979): 123–57; and Monroe Lee Billington, *New Mexico's Buffalo Soldiers, 1866–1900* (Boulder: University Press of Colorado, 1996).

The anthropological literature about Apaches is vast and valuable. Two classic works are Morris Edward Opler, *An Apache Life-Way: The Economic, Social, and Religious Institutions of the Chiricahua Indians* (Chicago: University of Chicago Press, 1941), and Grenville Goodwin, *The Social Organization of the Western Apache* (Chicago: University of Chicago Press, 1942). See also Keith H. Basso and Morris E. Opler, eds., *Apachean Culture, History, and Ethnology* (Tucson: University of Arizona Press, 1971).

In addition, studies of other Apache leaders with close ties to Victorio are helpful: Dan L. Thrapp, *Juh: An Incredible Indian* (El Paso: University of Texas, Southwestern Studies No. 39, 1973); Angie Debo, *Geronimo: The Man, His Time, His Place* (Norman: University of Oklahoma Press, 1976); Stephen H. Lekson, *Nana's Raid: Apache Warfare in Southern New Mexico, 1881* (El Paso: University of Texas, Southwestern Studies Series No. 81, 1987); Edwin R. Sweeney, *Cochise: Chiricahua Apache Chief* (Norman: University of Oklahoma Press, 1991); Edwin R. Sweeney, *Mangas Coloradas: Chief of the Chiricahua Apaches* (Norman: University of Oklahoma Press, 1998); and Almer N. Blazer, edited by A. R. Pruit, *Santana: War Chief of the Mescalero Apache* (Taos, N.Mex.: Dog Soldier Press, 1999).

Finally, two works of creative nonfiction examine Apache culture and attitudes. They are Keith H. Basso, *Wisdom Sits in Places: Landscape and Language Among the Western Apache* (Albuquerque: University of New Mexico Press, 1996), and Grenville Goodwin and Neil Goodwin, *The Apache Diaries: A Father-Son Journey* (Lincoln: University of Nebraska Press, 2000).

CHAPTER 3: CHIEF JOSEPH OF THE NEZ PERCE

Writers of the late nineteenth and early twentieth centuries paid much less attention to Chief Joseph and the Nez Perce than to other Indian leaders such as Sitting Bull, Crazy Horse, and Geronimo and the Sioux and Apache tribes. Perhaps Joseph seemed less heroic and valiant than the other Native

American leaders. Since the 1950s, however, historians have devoted many essays and several books to the Nez Perce chief and his people.

Not surprisingly, the earliest accounts are from participant observers in the war of 1877. Less than two years after the conflict at Bear's Paw, Chief Joseph published a widely cited essay, "An Indian's Views of Indian Affairs," *North American Review* 128 (April 1879): 412–33. The article explained and defended his tenacious attachment to the Wallowa country and pinpointed the failures of American military and political leaders to fulfill their promises to the Nez Perce. Important as the essay is for understanding Joseph's position, it must be used with caution. The Nez Perce leader neither read nor wrote English, so his piece passed through an interpreter and probably the hands of at least one editor before it was published. Before the turn of the century, General Howard (*Nez Perce Joseph* [Boston: Lee and Shepard, 1881]), Colonel Miles (*Personal Recollections and Observations of General Nelson A. Miles* [Chicago: Werner, 1896]), and Lieutenant Wood ("Chief Joseph, the Nez Perce," *Century Magazine* [May 1884]) presented their perspectives on the chief and the war, with Howard especially disagreeing with Joseph's viewpoint. Two journalists, Duncan MacDonald, in *New Northwest* (Deer Lodge, Mont., April 26–December 20, 1878), and Thomas A. Sutherland, *Howard's Campaign Against the Nez Perce Indians* (Portland, Ore.: A. G. Walling, 1878), also provided valuable first-hand accounts of the fight of 1877.

After the 1890s, there was a long hiatus in writings about Chief Joseph. More than three decades elapsed before the next noteworthy publications on the Native leader appeared. Not all these works were entirely satisfactory, however. For example, although Chester Anders Fee's biography, *Chief Joseph: The Biography of a Great Indian* (New York: Wilson-Erickson, 1936), contained new information, the author unfortunately chose to fictionalize some of his account. Two other authors, Helen Addison Howard (*War Chief Joseph* [Caldwell, Idaho: Caxton, 1941], written with Dan L. McGrath) and Francis D. Haines (*Red Eagles of the Northwest: The Story of Chief Joseph and His People* [Portland: Scholastic Press, 1939]), provided preliminary book-length accounts that they later revised to incorporate new information and interpretations. Haines's account, especially his revised work, *The Nez Perces: Tribesmen of the Columbia Plateau* (Norman: University of Oklahoma Press, 1955), was an early scholarly, pro-Indian account.

In the 1960s, three other important works appeared. Merrill D. Beal, drawing on his background as a park ranger and a scholar, furnished new information on Chief Joseph and the battle at Big Hole in his *"I Will Fight No More Forever": Chief Joseph and the Nez Perce War* (Seattle: University of

Washington Press, 1963). Four years later, Mark H. Brown, a military intelligence specialist and historian, produced a sturdy, thorough examination of military operations in his *Flight of the Nez Perce* (New York: G. P. Putnam's Sons, 1967). Brown's work, however, is limited in its contributions as the author concluded that "Indian accounts" of the Nez Perce conflict "merited very little trust" (p. 15). The third volume, Alvin M. Josephy Jr.'s *The Nez Perce Indians and the Opening of the Northwest* (New Haven: Yale University Press, 1965), remains the most extensive book on the subject. Invitingly written and thoroughly researched, this 700-page volume is particularly complete on the pre-1877 period of Nez Perce history.

A new round of books in the 1990s added much to the story. David Lavender's prize-winning *Let Me Be Free: The Nez Perce Tragedy* (New York: HarperCollins, 1992) and Bruce Hampton's *Children of Grace: The Nez Perce War of 1877* (New York: Henry Holt, 1994) are well-told stories based on strong research. The most recent book on the war, Jerome A. Greene's *Nez Perce Summer, 1877: The U.S. Army and the Nee-Me-Poo Crisis* (Missoula: Montana Historical Society Press, 2000), is also the most thorough military history of the conflict. No one has dug more deeply or widely into the military sources than Greene. For a list of important sources on General Howard, Colonel Miles, and other military figures, see the bibliographies on Howard and Miles in this section.

Several other volumes are useful sources for those wishing to see the Indian side of the Chief Joseph and Nez Perce story. Besides the previously mentioned essay by Joseph and the revised book by Francis Haines, one should consult the valuable works of Lucullus V. McWhorter, a lay anthropologist who gathered oral histories and other materials from several participants in the events of 1877. The revealing memories of one Nez Perce warrior are published in McWhorter, *Yellow Wolf: His Own Story* (Caldwell, Idaho: Caxton Printers, 1940), and reminiscences of other Native participants appear in his *Hear Me, My Chiefs! Nez Perce History and Legend*, ed. Ruth Bordin (Caldwell, Idaho: Caxton Printers, 1952). A later history of the Nez Perce, written by a tribal historian, is Allen P. Slickpoo (with Deward E. Walker Jr.), *Noon Nee-Me-Po (We, the Nez Perces): Culture and History of the Nez Perces* (N.p.: Nez Perce Tribe of Idaho, 1973).

Cultural anthropologists and ethnologists have also added valuable insights in several of their works. A pioneering study is Herbert J. Spinden, *The Nez Perce Indians (Memoirs of the American Anthropological Association)* (Lancaster, Pa.: New Era Print Company, 1908). More recently, anthropologist Deward E. Walker Jr. has published a clutch of essays and books about the Nez Perce and other Indian tribes of Idaho and the Pacific Northwest.

His *Conflict and Schism in Nez Perce Acculturation: A Study of Religion and Politics* (1968; Moscow: University of Idaho Press, 1985) is a particularly good source on recent Nez Perce history.

Finally, if scholars and general readers wish to move beyond these published books, they should consult several important collections of manuscript sources. The L. V. McWhorter Papers at the Washington State University Library in Pullman and holdings at the Idaho State Historical Society in Boise contain much valuable information. The bibliographies in the volumes by Josephy, Hampton, and Greene mentioned above also include extensive listings of other archival materials. Diligent researchers will also want to consult the valuable information on file at the Nez Perce Reservation in Idaho and the Colville Indian Reservation at Nespelem, Washington.

CHAPTER 4: O. O. HOWARD

Any analysis of Gen. O. O. Howard's relations with the Nez Perce should begin with the official records of the War Department and the Bureau of Indian Affairs in the National Archives in Washington, D.C. These records are readily available in National Archives microfilm publications as Letters Received by the Office of Indian Affairs and Records of the Adjutant General. The latter material is organized into consolidated files whereby the available correspondence on specific subjects, such as relations with the Nez Perce, is collected together in one file. The microfilm publications are available for loan from the regional branches of the National Archives. Other official sources are the published annual reports of the Secretary of War and of the Commissioner of Indian Affairs, which include annual reports by departmental commanders such as General Howard and Indian agents such as Montieth. Maj. H. Clay Wood's study of the status of Joseph's band, which was prepared as part of his official duties and which is an essential document, was published by the Department of the Columbia as *The Status of Young Joseph and His Band of Nez-Perce Indians Under the Treaties Between the United States and the Nez-Perce Tribe of Indians, and the Indian Title to Land.* It is interesting to note that Howard's various publications made no reference to this important study.

General Howard often made reference to his official records as he wrote the several publications that touched on his involvement with the Nez Perce. He wrote a lot, much more than his generation of Civil War officers and more than his contemporaries who served in the West. The focus of his publications was his career in the Indian fighting army and particularly his relations with the Nez Perce. They are important as an account by a leading participant and also as a record of the general's increasingly defensive posture.

Howard wrote "The True Story of the Wallowa Campaign," *North American Review* 128 (July 1879), to correct what he perceived as inaccuracies in "An Indian's View of Indian Affairs" by Chief Joseph, *North American Review* 128 (April 1879). Both articles were reprinted in *Northwestern Fights and Fighters* by Cyrus T. Brady (Garden City, N.Y.: Doubleday, Page and Company, 1907), along with essays by other military personnel. Undoubtedly influenced by continued favorable attentions for the Nez Perce, Howard published *Nez Perce Joseph: An Account of His Ancestors, His Lands, His Confederates, His Enemies, His Murders, His War, His Pursuit and Capture* two years later (1881; New York: Da Capo Press, 1972). Howard accused the Nez Perce of treachery and of planning war, and here he introduced the ridiculous claim that Joseph and Ollokot inherited evil traits from their mother. Here and in later publications he also credited Joseph with great military skills, contributing in a major way to the image of the chief as the "Red Napoleon." See *My Life and Experiences Among Our Hostile Indians* (1907; New York: Da Capo Press, 1972) and *Famous Indian Chiefs I Have Known* (1908; Lincoln: University of Nebraska Press, 1989). Howard's papers are at Bowdoin College.

The valuable observations of Emily FitzGerald are available in *An Army Doctor's Wife on the Frontier: Letters from Alaska and the Far West,* 1874–1878, edited by Abe Laufe (Pittsburgh: University of Pittsburgh Press, 1962).

Published Nez Perce accounts are available from a number of sources. Most important is the work of Lucullus V. McWhorter, who collected numerous accounts from the Nez Perce and published two essential books, *Hear Me, My Chiefs! Nez Perce History and Legend* (Caldwell, Idaho: Caxton Printers, 1952) and *Yellow Wolf: His Own Story* (Caldwell, Idaho: Caxton Printers, 1940). Duncan MacDonald, who was part Nez Perce, collected Indian testimony soon after the surrender and published a series of articles in a Deer Lodge, Montana, newspaper, *The New North-West.* That material was made more readily available when it was included in *In Pursuit of the Nez Perces,* compiled by Linwood Laughy (Wrangell, Alaska: Mountain Meadow Press, 1993).

The story of Joseph and the Nez Perce has attracted scholars and resulted in a rather voluminous body of literature, partly because of the color and drama of the events, partly because of the dignity and honor of Joseph, and partly because of the feeling by many that the conflict should have been avoided. It is a sad commentary on American attitudes, government policy, and the workings of the nineteenth-century bureaucracy. Today our government would seek out the individuals who committed violent acts, but in the nineteenth century, at least when it came to Native Americans, the group was held accountable for the acts of its individual members, although similar standards were not applied to crimes by whites against Indians. Indeed, in most cases even the individual perpetrator avoided punishment.

A limited list of the most significant scholarly accounts includes tribal histories by Francis Haines, *The Nez Perces: Tribesmen of the Columbia Plateau* (Norman: University of Oklahoma Press, 1955), and Alvin M. Josephy Jr., *The Nez Perce Indians and the Opening of the Northwest* (New Haven: Yale University Press, 1965). The latter is a masterful study that is critical of General Howard.

A number of books focus on the military campaign. Among the most useful are Merrill D. Beal, *"I Will Fight No More Forever": Chief Joseph and the Nez Perce War* (Seattle: University of Washington Press, 1963); Mark H. Brown, *The Flight of the Nez Perce* (New York: G. P. Putnam's Sons, 1967); and Jerome A. Greene, *Nez Perce Summer, 1877: The U.S. Army and the Nee-Me-Poo Crisis* (Helena: Montana Historical Society Press, 2000). Beal noted that Joseph was less a military leader than previously thought, which Josephy develops more fully. Brown's experience as a military officer contributed to the value of this work. However, the recent book by Greene, a National Park Service historian, is without question the essential study of the campaign. *War Chief Joseph* by Helen Addison Howard and Dan L. McGrath (Caldwell, Idaho: Caxton Printers, 1941) is a biography of Joseph with an emphasis on the military campaign.

John A. Carpenter, Howard's biographer, presents a positive portrayal of the general in *Sword and Olive Branch: Oliver Otis Howard* (Pittsburgh: University of Pittsburgh Press, 1964) and "General Howard and the Nez Perce War of 1877," *Pacific Northwest Quarterly* 49 (October 1958). A short but insightful look at Howard's western career was published in *New Mexico Historical Review* 62 (January 1987) by Robert M. Utley, the most distinguished scholar of the frontier army.

William S. McFeely, in *Yankee Stepfather: General O. O. Howard and the Freedmen* (New Haven: Yale University Press, 1968), is a critic of Howard's administration of the Freedmen's Bureau. Edwin R. Sweeney offers insightful comments on Howard in *Making Peace with Cochise: The 1872 Journal of Joseph Alton Sladen* (Norman: University of Oklahoma Press, 1997). Those interested in the controversy between Howard and General Miles after the surrender should refer to the excellent study of Miles's career in the West by Robert Wooster, *Nelson Miles and the Twilight of the Frontier Army* (Lincoln: University of Nebraska Press, 1995).

CHAPTER 5: GERONIMO

Older biographies that remain credible places to begin an investigation of Geronimo's life are Samuel M. Barrett, ed., *Geronimo's Story of His Life* (New York: Duffield, 1906), and Angie Debo, *Geronimo: The Man, His Time, His Place* (Norman: University of Oklahoma Press, 1976). Far more valuable are her papers in special collections at the Oklahoma State University Library. One may yet garner insights from her research notes.

John Anthony Turcheneske Jr.'s *The Chiricahua Apache Prisoners of War: Fort Sill, 1894–1914* (Niwot: University Press of Colorado, 1997), passionately written and occasionally fiercely partisan, is a remarkable history of a people's tragic removal from Arizona. James L. Haley, *Apaches: A History and Culture Portrait* (Norman: University of Oklahoma Press, 1981), is richly informed, even discounting his political asides about academic "revisionists." Likewise, Donald E. Worcester, *The Apaches: Eagles of the Southwest* (Norman: University of Oklahoma Press, 1979), is a splendid introduction to Apache cultural history. Still useful, and animated by lively prose, are Odie B. Faulk, *Crimson Desert: Indian Wars of the American Southwest* (New York: Oxford University Press, 1974), and the older *The Geronimo Campaign* (New York: Oxford University Press, 1969).

Other more specialized Apache cultural studies—but ones that specifically enrich any understanding of Geronimo's life—are the indispensable works by Edwin R. Sweeney, *Cochise: Chiricahua Apache Chief* (Norman: University of Oklahoma Press, 1991), and *Mangas Coloradas: Chief of the Chiricahua Apaches* (Norman: University of Oklahoma Press, 1998); and the truly ethnohistorical works by H. Henrietta Stockel, *Chiricahua Apache Women and Children: Safekeepers of the Heritage* (College Station: Texas A&M University Press, 2000), and *Survival of the Spirit: Chiricahua Apaches in Captivity* (Reno: University of Nevada Press, 1993). The latter work especially complements Turcheneske's. Eve Ball's oral history collecting among the Chiricahuas and other bands is reproduced in *Indeh: An Apache Odyssey*, with Nora Henn and Lynda Sánchez (Provo, Utah: Brigham Young University Press, 1980), and *Apache Voices: Their Stories of Survival as Told to Eve Ball* (Albuquerque: University of New Mexico Press, 2000). Ball's *In the Days of Victorio: Recollections of a Warm Springs Apache* (Tucson: University of Arizona Press, 1970) is also quite useful in understanding late nineteenth-century U.S.-Apache relations. Finally, there is no better place to begin one's immersion in the ethnohistory of Apacheria than Volumes 9 (1979) and 10 (1983) of the Smithsonian Institution's *Handbook of North American Indians*, both edited by Alfonso Ortíz. The works of such outstanding scholars as Keith H. Basso, James H. Gunnerson, Morris E. Opler, Robert W. Young, William B. Griffen, and Veronica E. Tiller are admirably highlighted.

More specialized primary investigation should begin in the Indian Archives Division of the Oklahoma Historical Society, Oklahoma City. Significant federal records pertaining to the Indian people of Oklahoma were deposited from the National Archives system in the 1930s. The Fort Sill Museum also contains important materials pertaining to the Apache prisoners of war. From there one need only follow the paper trails that lead elsewhere to American Indian and western history collections.

CHAPTER 6: GEORGE CROOK

The standard work on George Crook is *General George Crook: His Autobiography*, edited and annotated by Martin F. Schmitt (1946; Norman: University of Oklahoma Press, 1960). With extensive research and writing, Schmitt turned this unfinished memoir into a well-rounded biography. The most recent study of Crook is Charles M. Robinson's *General Crook and the Western Frontier* (Norman: University of Oklahoma Press, 2001). The bulk of surviving Crook papers are deposited at the Military History Institute, Carlisle Barracks, Pennsylvania; the Rutherford B. Hayes Library, Freemont, Ohio; and the Knight Library, University of Oregon, Eugene. Other pertinent material is in the Arizona Historical Society Library, Tucson, and the Huntington Library, San Marino, California. Readers interested in official reports, published and unpublished, pertaining to Crook's military commands should check the bibliographies in the Schmitt and Robinson volumes.

The most important contemporary work on Crook is John G. Bourke's *On the Border with Crook* (1891; Lincoln: University of Nebraska Press, 1971). Azor H. Nickerson's unpublished essay, "Major General George Crook and the Indians," is found in the Walter S. Schuyler Papers at the Huntington Library. Other significant primary sources are John G. Bourke, *An Apache Campaign in the Sierra Madre* (1886; Lincoln: University of Nebraska Press, 1987); Britton Davis, *The Truth About Geronimo* (1929; Lincoln: University of Nebraska Press, 1976); John F. Finerty, *War-Path and Bivouac, or, The Conquest of the Sioux* (1955; Lincoln: University of Nebraska Press, 1966); Charles King, *Campaigning with Crook* (Norman: University of Oklahoma Press, 1964); and Dan L. Thrapp, ed., *Dateline Fort Bowie: Charles Fletcher Lummis Reports on an Apache War* (Norman: University of Oklahoma Press, 1979).

Indispensable to any study of the Indian-fighting army is Robert M. Utley's *Frontier Regulars: The United States Army and the Indian, 1866–1891* (1973; Lincoln: University of Nebraska Press, 1984). Three fine biographies of Crook's contemporaries also help to illuminate Crook affairs: Paul A. Hutton, *Phil Sheridan and His Army* (Lincoln: University of Nebraska Press, 1985); Joseph C. Porter, *Paper Medicine Man: John Gregory Bourke and His American West* (Norman: University of Oklahoma Press, 1986); and Robert Wooster, *Nelson A. Miles and the Twilight of the Frontier Army* (Lincoln: University of Nebraska Press, 1993). Specialized works on Indian-white battles abound, but see especially Dan L. Thrapp, *The Conquest of Apacheria* (Norman: University of Oklahoma Press, 1967); Thrapp, *General Crook and the Sierra Madre Adventure* (Norman: University of Oklahoma Press, 1972); and J. W. Vaughn, *With Crook at the Rosebud* (1956; Lincoln: University of Nebraska Press, 1988). For the importance of army wives to their husbands' careers, see Patricia Y. Stallard, *Glittering Misery: Dependents of the Indian Fighting Army* (1978; Norman: University of Oklahoma Press, 1992).

Several shorter works help to assess Crook's importance to western history, including Richard N. Ellis, "The Humanitarian Generals," *Western Historical Quarterly* 3 (April 1972): 169–78; Jerome A. Greene, "George Crook," in *Soldiers West, Biographies from the Military Frontier*, ed. Paul A. Hutton (Lincoln: University of Nebraska Press, 1987), 115–36; James T. King, "'A Better Way': General George Crook and the Ponca Indians," *Nebraska History* 50 (Fall 1969): 239–56; King, "George Crook: Indian Fighter and Humanitarian," *Arizona and the West* 9 (Winter 1967): 333–48; and King, "Needed: A Re-evaluation of General George Crook," *Nebraska History* 45 (September 1964): 223–35. For an intriguing account of the missing Crook papers, see George D. McGeary, "My Search for General George Crook: The Interrupted Autobiography and the Mystery of the Missing Papers," *Journal of Arizona History* 41 (Autumn 2000): 289–306.

CHAPTER 7: GENERAL GEORGE ARMSTRONG CUSTER

The primary sources for studying George Armstrong Custer are extensive, but some, unfortunately, remain in private rather than archival holdings. The main collections open to all are the Marguerite Merington Collection at the New York Public Library, the Elizabeth B. Custer Manuscript Collection and the George A. Custer Manuscript Collection in the Western Americana Collection at the Beinecke Rare Book and Manuscript Library at Yale University, and the Elizabeth B. Custer Collection in the Little Bighorn Battlefield National Monument in Crow Agency, Montana. The Monroe

County Historical Commission Archives in the Monroe County Historical Museum in Monroe, Michigan, holds the Custer Collection and the Lawrence A. Frost Collection of Custeriana. The Ellis Reference and Information Center of the Monroe County Library System also houses a separate George Armstrong Custer Collection.

Merington collected some of the Custer letters and published them in edited form in *The Custer Story: The Life and Intimate Letters of General Custer and His Wife Elizabeth* (New York: Devin-Adair, 1950). A close friend of Elizabeth Custer's, Merington in some instances expurgated unflattering material from the correspondence. As a loyal wife, Libbie Custer wrote three works that provide, in subtle fashion, her answers to almost all the controversies of her husband's career. She also included excerpts from his letters, which she edited to show him in the best possible light. See *"Boots and Saddles"; or, Life in Dakota with General Custer* (New York: Harper & Brothers, 1885); *Tenting on the Plains; or, General Custer in Kansas and Texas* (New York: Charles L. Webster, 1887); and *Following the Guidon* (New York: Harper & Brothers, 1887).

For readers unfamiliar with Custer's life and the significance of his career, the best biography and one that the present writer finds most persuasive and is deeply indebted to is Robert M. Utley, *Cavalier in Buckskin: George Armstrong Custer and the Western Military Frontier*, rev. ed. (Norman: University of Oklahoma Press, 2001). A biography that stresses Custer's Civil War career is Jeffrey D. Wert, *Custer: The Controversial Life of George Armstrong Custer* (New York: Simon & Schuster, 1996). Louise Barnett, *Touched by Fire: The Life, Death, and Mythic Afterlife of George Armstrong Custer* (New York: Henry Holt, 1996), places Custer in the wider social world of the frontier army and argues that the debate on the Battle of the Little Bighorn continues because racism prevents many Americans from accepting the idea that Indians could have won on their own a victory over the Seventh Cavalry. Finally, Shirley A. Leckie, *Elizabeth Bacon Custer and the Making of a Myth* (Norman: University of Oklahoma Press, 1993), explores the Custer marriage and Elizabeth's role in advancing his career as well as her exploitation of middle-class gender roles as a means of transforming him into a hero for boys and also justifying the war against American Indians.

A specific account that deals with periods of Custer's life and career is Charles B. Wallace, *Custer's Ohio Boyhood* (Cadiz, Ohio: Harrison County Historical Society, 1987). An important work on Custer's role in the Civil War is Gregory J. W. Urwin, *Custer Victorious: The Civil War Battles of General George Armstrong Custer* (East Brunswick, N.J.: Associated

University Presses, 1983). For this same period, but covering political rather than military questions, also see Shirley A. Leckie, "The Civil War Partnership of Elizabeth and George A. Custer," *Intimate Strategies of the Civil War: Military Commanders and Their Wives*, eds. Carol K. Bleser and Lesley J. Gordon (New York: Oxford University Press, 2001), 178–98. I am also indebted to Stephen Ambrose for his insights on Custer's willingness to take often staggering casualties. See "Custer's Civil War," *Timeline* 7 (August–September 1990): 16–23, 27–31. For material on Custer's post–Civil War career prior to joining the Seventh Cavalry, see Minnie Dubs Millbrook's excellent "The Boy General and How He Grew: George Custer After Appomattox," *Montana: The Magazine of Western History* 23 (Spring 1973): 34–43 and "Custer's March to Texas," *Prairie Scout: The Kansas Corral of the Westerners* 1 (1973): 31–69. In two other essays, Millbrook provides revealing insights into Custer's introduction to the West after he joined the Seventh Cavalry based on official records from the National Archives and War Department publications. See "The West Breaks in General Custer," *Kansas Historical Quarterly* 36 (Summer 1970): 113–48, and "Custer's First Scout in the West," *Kansas Historical Quarterly* 39 (Summer 1973): 75–95.

A firsthand account of life in the Seventh Cavalry is Robert M. Utley, ed., *Life in Custer's Cavalry: Diaries and Letters of Albert and Jennie Barnitz, 1867–1868* (New Haven: Yale University Press, 1977). For Custer's court-martial, see Lawrence A. Frost, *The Court-Martial of General George A. Custer* (Norman: University of Oklahoma Press, 1968). Custer's version of the events leading up to the court-martial is found in *My Life on the Plains, or, Personal Experiences with Indians* (New York: Sheldon, 1875). Edward S. Godfrey presents an eyewitness account of the Battle of the Washita in "Some Reminiscences, Including the Washita Battle, November 29, 1868," *Cavalry Journal* 37 (October 1928): 481–506. The best work on the Battle of the Washita is still Stan Hoig, *The Battle of the Washita: The Sheridan-Custer Indian Campaign of 1867–69* (Garden City, N.Y.: Doubleday & Company, 1976). For general background on the destructive environmental changes that non-Indians introduced into the world of the Plains Indians, see Elliott West, *The Way to the West: Essays on the Central Plains* (Albuquerque: University of New Mexico Press, 1995), and *The Contested Plains: Indians, Goldseekers, and the Rush to Colorado* (Lawrence: University Press of Kansas, 1998).

For information on the Yellowstone and Black Hills Expeditions, see George A. Custer, "Battling with the Sioux on the Yellowstone," *Galaxy* 22 (July 1876): 91–102; Donald Jackson, *Custer's Gold: The United States Cavalry Expedition of 1874* (New Haven, Conn.: Yale University Press, 1966); and

Watson Parker, *Gold in the Black Hills* (Lincoln: University of Nebraska Press, 1982). An excellent overview of the Sioux effort to win compensation for the Black Hills (which they relinquished once the Supreme Court ruled in their favor) is Edward Lazarus, *Black Hills/White Justice: The Sioux Nation Versus the United States, 1775 to the Present* (New York: HarperCollins, 1991).

The question of why Custer was defeated at the Little Bighorn has generated almost innumerable studies. The starting place is Edward S. Godfrey's firsthand account as a lieutenant serving under Frederick Benteen. See "Custer's Last Battle," *Century Illustrated Monthly Magazine* 43 (January 1892): 358–84. Two authoritative studies are by John S. Gray: *Centennial Campaign: The Sioux War of 1876* (Ft. Collins, Colo.: Old Army Press, 1976) and *Custer's Last Campaign: Mitch Boyer and the Little Bighorn Reconstructed* (Lincoln: University of Nebraska Press, 1994). Larry Sklenar, *To Hell with Honor: Custer and the Little Bighorn* (Norman: University of Oklahoma Press, 2000), offers a new interpretation of Custer's battle plan at the Little Bighorn.

Richard Slotkin, *The Fatal Environment: The Myth of the Frontier in the Age of Industrialization, 1800–1890* (New York: Atheneum, 1985), describes the new meaning of the frontier in a period of rising labor and class conflict and Custer's role in advancing such interests. Robert M. Utley's *Custer and the Great Controversy: Origin and Development of a Legend* (Los Angeles: Westernlore Press, 1962) presents a lucid overview of the historical and literary responses to the Battle of the Little Bighorn and the debate over Custer's culpability for the battle's outcome. Brian W. Dippie, *Custer's Last Stand: The Anatomy of an American Myth* (Missoula: University of Montana Publications in History, 1976), describes the unfolding debate and the changing ways that literature, movies, and television have presented that battle. Bruce A. Rosenberg, *Custer and the Epic of Defeat* (University Park: Pennsylvania State University Press, 1974), demonstrates that Custer's Last Stand derives its power from its roots in similar narratives in the Bible and from the ancient Greeks and the medieval *Song of Roland*. Finally, Paul Hutton, "From Little Bighorn to Little Big Man: The Changing Image of a Western Hero in Popular Culture," *Western Historical Quarterly* 7 (January 1976): 19–45, traces the changing perceptions of Custer to historical developments and changes within the larger American culture.

For Indian perspectives on the Battle of the Little Bighorn, the best compilation of the Indian accounts in narrative form is Gregory F. Michno, *Lakota Noon: The Indian Narrative of Custer's Defeat* (Missoula, Mont.: Mountain Press, 1997). Indian testimony indicates that Custer confronted a village that was nowhere near as large as historians estimated in the past. It also provides evidence that in hand-to-hand combat the Indians proved more able fighters than the soldiers. Herman J. Viola, *Little Bighorn Remembered: The Untold Indian Story of Custer's Last Stand* (New York: Times Books, 1999), emphasizes the Indian-against-Indian nature of the 1876 campaign. Viola also introduces intriguing testimony that Crow scouts gave photographer Edward S. Curtis in 1907. They maintained that they informed Custer that Reno's attack had failed, but he refused to go to the major's aid. These and other recent works on the Indian perceptions of the Battle of the Little Bighorn indicate clearly that new scholarship from different perspectives will alter historical opinion in coming decades. Despite all the ink that has been spilled on this battle, more studies will emerge in the future, and historical opinion on the battle and on Custer will continue to evolve and change.

CHAPTER 8: RANALD MACKENZIE

Ranald Mackenzie's personal papers have been lost. This essay reconstructs his life and career from published primary sources and secondary sources. Biographies of Mackenzie are Lessing H. Nohl Jr., "Bad Hand: The Military Career of Ranald Slidell Mackenzie, 1871–1889" (Ph.D. diss., University of New Mexico, 1962); Ernest Wallace, *Ranald S. Mackenzie on the Texas Frontier* (Lubbock, Tex.: West Texas Museum Association, 1964); Michael D. Pierce, *The Most Promising Young Officer: A Life of Ranald Slidell Mackenzie* (Norman: University of Oklahoma Press, 1993); J'Nell L. Pate, "Ranald S. Mackenzie," in *Soldiers West: Biographies from the Military Frontier*, ed. Paul Andrew Hutton (Lincoln: University of Nebraska Press, 1987), 177–92; and Joseph H. Dorst, "Ranald Slidell Mackenzie," *Twentieth Annual Reunion of the Association of Graduates of the United States Military Academy at West Point, New York* (East Saginaw, Mich.: Evening News Printing and Binding House, 1889).

Professional peers wrote on Mackenzie's career or their experiences under his command. Capt. Robert G. Carter was the Fourth Cavalry's devoted memoirist. See his *On the Border with Mackenzie*, or, *Winning West Texas from the Comanches* (New York: Antiquarian Press, 1961), *The Mackenzie Raid into Mexico* (Washington, D.C.: Gibson Bros., 1919), and *The Old Sergeant's Story: Winning the West from the Indians and Bad Men in 1870 to 1876* (New York: F. H. Hitchcock, 1926). Four other memoirists who served in the Fourth are E[ugene] B. Beaumont ("Over the Border with Mackenzie," *United Service* 12 [March 1885]), George A. Forsyth (*Thrilling*

Days in Army Life [(New York: Harper & Brothers, 1900]), James Parker (*The Old Army: Memories, 1872–1918* [Philadelphia: Dorrance, 1929]), and William A. Thompson ("Scouting with Mackenzie," *Cavalry Journal* 10 [1897]). John G. Bourke, Crook's greatest promoter, recalls the Powder River Campaign in *Mackenzie's Last Fight with the Cheyennes* (Governor's Island, N.Y.: New York Headquarters, 1890). Service with Mackenzie figures in the accounts of Col. Homer W. Wheeler, *Buffalo Days: Forty Years in the Old West* (New York: A. L. Burt, 1923, 1925); Donald F. Danker, ed., *Man of the Plains: Recollections of Luther North* (Lincoln: University of Nebraska Press, 1961); and Henry W. Strong, *My Frontier Days and Indian Fights on the Plains of Texas* (Dallas: Henry W. Strong, 1925).

Published primary sources dealing with operations of Mackenzie and the Fourth Cavalry include the Secretary of War's *Annual Reports*, which contain official reports and correspondence, from 1870–1883. For letters, reports, and iteneraries dealing with Mackenzie's Texas operations, see Ernest Wallace, ed., *Ranald S. Mackenzie's Official Correspondence Relating to Texas, 1871–1879*, 2 vols. (Lubbock, Tex.: West Texas Museum Association, 1967–1968), and Joe F. Taylor, "The Indian Campaign on the Staked Plains, 1874–1875: Military Correspondence from the War Department Adjutant General's File, 1874-1875," *Panhandle-Plains Historical Review* 34 (1961): 1–216, and 35 (1962): 215–357.

Historical overviews of the army and the southern plains are Robert M. Utley, *Frontier Regulars: The United States Army and the Indian, 1866-1891* (Bloomington: Indiana University Press, 1973); Paul Andrew Hutton, *Phil Sheridan and His Army* (Lincoln: University of Nebraska Press, 1985); William H. Leckie, *The Military Conquest of the Southern Plains* (Norman: University of Oklahoma Press, 1963); and Edward M. Coffman, *The Old Army: A Portrait of the American Army in Peacetime, 1784–1898* (New York: Oxford University Press, 1986).

CHAPTER 9: NELSON A. MILES

A wealth of primary materials document the life and career of Nelson Appleton Miles. He wrote three books about his experiences: *Personal Recollections and Observations of General Nelson A. Miles, Embracing a Brief View of the Civil War; or, From New England to the Golden Gate, and the Story of His Indian Campaigns, with Comments on the Exploration, Development and Progress of Our Great Western Empire* (1896; Lincoln: University of Nebraska Press, 1992); *Military Europe: A Narrative of Personal Observation and Personal Experience* (New York: Doubleday and McClure, 1898); and *Serving the*

Republic: Memoirs of the Civil and Military Life of Nelson A. Miles,
Lieutenant-General, United States Army (New York: Harper Brothers, 1911).
For his early life, essential are his papers at the U.S. Army Military History
Institute, Carlisle Barracks, Pennsylvania. Another set of Miles papers at the
Library of Congress concentrates largely on his post–Civil War career. A
typed copy of his correspondence with his wife, assembled by his son,
Sherman, was provided to the author courtesy of Robert M. Utley. Smaller
Miles collections are also found at the Rutherford B. Hayes Presidential
Center, Fremont, Ohio, and the Forbush Memorial Library, Westminster,
Massachusetts.

Miles also published a number of articles for contemporary journals.
The most important are "Our Unwatered Empire," *North American Review*
150 (March 1890): 570–81; "The Future of the Indian Question," *North*
American Review 152 (January 1891): 1–10; "The Lesson of the Recent
Strikes," *North American Review* 159 (August 1894): 180–88; "Hunting
Large Game," *North American Review* 161 (October 1895): 484–92; "Our
Indian Question," *Journal of the Military Service Institution of the United*
States 2 (no. 7, 1881): 278–92; "War," *Cosmopolitan* 21 (June 1896): 142–48;
"My Treatment of Jefferson Davis," *Independent* 58 (February 23, 1905):
413–17; "The Necessity of the Isthmus Canal," *Independent* 52 (February 14,
1900): 409; "Our Coast Defences," *Forum* 24 (January 1898): 513–19; and
"The Political Situation in Europe and the East," *Forum* 24 (April 1898):
159–65.

Of the biographies of Miles, Robert Wooster, *Nelson A. Miles and the*
Twilight of the Frontier Army (Lincoln: University of Nebraska Press, 1993),
is the most analytical. More favorable to its subject is Peter R. DeMontravel,
A Hero to His Fighting Men: Nelson A. Miles, 1839–1925 (Kent, Ohio: Kent
State University Press, 1998). Less scholarly works include Virginia Weisel
Johnson's authorized biography, *The Unregimented General: A Biography of*
Nelson A. Miles (Boston: Houghton Mifflin, 1962); Newton F. Tolman, *The*
Search for General Miles (New York: G. P. Putnam, 1968); and Arthur J.
Amchan, *The Most Famous Soldier in America: A Biography of Lt. Gen. Nelson*
A. Miles, 1839–1925 (Alexandria, Va.: Amchan Publications, 1989). Brian C.
Pohanka, *Nelson A. Miles: A Documentary Biography of His Military Career,*
1861–1903 (Glendale, Calif.: Arthur H. Clark, 1985), provides a handy com-
pilation of many primary sources.

Robert M. Utley, "Nelson A. Miles," in *Soldiers West: Biographies from*
the Military Frontier, ed. Paul Andrew Hutton (Lincoln: University of
Nebraska Press, 1987), is the best brief analysis of the general's career. For
more detailed studies of particular campaigns in which Miles was involved,

see two excellent books by Jerome A. Greene: *Yellowstone Command: Colonel Nelson A. Miles and the Great Sioux War, 1876–1877* (Lincoln: University of Nebraska Press, 1992), and *Nez Perce Summer, 1877: The U.S. Army and the Nee-Me-Poo Crisis* (Helena: Montana Historical Society Press, 2000).

To place Miles's life in a larger context, Robert M. Utley, *Frontier Regulars: The United States Army and the Indian, 1866–1891* (1973; Lincoln: University of Nebraska Press, 1984), remains the best one-volume account of the post–Civil War campaigns against the Indians. Robert Wooster, *The Military and United States Indian Policy, 1865–1903* (1988; Lincoln: University of Nebraska Press, 1995), focuses on questions of policy and strategy. Michael L. Tate, *The Frontier Army in the Settlement of the West* (Norman: University of Oklahoma Press, 1999), describes the army's role in western development. Joe Frantz's influential essay on this theme may be found in *Aspects of the American West: Three Essays by Joe B. Frantz* (College Station: Texas A&M University Press, 1976). For a more detailed and systematic assessment of the military's economic impact, see Thomas T. Smith, *The U.S. Army and the Texas Frontier Economy 1845–1900* (College Station: Texas A&M University Press, 1999). Francis Paul Prucha, *The Great Father: The United States Government and the American Indians*, abr. ed. (Lincoln: University of Nebraska Press, 1986), ably traces the development of Indian policy.

 Contributors

Durwood Ball is associate professor of history and editor of the *New Mexico Historical Review* at the University of New Mexico. He is author of *Army Regulars on the Western Frontier, 1848–1861* (2001).

Richard N. Ellis is most proud of the approximately thirty doctoral students he trained at the University of New Mexico. He is chair of the Department of Southwest Studies at Fort Lewis College after serving as director of the Center of Southwest Studies at that institution. He directed the first phase of the search for the site of the Sand Creek Massacre. He is author of *General Pope and U.S. Indian Policy* (1970) and coauthor of *Colorado: A History in Photographs* (1991) and *Cheyenne Dog Soldiers: A Ledgerbook History of Coups and Combat* (1997) and other publications.

Richard W. Etulain is professor emeritus of history at the University of New Mexico, where he taught from 1979 to 2001 and directed the Center for the American West. A specialist in the history and literature of the American West, he is author or editor of more than forty books. His latest volumes are *New Mexican Lives* (2002), *César Chávez: A Brief Biography with Documents* (2002), *Wild Women of the Old West* (coedited with Glenda Riley, 2003), and *Western Lives: A Biographical History of the American West* (2004). He is at work on a general narrative history of the American West.

Robert W. Larson, professor emeritus of history at the University of Northern Colorado, is author of *Red Cloud: Warrior-Statesman of the Lakota Sioux* (1997), which was a History Book Club selection and won second prize in the Westerners International Co-Founders Book Awards. His other publications are *New Mexico's Quest for Statehood* (1968), *New Mexico Populism* (1974), *Populism in the Mountain West* (1986), and *Shaping*

Educational Change: The First Century of the University of Northern Colorado at Greeley (1989). He is working on a biography of Hunkpapa Sioux war chief Gall.

Shirley A. Leckie teaches at the University of Central Florida, where she offers courses in women in American history, the history of the Trans-Mississippi West, and the Gilded Age and Progressivism. She is author of *Elizabeth Bacon Custer and the Making of a Myth* (1993) and *Angie Debo: Pioneering Historian* (2000). She and William H. Leckie have revised *The Buffalo Soldiers: A Narrative of the Black Cavalry in the West*, which appeared in 2003.

Darlis A. Miller is professor emerita of history at New Mexico State University, where she taught courses on the American West and Southwest. Her special research interests are the frontier army, western women, and biography. Her most recent publications are *Above a Common Soldier: Frank and Mary Clarke in the American West and Civil War, 1847–1872* (1997) and *Mary Hallock Foote: Author-Illustrator of the American West* (2002).

L. G. Moses teaches American Indian history and the history of the American West at Oklahoma State University. He is author or editor of a number of books, among them *The Indian Man: A Biography of James Mooney* (1984, 2002). He is at work on a history of the Pueblo Lands Board of the 1920s.

Glenda Riley is Alexander M. Bracken professor emerita of history at Ball State University. She is author of many books and articles, especially regarding women in the American West. Riley is past president of the Western History Association and the recipient of numerous awards, including two Fulbright grants. Her latest book is *Taking Land, Breaking Land: Women Colonizing the American West and Kenya, 1840–1940* (2003).

Robert Wooster is professor of history at Texas A&M University—Corpus Christi. Named a Piper Professor for his teaching excellence, he specializes in Civil War and U.S. military history. He has written or edited eight books, including *Nelson A Miles and the Twilight of the Frontier Army* (1993), *The Civil War 100: A Ranking of the Most Influential People in the War Between the States* (1998), and *The Civil War Bookshelf: 50 Must-Read Books About the War Between the States* (2001). His current projects include a biography of John M. Schofield, commanding general of the U.S. Army.

INDEX

Page numbers in *italics* indicate illustrations. In the text, numerically designated military units are spelled out rather than marked with numerals. In the index, an individual's highest military rank is used.

INDEX

INDEX

INDEX